Cambridge English

MINDSET

FOR IELTS

An Official Cambridge IELTS Course

TEACHER'S BOOK 3

Cambridge University Press
www.cambridge.org/elt

Cambridge Assessment English
www.cambridgeenglish.org

Information on this title: www.cambridge.org/9781316649336

First published 2018

20 19 18 17 16 15 14 13 12 11 10 9 8 7 6 5 4 3 2 1

Printed in Malaysia by Vivar Printing

A catalogue record for this publication is available from the British Library

Library of Congress Cataloging-in-Publication data
NAMES: Womack, Brantly, 1947–
TITLE: Asymmetry and international relationships / Brantly Womack.
DESCRIPTION: New York, NY: Cambridge University Press, 2015 | Includes
    bibliographical references and index
INDENTIFIERS: LCCN 2015033495 | ISBN: 9781107132895 (hardback)
SUBJECTS: LCSH: International relations. | Diplomacy.
CLASSIFICATION: LCC JZ1305 . W63 2015 | DDC327.101--DC23 LC record
available at http://lccn.loc.gov/2015033495

ISBN 978-1-316-64933-6 Hardback

Additional resources for this publication at www.cambridge.org/mindsetforielts

About the authors

Lucy Passmore

Lucy began teaching English in 2002 in the UK and Spain, where she prepared young learners for the Cambridge Main Suite examinations. She has been a tutor of English for Academic Purposes since 2008, and has taught on IELTS preparation courses in addition to preparing international students to start degree courses at Brunel University and King's College London. Lucy is currently based at King's College London, where she teaches on foundation programmes for international students, provides in-sessional support in academic writing for current students and contributes to materials and course design.

Jishan Uddin

Jishan has been an English teacher since 2001 and in that time, he has taught on a range of courses in the UK and Spain including general English, exam preparation and academic English courses (EAP). He is currently an EAP lecturer and academic module leader at King's College London. He has an extensive experience in IELTS preparation classes for groups of students from many parts of the world, particularly China, Saudi Arabia and Kazakhstan.

The authors and publishers would like to thank the following people for their work on this level of the Student's Book.

Bryan Stephens and Jock Graham for their editing and proof reading.

Design and typeset by emc design.

Audio produced by Leon Chambers at The Soundhouse Studios, London.

The publishers would like to thank the following people for their input and work on the digital materials that accompany this level.

Jonathan Birkin; Anthony Cosgrove; Peter Crosthwaite; Deborah Hobbs; Kate O'Toole; Bryan Stephens; Emina Tuzovic.

Cover and text design concept: Juice Creative Ltd.

Typesetting: emc design Ltd.

Cover illustration: MaryliaDesign/iStock/Getty Images Plus.

CONTENTS

UNIT: INTRODUCTION

Mindset for IELTS Level 3 is aimed at students who are at a B2-C1 level and want to achieve a Band 7 or Band 7.5 result in the Academic IELTS test. You can follow the book by topic and teach it lineally or alternatively you can focus on the different skills and papers that you would like your students to improve. It is designed for up to 90 hours classroom use, but you can be flexible and focus on key areas of your choice. The topics have been chosen based on common themes in the IELTS exam and the language and skills development is based on research in the corpus, by looking at the mistakes that students at this level commonly make in IELTS.

Mindset for IELTS Level 3 offers flexible ways of teaching. You can work through the units consecutively or choose the lessons that are important to your students.

- Topics have been chosen to suit the needs and abilities of students at this level. They are topics that occur in the IELTS test, but are tailored to the needs and interests of your students.
- There is full coverage of the test both in the book and in the online modules. However, there is an emphasis on the parts of the exam that will stretch students aiming to achieve the higher band scores.
- Grammar and vocabulary are built into the development of skills, so students improve their language skills as well as the skills they need to learn to achieve the desired band score.

How *Mindset for IELTS* develops each skill

- **Speaking** – *Mindset* gives students strategies for what happens if they don't know much about the topic. It also helps build vocabulary for each part of the test and allows students to grow in confidence.
- **Writing** – *Mindset* gives students tips on how to plan better and develop their ideas. There is coverage of all types of Task 1 and Task 2 and detailed help on how to approach each, as well as model answers.
- **Reading** – Strategies for dealing with Reading texts on difficult and unknown topics are developed, as well as coverage of all question types. Strategies are provided for improving reading skills in general, as well as skills needed in the exam, such as an awareness of distraction and the use of paraphrase.
- **Listening** – *Mindset* gives coverage of all the Listening tasks, but concentrates on how students can maximise their score. Vital skills for dealing with the paper like paraphrasing are practised and listening strategies that will help students in their everyday life are also developed.

Outcomes

At the start of each lesson you will see a list of outcomes.

> ### IN THIS UNIT YOU WILL LEARN HOW TO
>
> - successfully answer 'matching features' questions
>
> - develop whole-text understanding to enable you to answer global multiple-choice questions
>
> - consider the meaning and use of modals of obligation, past and present.

In the Teacher's Book you will see how these outcomes relate to each lesson and the skills that students need to develop in order to be successful in improving their English language and exam techniques. There are typically three or four outcomes per lesson which look at skills that can be used both in the IELTS test and for students' broader English language development; an IELTS strategy for dealing with a particular paper and a linguistic outcome that helps with vocabulary and grammar development.

Tip Boxes and Bullet Boxes

- Tip boxes help you and your students improve task awareness and language skills. You will find further information on how to get the most out of them in the Teacher's Book. Note that the number in the corner refers to the exercise that the tip relates to.

TIP | 0 | 4

For this essay task, it is important to be concise. Limit yourself to two, possibly three, main ideas for each paragraph and develop them properly.

- Bullet boxes tell you how the test works and how to get a better understanding of the test task being addressed.

 For this task, the correct answers are specific words from the recording in the same form as you hear them, and in the same order as the questions. Make sure you check your answers for errors like the following, which can lose marks:

- incorrect spelling
- exceeding the given word limit
- repeating words that are already in the table
- omitting key details such as measurements (km, grams).

Teacher's Book

The Teacher's Book has been designed to help you to teach the material effectively and to allow you to see how the language and skills development relate directly to the IELTS test. You will also find the following:

- Extension exercises — exercises that help you give students more practice with key skills.
- Alternative exercises — ideas that you can use to make the exercises more relevant for students.
- Definitions — to help you with some of the key terms that are used in IELTS.

How to use the online modules

As well as the Student's Book there are several online modules that each provide 6-8 hours of further study. These can be used for homework or to reinforce what has been studied in the classroom. The core modules are:

- **Reading**
- **Listening**
- **Writing**
- **Speaking**
- **Grammar and Vocabulary**

In the Reading and Listening modules there is more practice with the same skills that they have studied but based on a related but slightly different topic.

The Writing module builds on the skills that they have learnt in the unit and offers advice and model answers to help improve writing skills.

The Speaking module builds on knowledge of the topics that students have studied in the Student's Book. This helps them to speak about a range of topics with confidence and to develop the skills needed for the different parts of the test.

The Grammar and Vocabulary module reinforces and extends the vocabulary and grammar that has been studied in each unit of the book.

There are also a number of other online modules with specific learners in mind:

- **Chinese Pronunciation and Speaking**
- **Speaking Plus**

These modules look at the types of mistakes made by students from different language groups. The syllabus and exercises have been developed with insights from our corpus database of students speaking. Each module takes between 6-8 hours. Students can also analyse and view video content of Speaking Tests in the following modules:

- **Arabic Spelling and Vocabulary**
- **Arabic Writing**
- **Writing Plus**

These modules use our database of past writing IELTS papers and corpus research to look at the typical mistakes that students from different language groups make on the Writing paper of the test. They are encouraged to improve their writing skills and also avoid the common pitfalls that students make. Each of these modules provides 6-8 hours of study.

- **Academic Study Skills**

The Academic Study Skills Module helps to bridge the gap between the skills that students learn studying IELTS and the ones that they need for the exam. The module shows students how they can use the knowledge they have and what they will need to work on when going to study in an English Language context for Higher Education.

About the IELTS Academic Module

Academic Reading

The Reading paper is made up of three different texts, which progress in level of difficulty. There is a total of 40 questions with one mark each. Candidates have one hour to complete the information; this includes the time needed to transfer answers to the answer sheet. (There is no extra time for this.)

The texts are authentic and academic, but written for a non-specialist audience. Candidates must use information that appears in the text to answer the questions. They cannot use outside knowledge if they know about the topic. The types of texts are similar to the texts you may find in a newspaper or a magazine, so it is important for your students to get as much practice reading of these types of text as possible.

Texts sometimes contain illustrations. If a text contains technical terms, a glossary is provided.

The different task types are:

Multiple-choice	Candidates will be asked to choose one answer from four options; choose two answers from five options or choose three answers from seven options.
Identifying information (True / False / Not Given)	Say if a statement given as a fact is True / False or Not Given
Identifying the writer's views or claims (Yes / No / Not Given	Say if a statement agrees with the opinions of the author of if it is not given in the text.
Matching information	Match information to paragraphs in a text
Matching headings	Match a heading from a list to the correct part of the text
Matching features	Match a list of statements to a list of possible answers (e.g. specific people or dates)
Matching sentence endings	Complete a sentence with a word or words from the text inside the word limit which is given.
Sentence completion	Complete a sentence with a word or words from the text inside the word limit which is given.
Notes/Summary/Table/Flow-chart completion	Complete with a suitable word or words from the text.
Labelling a diagram	Label a diagram with the correct word from a text. The words will be given in a box of possible answers.
Short-answer questions	Answers questions using words from the text inside the word limit

Academic Writing

There are two separate tasks. Candidates must answer both tasks.

Task 1

- Candidates should spend 20 minutes on this task.
- Candidates should write a minimum of 150 words. They will be penalised if they write less.
- Candidates need to describe and summarise a piece of visual information. The information may be presented in a diagram, map, graph or table.

Task 2

- Candidates should spend 40 minutes on this task.
- Candidates should write a minimum of 250 words. They will be penalised if they write less.
- Candidates need to write a discursive essay. They will be given an opinion, problem or issue that they need to respond to. They may be asked to provide a solution, evaluate a problem, compare and contrast different ideas or challenge an idea.

Listening

The Listening Paper is made up of four different texts. There are a total of 40 questions with 10 questions in each section. The paper lasts for approximately 30 minutes and candidates are given an extra 10 minutes to transfer their answers to the answer sheet. Each question is worth one mark.

In **Part 1** candidates hear a conversation between two people about a general topic with a transactional outcome (e.g. someone booking a holiday, finding out information about travel, returning a bought object to a shop).

In **Part 2** candidates hear a monologue or prompted monologue on a general topic with a transactional purpose (e.g. giving information about an event).

In **Part 3** candidates hear a conversation between two or three people in an academic setting (e.g. a student and a tutor discussing a study project).

In **Part 4** Candidates hear a monologue in an academic setting (e.g. a lecture)

There may be one to three different task types in each section of the paper, the task types are:

Notes/ Summary/ Table/ Flow-chart completion	Complete with a suitable word or words from the recording
Multiple-choice	Candidates will be asked to choose one answer from three alternatives or two answers from five alternatives.
Short-answer questions	Answer questions using words from the recording inside the word limit.
Labelling a diagram, plan or map	Label a diagram/ plan or map with a suitable word or words by choosing from a box with possible answers.
Classification	Classify the given information in the questions according to three different criteria (e.g. dates, names, etc.).
Matching	Match a list of statements to a list of possible answers in a box (e.g. people or dates).
Sentence completion	Complete a sentence with a word or words from the word limit which is given.

Speaking

The test is with an examiner and is recorded. The interview is made up of three parts.

Part 1

- Lasts for 4-5 minutes
- Candidates are asked questions on familiar topics like their hobbies, likes and dislikes.

Part 2

- Lasts for 3-4 minutes
- Candidates are given a task card with a topic (e.g. describe a special meal you have had) and are given suggestions to help them structure their talk. They have one minute to prepare their talk and then need to speak between 1 and 2 minutes on the topic.

Part 3

- Lasts for 4-5 minutes
- The examiner will ask candidates more detailed and more abstract questions about the topic in Part 2 (e.g. how are eating habits in your country now different from eating habits in the past?).

In the Speaking test candidates are marked on Fluency and Coherence; Lexical Resource; Grammatical Range; Pronunciation.

What your students will need to do to get the band they require

Academic Reading

Candidates need to score 30 to get a Band 7 on Academic Reading and 35 to receive a Band 8.

Listening

Candidates need to score 30 to get a Band 7 on Listening and 35 to get a Band 8.

Academic Writing and Speaking

Please see information from the band descriptors on Page 10–12

How to connect students' existing knowledge of English language with the exam

Students beginning this course should already have a good knowledge of English. It is important to let them know that this existing knowledge will be very useful for the IELTS test and will form the basis of developing further language knowledge and skills. The grammar, vocabulary and pronunciation they have already learned can be linked to different parts of the exam. In this book we help students to do this.

Vocabulary

Vocabulary is a key component in all four papers in the exam and at this level. Students are expected to have a fairly wide range of vocabulary and a good knowledge of collocation. In this course, students are encouraged to build on their existing vocabulary by expanding on what they already know. For example, candidates are shown that when noting a new item of vocabulary, they should also think about, synonyms, lexical sets and collocations.

An awareness of synonym and paraphrase is very important, as many of the tasks, across all papers, rely greatly on students knowing different words for the same thing. At this level, students should also be thinking about the style and register of the words that they are using in different contexts.

Grammar

At this level students will have a fairly good control of grammar and will have come across most tenses and aspects of verbs before, however, there may be some gaps in their knowledge and this course will help students plug these gaps. There is also an emphasis on the type of grammatical structures that aid students to get the higher band scores.

How to prepare your own materials for IELTS

There are many IELTS practice materials available, however you may want to create your own or use elements of practice tests to make lessons more communicative.

Reading

You can use texts from a number of sources: general English textbooks, the internet, practice tests or materials that you have written yourself. One important point to keep in mind, however, is that the reading is at the right level, not too easy or too difficult. In order to check the level of a text you can use an online tool called 'English Profile'. Here you can enter a word and it will tell you at what level of the CEFR students should know the word, so you can make a judgement about if you should be testing it or not.

As demonstrated throughout this course, skimming and scanning are two key skills needed for the Reading Paper. In order to practise and encourage the use of both of these techniques in a freer way you could try the following:

- Give groups of students the same reading text and ask them to race to find the information.
- Give students a very short deadline and tell them to skim read a text and then retell the main information to their partner.
- Give groups of students different texts and ask them to write questions / a quiz for other students. The groups then swap texts and questions and scan the text for answers, under a time limit.

Listening

For your own listening material, you can use recordings from other textbooks, record audios or use online materials. To get the higher band scores, it is important for students to get as much listening practice as possible, so encourage them to listen and watch material in English online. Also encourage students to listen to each other in class and use dictation and spoken instructions when appropriate.

Writing

For Writing Task 1, students need to write about graphs or a process. For this type of task you or your students, could easily create graphs based on information/ data which is of personal interest to the class. This can be done by searching, online for statistics that would be of interest to your students or creating the statistics from surveys done in class.

For a process diagram, you can demonstrate the language needed for this task, by showing a simple process that they are familiar or by finding interesting or amusing inventions that will be of interest.

For Part 2 of the writing you could exploit the use of sample answers found online, from other books or from students themselves (if they give you permission). With these sample essays you could do the following:

- Cut them into sections and ask students to order them appropriately (useful when teaching structure and coherence).
- Ask students to discuss what the sample answer does well and where it could be improved.
- Ask students to rewrite an essay from an opposing view.

Speaking

For the Speaking Part of the test, you can write your own questions or ask students to create questions they think will appear in each part of the exam. This will also gauge their understanding of the exam. At this level, it is also a good idea to try and discuss issues that are in the news and / or of global importance, as this will help them deal better with topics in Part 3. Dealing with topics in this part of the test is important for students who want to obtain a higher band score.

General

When producing your own material, it is important to ask yourself the following:

- Is this material the correct level for my students?
- Will it engage my students (personalizing the topics is often a good way to do this)?
- Are the instructions for the task clear and simple?

Using the band descriptors

It is a good idea to have a knowledge of the public version of the band descriptors, so that you and your students are aware of what they are aiming for in the speaking and writing parts of the test.

The full band descriptors can be found online at www.ielts.org , but here is a summary of the band scores in the area that students studying this course should be at.

Speaking band descriptors – selected bands

Band 8

Fluency and coherence

- Speaks fluently with only occasional repetition or self-correction; hesitation is usually content-related and only rarely to search for language
- Develops topics coherently and appropriately

Lexical resource

- Uses a wide vocabulary resource readily and flexibly to convey precise meaning
- Uses less common and idiomatic vocabulary skilfully, with occasional inaccuracies
- Uses paraphrase effectively as required

Grammatical range and accuracy

- Uses a wide range of structures flexibly
- Produces a majority of error-free sentences with only very occasional inappropriacies or basic/non-systematic errors

Pronunciation

- Uses a wide range of pronunciation features
- Sustains flexible use of features, with only occasional lapses
- Is easy to understand throughout; L1 accent has minimal effect on intelligibility

Band 7

Fluency and coherence

- Speaks at length without noticeable effort or loss of coherence
- May develop language-related hesitation at times, or some repetition and/or self-correction

Lexical resource

- Uses vocabulary resource flexibly to discuss a variety of topics
- Uses some less common and idiomatic vocabulary and shows some awareness of style and collocation, with some inappropriate choices
- Uses paraphrase effectively

Grammatical range and accuracy

- Uses a range of complex structures with some flexibility
- Frequently produces error-free sentences, though some grammatical mistakes persist

Pronunciation

- Shows all of the positive features of Band 6 and some, but not all of the positive features of Band 8

Band 6

Fluency and coherence

- Is willing to speak at length, though may lose coherence at times due to occasional repetition self-correction or hesitation
- Uses a range of connectives and discourse markers but not always appropriately

Lexical resource

- Has a wide enough vocabulary to discuss topics at length and make meaning clear in spite of inappropriacies
- Generally paraphrases effectively

Grammatical range and accuracy

- Uses a mix of simple and complex structures, but with limited flexibility
- May make frequent mistakes with complex structures though these rarely cause comprehension problems

Pronunciation

- Uses a range of pronunciation features with mixed control
- Shows some effective use of features but this is not sustained
- Can generally be understood throughout, though mispronunciation of individual words or sounds reduces clarity at times

Academic Writing Part 1 – selected bands

Band 8

Task achievement

- Covers all requirements of the task sufficiently
- Presents, highlights and ands illustrates key features/bullet points clearly and appropriately

Coherence and cohesion
- Sequence information and ideas logically
- Manages all aspects of cohesion well
- Uses paragraphing sufficiently and appropriately

Lexical resource
- Uses a wide range of vocabulary fluently and flexibly to convey precise meanings
- Skilfully uses uncommon lexical items but there may be occasional inaccuracies in word choice and collocation
- Produces rare errors in word choice, spelling and/or word formation

Grammatical range and accuracy
- Uses a wide range of structures
- The majority of sentences are error-free
- Makes only very occasional errors or inappropriacies

Band 7

Task Achievement
- Covers the requirements of the task
- Presents a clear overview of main trends, differences or stages
- Clearly presents and highlights key features/bullet points but could be more fully extended

Coherence and cohesion
- Logically organises information and ideas; there is clear progression throughout
- Uses a range of cohesive devices appropriately although there may be some under-/over-use

Lexical resource
- Uses a sufficient range of vocabulary to allow some flexibility and precision
- Uses less common lexical items with some awareness of style and collocation
- May produce occasional errors in word choice, spelling and/or word formation

Grammatical range and accuracy
- Uses a variety of complex structures
- Produces frequent error-free sentences
- Has good control of grammar and punctuation but may make a few errors

Band 6

Task achievement
- Addresses the requirements of the task
- Presents an overview with information appropriately selected
- Presents and adequately highlights key features/ bullet points but details may be irrelevant, inappropriate or inaccurate

Coherence and cohesion
- Arranges information and ideas coherently and there is a clear overall progression
- Uses cohesive devices effectively, but cohesion within and/or between sentences may be faulty or mechanical
- May not always use referencing clearly or appropriately

Lexical resource
- Uses an adequate range of vocabulary for the task
- Attempts to use less common vocabulary but with some inaccuracy
- Makes some errors in spelling and/or word formation, but they do not impeded communication

Grammatical range and accuracy
- Uses a mix of simple and complex sentence forms
- Makes some errors in grammar and punctuation but they rarely reduce communication

Academic writing part 2 – selected bands

Band 8

Task achievement
- Sufficiently addresses all parts of the task
- Presents a well-developed response to the question with relevant, extended and supported ideas

<u>Coherence and cohesion</u>

- Sequences information and ideas logically
- Manages all aspects of cohesion well
- Uses paragraphing sufficiently and appropriately

<u>Lexical resource</u>

- Uses a wide range of vocabulary fluently and flexibly to convey precise meanings
- Skilfully uses uncommon lexical items but there may be occasional inaccuracies in word choice and collocation
- Produces rare errors in spelling and/or word formation

<u>Grammatical range and accuracy</u>

- Uses a wide range of structures
- The majority of sentences are error-free
- Makes only very occasional errors or inappropriacies

Band 7

<u>Task achievement</u>

- Addresses all parts of the task
- Presents a clear position throughout the response
- Presents, extends and supports main ideas, but there may be a tendency to overgeneralise and/or supporting ideas may lack focus

<u>Coherence and cohesion</u>

- Logically organises information and ideas; there is a clear progression throughout
- Uses a range of cohesive devices appropriately although there may be some under-/over- use
- Presents a clear central topic within each paragraph

<u>Lexical resource</u>

- Uses a sufficient range of vocabulary to allow some flexibility and precision
- Uses less common lexical items with some awareness of style and collocation
- May produce occasional errors in word choice, spelling and/or word formation

<u>Grammatical range and accuracy</u>

- Uses a variety of complex structures
- Produces frequent error-free sentences
- Has good control of grammar and punctuation but make a few errors

Band 6

<u>Task achievement</u>

- Addresses all parts of the task although some parts may be more fully covered than others
- Presents a relevant position although the conclusions may become unclear or repetitive
- Presents relevant main ideas but some may be inadequately developed/unclear

<u>Coherence and cohesion</u>

- Arranges information and ideas coherently and there is a clear overall progression
- Uses cohesive devices effectively, but cohesion within and/or between sentences may be faulty or mechanical
- May not always use referencing clearly or appropriately
- Uses paragraphing, but not always logically

<u>Lexical resource</u>

- Uses an adequate range of vocabulary for the task
- Attempts to use less common vocabulary but with some inaccuracy
- Makes some errors in spelling and/or word formation, but they do not impeded communication

<u>Grammatical range and accuracy</u>

- Uses a mix of simple and complex sentence forms
- Makes some errors in grammar and punctuation but they rarely reduce communication

The following checklists can be used for you or your students to assess their work based on the descriptors and the bands that they are aiming for in this level. You may not always be looking at the paper as a whole, so you may wish to adapt them depending on the part of the paper that you are focusing on.

MINDSET FOR IELTS LEVEL 3 SPEAKING CHECKLIST

FLUENCY AND COHERENCE	
Did they speak at length without many pauses?	
Did they develop all of the topics?	
Did they answer the questions fully?	
Did they answer the questions naturally?	
LEXICAL RESOURCE	
Did they use a wide range of vocabulary?	
Did they use any less common or idiomatic phrases?	
Did they make very few mistakes?	
Did they paraphrase the questions or anything that they had already said?	
GRAMMATICAL RANGE AND ACCURACY	
Did they use a wide range of grammar structures?	
Did they avoid making many grammar mistakes?	
PRONUNCIATION	
Were they easy to understand?	

Notes

Good uses of vocabulary

....
....
....
....

Good uses of grammar

....
....
....
....

Areas for improvement

....
....
....

MINDSET FOR IELTS LEVEL 3 WRITING PART 1 CHECKLIST

TASK ACHIEVEMENT	
Have all points of the question been answered?	
Have all of the key points been covered?	
Has everything been covered in enough detail and not too much detail?	
Is there a clear overview?	
Has the writer avoided drawing conclusions that are not in the text?	
COHERENCE AND COHESION	
Are the ideas and information presented in an order that is clear to follow?	
Are linking words and phrases used well and without much repetition?	
Are paragraphs used and developed clearly?	
LEXICAL RESOURCE	
Has a wide range of vocabulary been used?	
Is the use of vocabulary accurate?	
Is there a good use of different collocations?	
GRAMMATICAL RANGE AND ACCURACY	
Has a wide range of structures been used?	
Has grammar been used accurately?	
Has punctuation been used well?	

Notes

Good uses of vocabulary

....

....

....

....

Good uses of grammar

....

....

....

....

Areas for improvement

....

....

MINDSET FOR IELTS LEVEL 3 WRITING PART 2 CHECKLIST

TASK ACHIEVEMENT	
Have all points of the question been answered?	
Is the argument fully developed?	
Is it clear to understand what the position of the writer is?	
Are all of the ideas relevant?	
Has the writer fully supported the points that they are making?	
COHERENCE AND COHESION	
Are the ideas and information presented in an order that is clear to follow?	
Are linking words and phrases used well and without much repetition?	
Are paragraphs used and developed clearly?	
LEXICAL RESOURCE	
Has a wide range of vocabulary been used?	
Is the use of vocabulary accurate?	
Is there a good use of different collocations?	
GRAMMATICAL RANGE AND ACCURACY	
Has a wide range of structures been used?	
Has grammar been used accurately?	
Has punctuation been used well?	

Notes

Good uses of vocabulary

....
....
....
....

Good uses of grammar

....
....
....
....

Areas for improvement

....
....

READING

OUTCOMES

- deal with matching headings tasks
- identify the main idea of a paragraph
- understand the meaning of prefixes

OUTCOMES

Ask students to focus on the outcomes of the lesson. Explain that the IELTS matching task requires them to choose a heading which correctly summarises the whole paragraph. To do this they need to identify the main idea in a paragraph. Explain that there will probably be some unknown words in IELTS reading texts, but that it is possible to 'guess' the meaning of some of these without using a dictionary. Students should also be aware of the use of prefixes, which can further help them to choose the correct paragraph headings.

LEAD-IN

To engage students in the topic, elicit where they would prefer to go on holiday (e.g. the beach, the mountains, the countryside, a city). Ask them to read the text and underline any places they chose that are mentioned in the text.

01 Elicit several examples of underlined nouns in the text which are preceded by *the*. Ask students if they know why. Do the same for underlined nouns with zero article.

Ask students to work in pairs and complete the exercise.

No article used for:
individual islands: e.g. Mallorca
names of most countries: e.g. Spain, France, Germany, China
names of beaches: Alcudia Beach
names of cities/towns/regions: Palma de Mallorca, Algaida, Binissalem
names of mountains: Mount Everest, Mont Blanc
Use 'the' for:
groups of islands: the Balearic Islands
coastal areas: the Valencian Coast
oceans and seas: the Mediterranean Sea, the Persian Gulf
nationalities: the Spanish, the Omanis, the Chinese
countries which are Republics, Kingdoms or Unions:
the Republic of China, the United Kingdom (the UK),
the United States of America (the USA)
mountain ranges: the Tramuntanas, the Himalayas
geographical areas: the north east, the south west
Other geographical features:
lakes: no article, usually begins with the word Lake
(Lake Windermere)
rivers: definite article before name of river. Capitalise
the word 'river' or it can be omitted (the Thames,
the River Thames).

02 Ask students to write a short paragraph about an area of their own country. Make it clear to students that the purpose of writing is to prepare them for the IELTS style texts that they will read in later exercises.

03 Draw students' attention to the title. Ask them to work in pairs and predict what the main text could be about.

04 Ask students to complete Exercise 04.

Students' own answers

Alternative

Write the first sentence of the paragraph on the board. Encourage students to identify the main ideas in the sentence by asking questions (e.g.'What is special or different about the city of Auroville?'). Before students do this exercise, ask them to read the Bullet Box.

Advice

Students will need to know what a topic sentence is in order to attempt IELTS matching tasks. Explain / elicit the definition below:

Definition

Topic sentence: The sentence which conveys the main idea of a whole paragraph

Heading B seems to fit best, as it contains paraphrases of the sentence: designed = planned and built an imperfect world = today's world of conflict, greed and constant struggles for power an urban ideal = the ultimate model of unity, peace and harmony
Heading A: There is nothing in the sentence that matches 'always fail'.
Heading C: The sentence talks about 'peace and harmony', which contradicts the idea of 'conflict' in the heading.

05 Ask students to read the full paragraph and to check in pairs whether they think the heading is still the same.

Heading B is correct.

06 Ask students to complete Exercise 06 following the same procedure as before.

At this point, the best heading appears to be B: A city at the top of the world

07 Ask students to read the whole paragraph and to decide whether they still agree with their original choice.

The best heading is C: An unusual approach to regulation, because the paragraph talks about other examples of rules and laws that could be seen as unusual. It is not A –

> An unwelcoming place to die – because the text tells us that it is forbidden to die there.

08 Encourage students to identify the sentence that gives the main idea of the whole paragraph and to compare their ideas in pairs. Make it clear that the topic sentence is often, but not always the first sentence.

> But what really sets it apart is that it can also lay claim to some of the world's strangest rules.

09 Tell students that they are going to read the first sentence of another paragraph and find words or phrases that match the words underlined in the three options. Explain that in the IELTS reading exam they will need to find information in the text that supports the key words in the headings.

> **A** *regulation* = not allowed to build fences around their houses
> **B** *dangers of the wild* = the constant threat of visits from wild animals
> **C** *humans and animals* = lions and hippopotamuses [and] anxious residents; co-exist = residents are not allowed to … keep out their neighbours

10 Ask students to focus on the underlined adjectives and adverbs and look for information in the sentence that matches the underlined words and to decide which of the headings could be eliminated. Emphasise that this is a strategy that they can use in the exam.

> **A** An <u>unusual</u> approach to regulation – still possible as a correct answer, and you would need to read more of the paragraph to be sure.
> **B** Dealing with the occasional dangers of the wild – no longer possible as it contradicts 'the constant threat'.
> **C** Where humans and animals cautiously co-exist – most likely to be correct as it paraphrases the sentence.

11 Ask students to read the whole paragraph and check which heading correctly matches the idea of the whole paragraph.

> Heading C is correct.

12 Ask students to identify the topic sentence of the paragraph.

> Everywhere in Marloth Park, a wary understanding exists between man and beast.

13 Tell students to read the paragraph and to take some brief notes on the main ideas.

> Students' own notes

14 Ask students to look at their notes and to use them to identify the main idea of the paragraph and write a sentence giving the main idea of the paragraph.

Extension

Ask students to come and write their headings on the board and decide as a class on the best one.

Students then complete Exercise 14.

> Heading A – A conflict between reality and imitation – is correct.

15 Write the word 'pre' on the board and elicit its meaning from students (i.e. that it means 'before'). Write the first heading – 'an unusual approach to regulation' on the board. Ask students to identify which word in the heading contains a prefix.

Ask them to discuss the possible meaning of each prefix.

> un- = not opposite;
> im- = not;
> co- = together

Ask students to complete the rest of the examples in pairs.

16 Use the first prefix as a quick example to work through with the whole class. Ask students to work in groups of 3. Give each group a prefix from the list and ask them to list words that contain it and to work out their meaning.

> *un* = not/opposite; *im* = not; *co* = together
> *post* = after, behind – postgraduate, post-mortem, postpone
> *for-/fore-* = before – forecast, forward, forehead
> *sub* = under, below – submarine, subway, subtitle
> *multi* = many, much – multinational, multiply, multicultural
> *anti* = against, opposite – antivirus, antiseptic, antiperspirant
> *mis* = wrong, bad, badly – misunderstand, misjudge, misspell
> *non* = not – non-profit, non- fiction, nonsense
> *pre* = before – preview, prepay, prejudge
> *over* = above, too much – overload, overtake, oversleep
> *under* = below, not enough – underwater, underwear, underage

17 Work through the first example as a class. Write the sentence on the board and ask students to volunteer which prefix they think would best fit the context of the sentence.

Ask students to work through the remaining examples.

> A forewarned / pre-warned   B overpopulated
> C misinformed   D anti-government(al)

EXAM SKILLS

18 Tell students to read through the text quickly to get a general idea. Tell them not to look at the headings yet, as this will encourage them to focus on specific words, which may appear in the paragraph, but will not necessarily represent the main idea.

Alternative

Go through the first paragraph as a whole class. Ask students to carefully read paragraph A again, and to write down what they think its main idea is. Then ask them to refer to the headings and to try to select the correct one for paragraph A.

Ask students to work individually through the paragraphs following the same procedure. Before students do this exercise, ask them to read the Bullet Box at the start of the Matching Headings section.

Advice

Make students aware that there are two 'distractor' headings. Emphasise that if they focus on the paragraphs before looking at the headings, they will be less likely to be confused by the distractors.

Definition

Distractors: Extra heading in the IELTS reading heading matching task which do not match with any of the paragraphs.

It is good practice to give students a time limit to complete IELTS practice tasks, so that they can get used to working under exam conditions. Monitor as they are working through the task, in order to get an idea of how easy or difficult students are finding it.

| 1 ii | 2 vi | 3 iii | 4 v | 5 viii | 6 vii |

WRITING

OUTCOMES

- identify the main features of a line graph
- achieve a high score for Task Achievement
- describe and compare with adjectives and adverbs.

OUTCOMES

This lesson is linked to Part 1 of the IELTS writing test, which involves giving a written description of a graph, chart, map or process diagram. The first outcome is linked to one of the graphs that students may be asked to describe. The second outcome focuses on Task Achievement – one of the four criteria that will be used to measure students' performance in Writing Part 1. The third outcome concerns some of the key language that is frequently used for describing graphs and charts. These outcomes are all key requirements for IELTS Task 1.

LEAD-IN

01 Project an image of the simple chart in Exercise 1 onto the board. Ask students to work in pairs and discuss information about the chart (e.g. 'What type of chart is it?' 'What does it show' etc.). This will give you an idea of how familiar your students are with reading and interpreting information in charts. Ask students to work in pairs and complete the remaining tasks.

---

2 Between 1980 and 1990 sales grew rapidly to 90,000.

3 From 2020 to 2030 sales *will / are predicted to / are expected to grow rapidly* to 90,000.

4 By the year 2000, sales had grown rapidly to 90,000

5 By the year 2020, sales will have grown rapidly to 90,000.

---

02 Ask students to complete the next task as a pair activity.

Draw students' attention to the advice box on Part 1 Task Achievement. Ask them to read through it and then elicit the types of common mistake that may stop students from getting high marks. Then ask students to focus on the main questions that they should ask themselves when looking at a Part 1 task.

03 Ask students to work in pairs and complete Exercise 03.

Suggested answers

All three reasons have risen over the period. Overall, the number of people moving away from the capital city is on the up.

Traffic saw the steepest rise, particularly from 2000 to 2010.

Rising cost of living rose the least over the whole period and this reason was the only one to show any fall (2000–2010). However, in terms of numbers it was the main reason for moving to the countryside across the whole period by a significant margin.

The increase in people leaving for lifestyle reasons was steady across the whole period but relatively low.

---

04 Ask students to read the example answer, and to discuss with a partner why it would not have received a good mark for Task Achievement. Remind students to look back at the reasons students lose marks for this task from the previous exercise. Before students do this exercise, ask them to read the Tip for exercise 03

Advice

A good answer to Task 1 should include the following:

- A brief overview of the information shown in the graph, chart, map or process diagram.
- Several paragraphs highlighting key information or trends.
- A concluding paragraph which summarizes the main features.

Emphasize to students that they are not expected to speculate reasons why changes have occurred; they only need to comment on the data that appears in the task.

Suggested answers

Some of the data and categories are incorrectly reported. (Incorrect: The main reason was tra ic; 70,000 le in 2010)

The third paragraph does not include any data to support its arguments.

There is no concluding paragraph.

The answer is considerably less than 150 words.

The level of language is OK, but unlikely to impress the examiner.

Note: it is also recommended that when you write your introduction, you put it in your own words as this demonstrates the ability to paraphrase (Lexical Resource). This introduction borrows heavily from the question.

05 Ask students to read the second sample essay and to complete the task.

1 B	2 A	3 D	4 C

06 Students discuss the best summary in pairs, giving reasons for their choice.

A This is not a good conclusion: (a) to say 'people left the city for three main reasons' is not necessarily true: the graph did supply three reasons – however, there may have been others that were not included in the graph; (b) there is incorrect reporting of data, which should be 'between 1990 and 2010', not '1990 and 2000'. Also, life style did not change the least, given the fall between 2000 and 2010, rising cost of living changed the least for the whole period.

B This is the best conclusion. It is less mechanical than A, mentions the main features and expresses what had started to happen by the end of the period.

C The worst conclusion of all three. Not only has the candidate included data in their concluding paragraph, but it also repeats what has already been stated in the main body. The candidate does not 'step back' and present a summary of the main trends or features.

07 Encourage students to check the meaning of any unknown vocabulary, and then complete Exercise 07.

1 highest	2 overall	3 notable	4 consistent
5 stable	6 lowest	7 joint-lowest	

08 This task requires students to distinguish between objective and subjective adverbs for describing manner of change. Before students do this exercise, ask them to read the Tip.

Advice

It is important to encourage students to use appropriate academic register when responding to Writing Task 1, as this is linked to the Task Achievement criterion. A simple explanation would be that objective language concerns 'facts' whereas subjective language brings in the writer's feelings. An example could be demonstrated to clarify the difference e.g. numbers rose *abruptly* vs numbers rose *shockingly*. Ask students which of these adverbs represents a feeling, and then explain that this makes the language subjective.

Ask students to complete the exercise in pairs, and then nominate individuals to answer.

Inappropriate adverbs for a Task 1 essay: *amazingly, shockingly, surprisingly, predictably.*

The adverbs *significantly* and *noticeably* are arguably subjective, but *inconsistently* used in the correct way are not necessarily so:

The increase in people moving for a better quality of life is *significantly* higher than in the other categories.

The rise in people moving for a better quality of life is *noticeably* higher than in the other categories.

09 Turn students' attention to the example sentence in the students' book, then ask them to produce written descriptions in pairs. This will help to familiarise students with vocabulary that may be new to them, but which will be frequently used in writing Task 1.

Alternative

Provide students with some simple visual representations of line charts (these can be drawn on the board). Ask students to work in pairs. One student sits with their back to the board, while the other describes the line (not using the adverbs from Exercise 08). The students with their backs to the board have to work out which adverb from Exercise 08 is being described.

inconsistently: the line changes in a way that doesn't demonstrate an obvious pattern

significantly: the change showed by the line is marked or major, perhaps in comparison to another line on the graph

progressively: the change is slow and consistent

noticeably: the change showed by the line is clearly visible, especially in comparison to another line on the graph

gradually: the tendency to change on the graph is slow

sharply: the change indicated by the line is fast and dramatic

markedly: the change showed by the line is clearly visible, especially in comparison to another line on the graph

abruptly: the change indicated by the line is fast and dramatic

10 Emphasize the importance of using a range of grammatical structures in the response to Task 1, as this will result in achieving a better score for *Grammatical Range and Accuracy*. Turn students' attention to the example exercise. Ask them to identify the parts of speech in the second sentence, and whether it is necessary to add any other words (e.g. *The*).

Ask students to work in pairs and complete the rest of the exercise.

Sample answers

2 Traffic experienced a steady rise as a reason for moving to the countryside between 1990 and 2000

3 but then increased markedly between 2000 and 2010.

4 The number of people moving to the countryside for lifestyle reasons saw a consistent growth across the whole period shown in the graph.

EXAM SKILLS

11 Tell students that they are going to attempt an IELTS Task 1 response to a line chart.

Remind students of the 4 questions that they should ask themselves about the information in the line chart that they read about in the tip box in Exercise 03. Elicit that these questions relate to the Task Achievement criterion. Set a time limit and ask students to complete the task individually. Before students do this exercise, ask them to read the Tip from Exercise 10.

Advice

It is good practice to ask students to work individually on the task and to give them a time limit, as this will give them a more authentic experience of exam practice. Tell students that they will be penalized for being over or under the word limit of 150 words.

Feedback

If there is time before taking the papers in, you could ask students to peer-assess a partner's answer. Peer assessment is a useful way of raising students' awareness of the strengths and weaknesses of a particular piece of writing, which will help them to develop their own writing skills. As students can find peer-assessment difficult if they are unused to it, it may be useful to provide them with a checklist.

e.g.

- Has the writer described the information in the chart accurately?
- Has the writer identified key trends?
- Has the writer used a good range of vocabulary for describing trends?
- Has the writer used a range of grammatical structures?

Refer students to the IELTS criteria specifically for bands 7 and 8 in the introduction to the Teachers' Book. Tell them to firstly determine whether they fully meet the criteria for band 7 and then check if they surpass it and can be judged to meet the grade 8 criteria.

Sample answer

The line graph sets out the key motivations for people relocating to the capital of a specific country between 2000 and 2015.

Moving for the purpose of study saw the greatest rise overall, with a jump of approximately 62,000. It rose considerably in two periods – from 2000 to 2005 (by 22,000), and then again from 2010 to 2015 (by 33,000), with a more gentle growth of around 7,000 in between.

Elsewhere, the figure of people relocating for work began at 61,000 in 2000, then peaked at 92,000 in 2010 – the highest of any reason, in any year – before finishing as the joint-highest in 2015 (87,000 – on a level with those relocating in order to study). Notably, this category was the only one of the four that underwent a downturn.

Turning to 'adventure', this category rose the most stably and steadily of all four categories, from 11,000 to 15,000 over the fifteen-year period. Meanwhile, the number of people relocating for 'family and friends' reasons climbed gently in the first five years (12,000 to 14,000), followed by an upswing to 22,000, before eventually levelling o at around 23,000 in 2015.

All in all, the graph tells us that, 'employment' aside, there was an increase in each of the four reasons for moving over the period in question, with the greatest rise occurring in those citing study as the main motivating factor. (212 words)

Extension

Ask students to work in pairs and look at the sample answer. Go over the three criteria that students considered in the lesson (*Task Achievement*, *Lexical Resource* and *Grammatical Range and Accuracy*) and ask students to apply these criteria to the sample answer.

LISTENING

OUTCOMES

- successfully deal with Part 1 form completion tasks
- correctly understand names and numbers
- develop your paraphrasing skills for multiple-choice questions
- understand and use future time conditionals.

OUTCOMES

Ask students to focus on the outcomes. The first outcome helps students with the form completion task in Part 1 of the listening test. This lesson will help students develop strategies to best complete this task. The second outcome focuses on correctly identifying names and numbers when listening. Remind students that spelling is very important in IELTS exams and that there are certain ways of expressing information in English. This lesson will help students do this better. The third outcome helps students to recognise paraphrases and synonyms for multiple-choice questions. In IELTS listening tasks, it is common for the recording to use different words to the questions and students need to be able to cope with this. The final outcome helps students to understand future time conditionals when they hear them. This will also make it easier for students to be able to use this grammatical structure.

LEAD-IN

01 This exercise helps to prepare students for the topic of the lesson. Give students a few minutes to discuss this and generate class discussion during feedback. Ask students to give reasons and to comment on other students' answers.

02 The focus on city tour vocabulary will help students identify the differences between similar words. This will help when students need to identify synonyms or paraphrases when listening. After students discuss this in pairs, encourage student discussion during feedback before you confirm the answers.

1 *book* and *reserve* are synonyms; *select* means to choose or decide.
2 *discount* and *reduction* are synonyms; *bargain* means that you get something for a very favourable price.

3 There are no synonyms here; a *curator* is someone who organises the exhibits in a gallery or museum; a *presenter* is someone who introduces a television or radio show; a *guide* is someone whose job is to show a place to visitors or tourists.

4 *visitors* and *guests* are synonyms; *explorers* travel to new and unknown places. You can explore a museum, but you cannot be a museum explorer.

5 the *front desk* and *main entrance* are synonyms here; the guard room is more likely to be in a prison and not a place where you show your tickets.

6 *explore* and *wander* around are synonyms here; *navigate* means to direct the course of a vehicle, such as a ship.

7 *pick us up* and *collect us* are synonyms; *let us* on means allow us to board the bus.

03 Ask students to look at the advice given. Make sure students are aware that they may need to identify when an idea is expressed differently when listening compared to the questions but that students must use the exact word they hear. Highlight the need for correct spelling. This exercise prepares students for the listening task in the next exercise by allowing them to discuss possible answers and synonyms for each gap.

Suggested answers
1 adjective (the earliest, ancient, prehistoric)
2 adjective (ancient, prehistoric, early)
3 plural or collective noun (treasure, objects, items, scenes, displays)
4 adjective or noun (present day, contemporary, current day)
5 ordinal number or adjective (22nd, twenty-second, next, forthcoming)

04 Students now have the opportunity to practise identifying synonyms and paraphrases when listening. Make sure students are aware that they cannot write more than two words for each answer.

1 ancient   2 prehistoric   3 objects
4 Contemporary   5 22nd / twenty-second

Transcript 02

Guide: Ladies and gentlemen, welcome to the Museum of London Life. My name's Peter, and I'll be your guide taking you through your exciting visit, which lasts for approximately ninety minutes, and traces the history of this vast and ever-changing city. But before we eventually arrive back here in the present, we begin our walk in ancient London, where we're going to take a look at life from the point of view of prehistoric men, women and children, looking at how they lived thousands of years ago, when all this around us was fields. At this point, London was little more than a few settlements dotted about here and there. Certainly nothing like the metropolis you see surrounding you today. So, from there, the walk allows you to see the city grow as you progress through the exhibits and take in the fascinating pieces of history that have been found and donated to the museum over the years – including maps, photos, images and thousands of other objects here. And finally, when we leave the part of the exhibition called 'Contemporary London', we'll move away from our present, here in the 21st century and head o into the 22nd.

05 Students can now read the script as well as listen again. This will help them to identify what words have been paraphrased and what synonyms have been used. This is a good way for students to see the actual different expressions used.

1 *exciting visit, which … traces the history of this vast and ever-changing city*
2 *life from the point of view of prehistoric men, women and children*
3 *when all this around us was fields*
4 *take in the fascinating pieces of history*
5 *we'll move away from our present, here in the 21st century and head off into the 22nd*

06 Ask students to read the advice box. Make sure they are aware that Part/Section 1 of the listening test is the least difficult and that they should aim to score as much as possible as the later sections of the test will be more challenging. This exercise allows students to prepare for the listening and you should recommend that they should try to predict the missing words in the test. During feedback, you don't need to confirm answers but it is a good idea to see if other students agree or not.

07 Students have the opportunity to practise filling in the form. Ask students to compare their answers before you give feedback. Remind students that spelling is important here.

1 James Graeme	2 16 Mount Hill	3 E15 2TP
4 770 464	5 15/fifteen	6 15/fifteen
7 4/four	8 (£)4.25	9 Underground
10 12/12th/twelfth		

Transcript 03

Museum employee:	Hello, The Museum of London Life. How can I help?
James:	Oh, hi, I was wondering if I you could send me some information. I've been looking on your website and can't seem to find what I need to know.
Museum employee:	Certainly, sir. Can I take your name first of all?
James:	Yes, it's James Graeme.
Museum employee:	Ah, okay…so that's G-R-A-H-A-M, correct?
James:	No, it's G-R-A-E-M-E.
Museum employee:	OK, great. Got there in the end. So, how can I help?
James:	Well, it says that I can print off some vouchers for reduced entry, but I haven't got a printer. Could you send me some through the post?

Museum employee:	Sure. What's your address?
James:	16, Mount Hill Road, – that's M-O-U-N-T Hill Road, London, E-fifteen-2-T-P.
Museum employee:	Okay. Can I take a contact number for you for our records?
James:	Yes, it's -Double 7-Oh, 3-6-4. Sorry, I mean Double 7-7-Oh, 4-6-4
Museum employee:	OK, great. I'll get some vouchers sent out to you.
James:	Thanks. Could you just clarify what the discount structure is?
Museum employee:	Of course. So, for groups of four or more there is a ten percent discount applied. If you manage to get together a larger gang of people – ten or more, to be precise – then that figure goes up to fifteen percent.
James:	And what about students like me? Anything extra?
Museum employee:	Yes, all students get that same 15 percent discount automatically, but in groups of four or more that goes up by another 5 to 20%. Would you be coming with friends?
James:	No, I think the likelihood is that I'll be on my own. So how much exactly would that cost me for entry?
Museum employee:	That's four twenty-five
James:	So with the discount that makes… three pounds sixty-one, doesn't it?
Museum employee:	No, sorry, that price was with the discount already applied.
James:	Oh, OK. And are there any special exhibitions at the moment? I'll book tickets for that as well today, provided there's something special that I'm particularly interested in.
Museum employee:	There is, actually. You've just missed a really popular one that took in the Viking period, and coming up we've got the period known as 'The Industrial Revolution', but the one we're currently running one called Underground London, which looks at the tunnels, sewers, and catacombs beneath the streets of the city.
James:	Great! Ideally, I'd like to visit on my birthday, the thirteenth of July.
Museum employee:	Let me check…No, that's a Monday. We're closed on Mondays.
James:	Ah, that's a shame. Never mind, I'll come the day before. Can I book over the phone now?
Museum employee:	Certainly, so that's one student ticket for the 12th. Let me take your payment details.

08 Ask students to read the tip. Tell students that there are certain ways that information is expressed in English and by knowing this that they can get higher marks and not make as many mistakes. The exercise tests students' existing knowledge of this. Put students into pairs or small groups to do this and encourage discussion during feedback before confirming answers.

1 B	2 A,C	3 A	4 C	5 B	6 C	7 A,B	8 B

Extension

Prepare a document with the following – you can choose alternatives but try to use the categories in Exercise 08. Ask students to work in pairs to say how they should be said in English.

Telephone Number

662 005 005

Period

21st Century

Year

1978

Date

31/10/80

Name

Smith-Peters

Price

£12.99

citybreaks@travel.com

Time

16.00

09 This exercise focuses again on identifying synonyms or paraphrased information but this time within a multiple-choice question context. Ask students to read the Bullet Box. Tell students that it's a good idea to think about how the possible answers could be rephrased before students start to listen. This exercise gives students practice of this. Tell students to read the example to help them.

Suggested answers

1 *show to collect his ticket* – produce in order to be able to enter, have as proof of identity to get his ticket
passport – identification document, ID
debit card – bank card, payment card
smartphone – no obvious synonym except telephone/phone

2 *most appreciates* – likes the most/best, thinks is the most important, is most impressed by, thinks is key
designed – structured, put together, connected, linked, built talks about *the city's inhabitants* – shows/paints a picture of the life of city dwellers / citizens / the local people *is involved in fundraising for the local community* – does local charity work, raises money for local causes, donates money to worthwhile community organisations

10 Before students listen to check their answers, ask them to read the exam advice. Tell students not to write down the first answer they hear as the speaker may change what they say. Ask students to compare their answers in pairs before class feedback is provided.

1 B	2 B

Transcript 04

Museum employee:	Your pre-printed ticket will be available to collect as soon as you arrive at the front desk.
James:	So, I should bring my passport, then, for proof of ID?
Museum employee:	People usually have a copy of their booking on their email, and they just show this on their smartphones and go straight through. But if, for some reason, you can't get any internet connection here, you obviously can't pull up your ticket details to show the museum assistant. But you'll get your tickets fine, as long as you can produce the payment card you bought the tickets with. That's the only ID we need to see.
James:	Great. Well, thanks for all your help today. Anything you'd recommend personally? What do you like most about the museum?
Museum employee:	One very important thing is that the museum here has formed some extremely worthwhile partnerships with a wide range of local charities. In London, like any capital city, there are a lot of social problems, and the museum's help in reaching out to the world outside is greatly appreciated by so many. But what is so good for visitors – and is absolutely key for me – is that, as you walk through from one room to another, you always, always get a real sense of who has lived here over the years, and what sort of people they are, or have been. And that's really easy to do, because the way the exhibition designers have connected each section to the next with a real sense of development and design. It just flows so well from one room to the next, better than any other museum I've been into, certainly.
James:	Wow. You really like it there, don't you?
Museum employee:	Absolutely. Unless something dramatic happens, I should be working here for a long time.

11 This exercise gives students the opportunity to analyse the language structures used and order of information given by the speaker. This will help students to understand more about how this particular task in the listening test may be structured.

> *Question 1*
>
> 1 The options are mentioned in the order A C B.
> 2 Option A: 'So, I should bring my passport, then, for proof of ID?' Option B: 'But you'll get your tickets fine as long as you can produce the payment card you bought the tickets with. That's the only ID we need to see.' Option C: 'People usually have a copy of their booking on their email, and they just show this on their smartphones and go straight through.
>
> *Question 2*
>
> 1 The options are mentioned in the following order: C B A
> 2 Option A: *because of the way the exhibition designers have connected each section to the next with a real sense of development and design. It just flows so well from one room to the next. Better than any other museum I've been into, certainly.*
>
> Option B: *But what's so good for visitors – and is absolutely key for me – is that, as you walk through from one room to another, you always, always get a real sense of who has lived here over the years, and what sort of people they are, or have been.*
>
> Option C: *One important thing is that the museum here has formed some extremely worthwhile partnerships with a wide range of local charities. In London, like any capital city, there are a lot of social problems, and the museum's help in reaching out to the world outside is greatly appreciated by so many.*

12 This exercise uses sentences from the unit in order to analyse them in terms of grammatical structure. This is a good idea as students already understand the context. If you feel students need more help with this, write the first question on the board and invite answers from the class.

> Cause underlined
>
> 1 <u>I'll book tickets for that as well today</u>, provided there is something special that I'm particularly interested in.
> 2 <u>You'll get your tickets fine</u>, as long as you can produce the payment card you bought the tickets with.
> 3 Once we leave the part of the exhibition called 'Contemporary London', <u>we will move into the 22nd century</u>.
> 4 <u>Unless something dramatic happens</u>, I should be working here for a long time.

13 This exercise provides further linguistic analysis – this time focusing on the future time word. Ask students to do this in pairs and then provide feedback and confirmation of answers after encouraging class discussion of the possible answers.

14 Students now can use their existing knowledge of the examples from the sentences in the previous 2 exercises to identify the grammatical patterns for first conditional. You may want to confirm that students are aware of what is meant by both terms by providing examples. In addition, you may want to ask students to create example sentences and you can then concept check that all students are aware of the correct structure and usage.

> Future time conditionals follow the same structure as the *first* conditional:
>
> *If* + present simple … / … *will* + bare infinitive.
>
> Note that all present tenses are possible in the *If* clause, although the present simple is the most commonly used. In the result clause, instead of *will* we can use *be going to* and other modal verbs such as *can, should* and *must*. We can also use an imperative in the result clause.

15 This exercise provides students with practice of this language structure. Ask students to complete this exercise in pairs before providing class feedback. Ask students to comment on their classmate's answers before you confirm if they are correct or not.

> Sample answers
> 1 You can get a discounted ticket as long as you show your student card.
> 2 Once everybody has bought their ticket, we will go to the first exhibit room.
> 3 You won't get lost provided you use the map you were given.
> 4 Now everybody is free to explore the museum. You can go wherever you like as long as you return to the main entrance for 4 pm.
> 5 Your bus back to the hotel will depart as soon as everybody is on board.
> 6 Do not touch or take photos of the exhibits unless there is a sign saying that it is allowed.

Extension

You can provide students with further practice of this by recording your own answers and then playing these full sentences for students to listen to and note down. Alternatively, you can ask other students to read out their sentences while students note down the answer. You can vary this by using the same language structures in different contexts.

EXAM SKILLS

16 Students now have the opportunity to practise the skills they have developed in this unit. You can do this under conditions similar to the listening test and then ask students to compare their answers after or you can ask students to discuss strategies before doing the exercise.

Transcript 05

You will hear a conversation between an employee at a removals company and a man who is planning to move to London. First you have some time to look at questions 1 to 6.

[pause]

Now listen carefully and answer questions 1 to 6.

Woman:	Good afternoon, We-Move-U, how can I help you?
Man:	Hello, there. I'd like some help with my move to London. I'm currently living a long way away in the southwest of the UK, is that an area you cover?
Woman:	Yes, we cover all of the UK, so that is no problem. Can I take your name first, please?
Man:	Yes, it's Mr. David Cottenham.
Woman:	C-O-T-N-A-M?
Man:	No, it's <u>C-O-T-T-E-N-H-A-M</u>.
Woman:	Okay, Mr. Cottenham, you said that you live in Devon…
Man:	Yes, at 4 West Cottage in Humblington. It's a small town near Exton. Well, it's more of a village really.
Woman:	Mm-hm, and the postcode there, please, so I can look up exactly where you are?
Man:	<u>D-V-12 8-H-A</u>.
Woman:	Okay, I've found your home on the system here. My goodness, that is very much in the countryside, isn't it?
Man:	Yes, it is. London is going to be a bit of a shock for me. It's so crowded.
Woman:	Well, it can be, but it depends where you live. What address are you moving to?
Man:	<u>8b Greenend</u> Road, E19 4RR. 'Greenend' is one word.
Woman:	Well, that area is one of the quieter parts of London, at least. Not as busy as other places, certainly. When are you looking to move?
Man:	30th August.
Woman:	That's good for us. People are on their summer holidays, children are not at school…so there is less traffic on the roads. What sort of time are you thinking of leaving?
Man:	Around half seven would be good.
Woman:	That may be difficult, because our staff need a lot of time to pack your things into the van.

	They will need to start in the middle of the night if you want to leave that early…
Man:	No, no, I mean <u>half seven in the evening</u>.
Woman:	Oh, I see. We can do that. And do you want to take out insurance, in case there is any damage to your property?
Man:	Yes, I think so. I've looked at everything I own, and I think that it's all worth about forty thousand pounds in total.
Woman:	Shall we say a little bit more, just in case? I know you probably think it will be much more expensive to take a higher amount, but the difference in what you pay for forty thousand or fifty thousand in insurance is actually just a few pounds. It's ten pounds higher for fifty thousand, and fifteen pounds higher for sixty thousand.
Man:	Yes, OK. Make it fifty thousand. <u>No, on second thoughts sixty thousand</u>. So, how much do you think the relocation will cost in total?
Woman:	Let me check…I think we can do everything for approximately £2,000. That figure may change, of course – it's just an estimate for now – but it gives you a good idea of the price you will have to pay.
Man:	That's pretty good, actually. I was expecting a lot more?
Woman:	Would you like to book now? Or shall I take your mobile number? I can call you back tomorrow, after you've had some time to think about it, maybe?
Man:	Sure, it's oh-seven-two-three-eight, <u>two double-four, five-one-oh</u>.
Woman:	Great. I'll speak to you tomorrow. And if you have any other questions, either call us back on the number you first dialled, or have a look at our website.
Man:	What's the website address, please?
Woman:	<u>www-dot, we-hyphen-move-hyphen-u, (that's the letter u, not the word 'you')</u> dot-co-dot-uk.
Man:	Okay, thanks for your help. I'll speak to you tomorrow.

Before you hear the rest of the conversation you have some time to look at questions 7 to 9.

[pause]

Now listen and answer questions 7 to 9.

Woman:	Hello, Mr Cottenham, it's Maria here from We-Move-You. How are you?
Man:	Oh, hi there. Yes, I'm very well. I've actually been thinking about our conversation yesterday. You said that the total cost of the package with insurance would be around £2,000. Does that insurance cover everything?
Woman:	It depends what you mean by 'everything'. That is how much our 'Silver' package would cost, and as well as insurance for anything that gets broken or damaged, it also covers your costs if our delivery drivers are late getting to London.
Man:	Are there any other packages?
Woman:	Yes, our 'Economy' cover is the same as 'Silver', but without the cover for late arrival, and that would cost you around £1,800. Our 'Premium' package has the same insurance as 'Silver', but on top of that our removals team men come and pack all your things, put everything into boxes for you.
Man:	And that's the 'Premium'? Hmm, I guess that's quite a benefit. How much is that?
Woman:	It would be £2,500 for this job. So shall we agree on 'Premium'?
Man:	Hmmm…no, <u>let's stick with 'Silver'</u>. If your drivers are late, it doesn't affect us. Actually, I've been looking at some reviews of your company online. Generally very good – the thing that seems to impress most people is the cost.
Woman:	Well, yes, I think most people are surprised by our low prices. Others believe that our level of customer care is the best thing about us, and I have also seen some reviews where people are most impressed by how quickly we complete the job. I agree with everything they say, of course, <u>but I am probably most proud of our reputation for customer care and satisfaction</u>.
Man:	Great. Well, I think that's everything. Oh, one final question – once I make the booking, will I have to pay more if I need to make any changes?
Woman:	In most cases, there is nothing extra that you will need to pay once your initial payment is completed. Unless, that is, you decide to cancel the booking completely – in that case, there will a charge of 10 percent of the total fee if you cancel less than 15 days before the date of the move. And if you need to move the date, for any reason, we will usually do that for a very low cost.
Man:	Fantastic. Great. Well, I think I'm ready to book.

Extension

As previously done in this unit, provide students with another opportunity to listen and read the tape script in order for students to analyse both the language used in terms of paraphrasing, synonyms and grammatical structures as well as order of information provided. This will help students better prepare for the listening test.

SPEAKING

OUTCOMES

Ask students to focus on the outcomes. This lesson is linked to Parts 1, 2 and 3 of the IELTS speaking test. The first outcome helps students to understand the structure and format of the test. The second outcome follows on from this and helps students to analyse examples of student responses in the test in order to understand what they should and should not do when answering. The final outcome focuses on a specific grammatical feature (future time conditionals). This will help students to respond more accurately and to gain greater marks for grammatical range when answering in the speaking test. Future time conditionals are a relatively complex and high level grammatical feature and accurate use of this will be rewarded in the test.

LEAD-IN

01 This exercise aims to identify what students already know about the IELTS speaking test and to help them understand what format the speaking test will have. In addition, it will help to familiarise what the examiner expectations are. If you feel that students need a little more time before they do this exercise, give students 3-4 minutes to discuss in pairs what they already know about the speaking test. After this time, invite student responses but do not confirm answers. Instead, ask students to comment on other students' contributions. This will generate a class debate. Then ask students to complete the exercise.

| 1 B | 2 C | 3 C | 4 B | 5 C | 6 C | 7 A | 8 A |

02 This exercise gives students the opportunity to give their own opinions about the test and encourages them to identify what they are good at and what they will need more support with when preparing for the speaking test. After pairs discuss this, invite students to give their opinions to the class and encourage other students to comment.

Students' own answers

03 This exercise focuses only on Part 1 of the speaking test. Before students do this exercise, explain to students that Part 1 questions focus on general familiar topics that reflect students' everyday life rather than complex or abstract questions. Ask students to complete this exercise in pairs. This will allow you to monitor.

The following questions would not be asked: 2, 3, 5, 7

04 Before students complete this exercise, ask them to work in pairs to think of 3-5 pieces of good advice for students doing Part 1. Before students do this exercise, ask them to read the Tip.

Advice

- Never memorise complete answers to questions BEFORE the exam. It is normally obvious to examiners when a candidate does this and it may affect your score.
- Aim to show a variety of verb forms and grammar structures – but they must be correct if you want a high score.
- Vary your vocabulary. Use synonyms and paraphrase to express your ideas using different words.

This will help students when doing this exercise. Ask students to listen first and then to discuss their answers in pairs afterwards. Tell students to focus on bad practice.

These answers are not likely to impress the examiner.

Question 1: The candidate repeats the word 'apartment' several times. She could improve this by using reference words like 'it' and 'one', and the flow of her answer would improve (along with her score for Fluency and Coherence).

Question 2: The language used is very good, but it doesn't answer the question. It is highly likely to be a memorised answer, which should be avoided completely – the vocabulary is not relevant to the topic at all. This limits the score for both Fluency and Coherence and Lexical Resource.

Question 3: There are several problems with the grammar used; these would limit the score the candidate might get for Grammatical Range and Accuracy.

Transcript 06

Examiner: In this first part of the exam, I'd like to ask you some questions about yourself. Let's talk about where you live. Do you live in a house or an apartment?

Candidate 1: Apartment. It's a small apartment in the centre of my home town, but it's still bigger than the apartment I live in now. My apartment now is just one room, really. I used to live in a huge apartment, but it was my parents' apartment and it was time for me to go to university. I left, found a place. And that's the apartment where I live now.

Examiner: What do you like about the area where you live?

Candidate 2: I used to live in Guangzhou, the capital city of Guangdong Province in south-eastern China. Once an important stop-off point on the maritime Silk Road, Guangzhou maintains to this day its importance as a major port and transportation hub.

Examiner: Do you often visit parks in your city?

Candidate 3: Actually, I have gone to my local park last week. I've really enjoyed it. I have a friend, he never been to my town, so yesterday we have decided to go together next week. We will go on next Tuesday, I think. As soon as we will finish class, we will go.

Extension

Ask students to take it in turns to role-play the same questions from the recording. Put students into pairs. Tell student A to ask the exact questions that the examiner asks. Ask student B to create their own answers. Then ask students to swap roles. Monitor as students do this and note down any common errors or points you wish to talk about in class feedback.

Feedback

Using the notes you made, you can write on the board examples good practice and not so good practice that you heard when monitoring. Mix these up and ask students to identify whether the examples are positive or negative. This is a good way to respond to emerging learners' needs.

05 This exercise focuses on Part 2 and helps students to familiarise themselves with the task required of them. Encourage students to discuss their answer and to give reasons.

Task card A

06 In this exercise, students evaluate an example response. This will help them to identify how to divide up their time when answering this task in the test. Before students do this exercise, ask them to read the Tip.

Advice

In each Part 2 question, you do not need to try and give equal time to each of the four prompts. Some prompts will be easier to expand on than others.

As before, play the recording and give students some time to discuss their answers in pairs or small groups.

> This candidate talked about all four points, exploring three of them in some detail. He used a good range of vocabulary and grammar; the organisation of the answer was also very good indeed, and the long turn flowed naturally from one idea to the next. It is not important that he spoke about the third prompt only very briefly, as he clearly had decided to spend more time on the points he felt he could expand on more easily, and in more detail.

Transcript 07

Candidate: So, I'm going to tell you about a town in the Lake District, which is a beautiful region in the north-west of England, pretty close to the border of Scotland. There are dozens of fantastic little villages and towns there, but the one that tops the rest is called Windermere. It sits on a huge lake and is surrounded by hills, trees and rocks. I've been lots of times already, and I can't wait to go back – as soon as I finish the second semester at university, I'm going to head up there again.

Being far up in the north, as you can imagine, it can get pretty cold in Windermere, particularly in winter. Too cold for some. Having said that, there is a real stark beauty to the town at that time, when your breath comes out like mist, and

the streets get white with the snow that falls. Summer is the opposite extreme – it can actually get pretty warm, comfortable enough to wear just a t-shirt and shorts – but if you wanted to visit at that time, you'd have to get yourself prepared for all the tourists. Other times? Autumn is pretty, I've been told, but I tend to visit in spring.

I go every year, just me; I have to say that I generally prefer not to go with anyone else. For one thing, you can make friends really easily if you stay in a hostel. There are young people from all over the world who make it their mission to spend a few days or a week there. As I say, it's an ideal place to go hiking or hill-walking, so that's the priority for me and for hundreds of others. There are also a really interesting variety of independent local shops, selling everything from cheap souvenirs to galleries full of extremely expensive art. When I go back, I'm going to do what I always do – browsing through the shops after a long day walking in the countryside.

Extension

Ask students to take it in turns to complete the example Part 2 test above. In pairs, ask student A to speak first and for student B to listen and give feedback after student A finishes. Encourage students to be constructive in their comments. Then ask students to swap. Monitor and make notes as students do this.

Feedback

Using the notes you made, you can write on the board examples good practice and not so good practice that you heard when monitoring. Mix these up and ask students to identify whether the examples are positive or negative.

07 This exercise gives students the opportunity to listen to a good example of responses to Part 3 of the speaking test in order to analyse them in more detail in the following exercise.

1 D	2 E	3 A	4 C	5 B

Transcript 08

Candidate: (Answer 1) For a number of reasons. Often, I think, because they are exhausted; capital cities in particular can be very demanding places to live – the noise, the traffic, the cost of living – and people o en grow tired of all that. It's just too over the top for some. They start to feel drawn to the peace and quiet that rural life might be able to give them. Generally speaking, though, I do think that it is the case that younger people – people like me – are more drawn to that vibrant, city lifestyle. As soon as you get older and have a family, you start thinking it's time to move.

(Answer 2) Well, one possibility that I can foresee is that buildings will keep getting taller and taller. This has been going on for some time, all over the world, and so many people now are moving to the city. Unless this changes, we are going to need more and more homes for everyone. We might even see a 500-storey skyscraper one day. That might sound ridiculous now, but cities are likely to keep expanding at the rate they are currently, so there will be no other option that I can think of.

(Answer 3) Oh, I think that would be a bit of a disaster, to be honest. Insisting that everyone uses public transport could create more problems than currently exist. Fine, if you were just visiting the city it probably wouldn't bother you too much, but if you were a resident there...then again, the streets would be safer for pedestrians. And it might do something about the levels of pollution. I do think it is bound to happen, to be honest. So, as long as people are happy to use buses and bikes instead of their cars, life will continue as normal.

(Answer 4) I can understand why people want a huge, old-fashioned house. In the similar way to living in the middle of the bright lights of the big city, there is something quite romantic about it. Having said that, I do think it does depend on your age. Most people of my age, for example, prefer the idea of coming home to a smart, modern apartment every day, high up in the sky, overlooking the city, well – it just sounds amazing. Providing I make enough money, I'll definitely be on a top floor myself one day.

(Answer 5) Well, in the old days, your whole life was in one place. You married someone from the same town, you had a job in the same village, and your family stayed around you. In some places, life is still like that – people only need to go next door or downstairs to see their parents, for example – but a er people were given the opportunity to move around from one town to another, on trains or even aeroplanes, the traditional family unit started to change, I think, and people are now much more spread out. Not just nationally, but internationally. By the time I'm a grandparent, I think it will be even more different.

08 Students are able to analyse the responses in more detail here. The specific focus of this exercise is to make students aware of the connection between the function of what is said and the grammar used. Before students do this exercise, ask them to read the Tip.

Advice

Thinking about the function of the question being asked will help you to develop your answer and decide what language and structures to use.

A iii	B v	C ii	D iv	E i

09 This exercise gives students the opportunity to understand some of the marking criteria and comments made about the example answer they have just listened to and read. This will help students to identify what they need to do to provide good responses in this part of the speaking test. Let students discuss this in pairs.

1 P	2 GRA	3 FC	4 GRA	5 LR	6 FC
7 P	8 LR	9 FC			

10 This exercise gives students another opportunity to listen and to better understand the feedback given.

Extension

Ask students to take it in turns to complete the example Part 3 test above. Put students into pairs. Tell student A to ask the exact questions that the examiner asks. Ask student B to create their own answers. Then ask students to swap roles. Monitor as students do this and note down any common errors or points you wish to talk about in class feedback.

Feedback

Using the notes you made, you can write on the board examples of good practice and not so good practice that you heard when monitoring. Mix these up and ask students to identify whether the examples are positive or negative.

11 This exercise links back to the student's answer from the example Part 1 response and connects to the grammar focus of this lesson. Encourage students to discuss this in pairs.

The grammar is incorrect: *As soon as we will finish class, we will go.*

This is the grammatical structure o en known as the first conditional (*If* + present tense, *will* + bare infinitive) but with *As soon as* instead of *If*.

12 This exercise connects back to the Part 3 example above and focuses on the grammar used for future conditionals. Ask students to discuss their answers in pairs first. Then play the recording for students to check their answers.

A As long as	**B** By the time	**C** Providing that
D As soon as	**E** Unless	

Transcript 09

A   As long as people are happy to use buses and bikes instead of their cars, life will continue as normal.

B   By the time I'm a grandparent, I think it will be even more different.

C   Providing I make enough money, I'll definitely be on a top floor myself one day.

D   As soon as you get older and have a family, you start thinking it's time to move.

E   Unless this changes, we are going to need more and more homes for everyone.

13 Students have the opportunity now to analyse the grammar used in order to be aware why certain language choices have been made in the recording and what would happen if alternative words were used. Ask students to do this in pairs

and then encourage a class discussion before confirming answers. After going through the answers, you may wish to ask concept check questions to make sure that all students understand.

> 1 *Unless* suggests that the speaker sees the changes as completely necessary, but they doubt whether the changes will ever happen. On the other hand, *Once* suggests that the speaker sees the changes as certain to happen, with a natural result (which they give). Using *Once* in this sentence is still grammatically correct and logical. However it wouldn't work in the answer given by the candidate.
>
> 2 *When* suggests the speaker believes that people will definitely, at some point, be happy to use buses and bikes instead of their cars (A), and that she will definitely, at some point, make enough money to buy a top-floor flat (C). *As long as* and *Provided that* both suggest that the speaker is not convinced that the result given in each case is definite – people may not be happy about using buses and bikes; she may not ever earn enough money to buy the top- floor flat.
>
> 3 Sentence D is different. The speaker is not thinking about the future in particular, but is stating something as a constant fact (in their opinion). The structure is a *zero conditional* (present simple / present simple), whereas the other sentences use the *first conditional* (present simple / *will* + bare infinitive).

14 This exercise uses the sentences from the previous exercise but the focus here is on pronunciation.

Advice

In order to get a high score for pronunciation, it is important to know how to use natural word and sentence stress. Normally the syllables of words which carry the main meaning are those which are stressed and grammar words which are not.

B By the time I'm a grandparent, I think it will be even more different.

C Providing that I make enough money, I'll definitely be on a top floor myself one day.

D As soon as you get older and have a family, you start thinking it's time to move.

E Unless this changes, we are going to need more and more homes for everyone.

15 This exercise gives students the opportunity to practise repeating the sentences with the correct pronunciation. Students can do this in pairs with the non-speaking partner giving feedback. Nominate students to try saying the sentences in front of the class and encourage other students to comment and correct if necessary.

Alternative

If students have smartphones, you could ask them to record their sentences and then to listen again at home and then try to improve the pronunciation by listening again to the model and re-recording.

EXAM SKILLS

16 Exercises 16-18 provide students with an opportunity to practise all 3 parts of the speaking test focusing on the topic of towns and cities. In this exercise, ask students to take it in turns to ask and answer Part 1 questions. Monitor as students do this and take notes of any common errors or points you wish to talk about in class feedback.

Feedback

Using the notes you made, you can write on the board examples of good practice and not so good practice that you heard when monitoring. Mix these up and ask students to identify whether the examples are positive or negative.

17 This exercise provides practice of Part 2 of the speaking exam. Make sure students are aware of the procedure and encourage them to spend one minute preparing notes. If you feel students would benefit from comparing notes, you can allow students to discuss their notes in pairs before speaking. Ask students to take turns completing this exercise and to give each other constructive feedback. As before, monitor as students do this and take notes of any common errors or points you wish to talk about in class feedback.

Feedback

Using the notes you made, you can write on the board examples of good practice and not so good practice that you heard when monitoring. Mix these up and ask students to identify whether the examples are positive or negative.

Refer students to the IELTS criteria specifically for bands 7 and 8 in the introduction to the Teachers' Book. Tell them to firstly determine whether they fully meet the criteria for band 7 and then check if they surpass it and can be judged vto meet the grade 8 criteria.

Extension

Ask students to record their answers on a smartphone and to re-record it at home. This can then be emailed to you and you can use example answers in future lessons in order to analyse them, show good practice or improve on a weaker model.

18 Students have exam practice of Part 3 questions here. Students should take it in turns to ask and answer the questions. Encourage students to focus on grammatical range and accuracy, including future conditionals, and pronunciation in terms of word and sentence stress. Follow the advice for feedback and extension above.

READING

OUTCOMES

- review skimming and scanning skills
- understand and correctly use determiners and quantifiers
- correctly answer flowchart and table completion questions
- use paraphrase to help you answer note completion questions

OUTCOMES

Ask students to focus on the outcomes of the lesson. This unit focuses on note completion tasks in the IELTS reading exam, which involves completing missing information in a flow chart, table or sentences which summarize part of a longer text. Tell students that in order to complete these tasks effectively, they will need to apply skimming and scanning skills, be aware of the correct use of determiners and quantifiers and be able to understand paraphrase in order to answer note completion questions.

LEAD-IN

01 This exercise introduces suffixes, and how they can be useful for identifying unknown words. Identifying suffixes is a useful skill for the IELTS exam, as it will often be necessary for candidates to work out the meaning of unknown words. Elicit from students what a suffix is, writing an example on the board if necessary. Then ask students to complete the exercise in pairs.

> **Noun:** -ism -tion -ian -er -ment
>
> **Adjective:** -ic -ful -less -al -ious -ative -ary -able

02 Ask students to look at the words that contain the suffixes in the exercises and to work out from context the meanings of the suffixes and parts of speech where relevant.

> 1 They are essentially antonyms. *-ful* derives from the word *full* meaning 'a lot of' and *-less* means 'without'. For example, *harmful* means 'causing harm' and *harmless* means 'not causing harm'.
> 2 It is possible or it can be done. For example, *treatable* means it can be treated.
> 3 Normally to a verb. For example, *treat* (v) + *-able*, *prevent* (v) + *-able*
> 4 They normally refer to people. For example, *doctor, technician, manager*.
> 5 They are common verb suffixes.

Emphasize to students the value of skimming as a reading strategy. Elicit how skimming a text can be helpful in the IELTS reading test. Before students do this exercise, ask them to read the Tip box.

Advice

Skim reading a text is not only useful for tasks that require students to identify a main idea of a paragraph. It is also useful for getting a general overview of the text before doing tasks that involve finding specific information in the text.

03 Focus students' attention on the two versions of the text. Elicit the types of words that students should focus on when skimming.

> The second sentence mimics the technique you should aim to use while skim reading. Aim to 'blank out' the grammar words (conjunctions, prepositions, auxiliaries, determiners) and concentrate on noticing the content words (nouns, verbs, adjectives).

04 Tell students that they are going to practise skimming a text for main ideas. Ask students to skim read the text individually, taking care to focus on the information carrying words only. Then ask students to discuss their answer to the matching task in pairs.

> | 1 paragraph C | 2 paragraph F | 3 paragraph A |
> | 4 paragraph D | 5 paragraph B | 6 paragraph E |

05 Students discuss in pairs which words from the paragraphs helped them to match the headings. Ask students to share their ideas with the group, and see if their ideas were similar to those of other students.

> 1 *Research suggests that there is an evolutionary reason as to why people compulsively overeat*
> 2 *it is difficult to see how … can ever be halted*
> 3 *have taken over the world […] levels of growth that show no signs of slowing down […] increasing body of evidence*
> 4 *causes the heart to pump faster while transporting blood through the veins […] immediately start […] Thereafter the body starts to digest the food […] the same process lasts at least three days.*
> 5 *While local authorities … have taken measures to combat the rise in this trend … critics argue that people have every right to make their own decisions*
> 6 *young people […] a child […] their parents […] a child […] children*

06 Explain to students that there are several different ways of skimming a text, but that not all will help them to take in the key information. Ask them to discuss the techniques in Exercise 06 and to compare ideas with a partner.

> All of these suggestions for scanning are useful apart from the first – moving your eyes from left to right along each line. By doing this, you are so closely copying the acts of reading for understanding or skimming that it becomes difficult for your brain to scan the text. Reading for understanding, skimming and scanning are all completely different skills.

07 Explain to students that now they have formed a 'mental map' of the text, they are going to scan for some specific information. It would be a good idea to set a time limit for them to do this, as they will be searching for specific information in the IELTS exam under timed conditions.

> 1 *dopamine* – paragraphs C and E; *sodium* – paragraphs C and D
> 2 *rose by 45 per cent* – paragraph A
> 3 *calorie* (as in 600-calorie burger) – paragraph C
> 4 *brain* – paragraphs C and E; *blood* – paragraphs C–D; *kidneys* – paragraph D; *veins* – paragraph D; *heart* – paragraph D

The next exercises prepare students for the flowchart completion task in the IELTS Reading test. Draw students' attention to the advice box, and ensure that they are familiar with the process for completing the task.

08 Explain to students that they are going to identify the sections of the text that contain the information in an incomplete flowchart. Use space number 1 as an example and elicit what key words students should identify to find in the text (Reward Response / activated). Elicit which paragraph contains this information (paragraph 3). Ask students which word is used in the text as a synonym for 'activated' (stimulates). Tell students that they do not need to complete the information in the gaps yet; they should just identify where in the text the information is located.

> Paragraphs C-E talk about the effects of fast food on the body.

09 Again, use space number 1 as an example. Ask students to look at the space, and to predict which type of information is missing. Elicit that students will be looking for a noun or noun phrase in the text. Ask students to return to paragraph 3 and to locate the words that would fit in the space (processed food). Ask students to complete the rest of the exercises individually and to check their answers in pairs.

> 1 processed food   2 (the) brain   3 surge
> 4 (The) kidneys   5 the elderly   6 hunger
> 7 three days / 3 days

10 Tell students that they are going to use the same text to do a table completion task. Ask them to look at the key words in the table, as they did for the flowchart and to identify the part of the text that contains the information.

> Paragraph E focuses on the different effects on adults and children

11 Ask students to complete the note completion task and then compare answers in pairs

> 8 maturity   9 urge   10 restraint

12 Introduce students to the sentence completion task. Explain that they are going to begin by identifying paraphrased version of the information in the text. This is an important skill

for the IELTS exam, as they will need to match information in the summary from the text.

Definition

Paraphrase: express the same idea using different words, for example synonyms, different word classes or different word order.

Focus students' attention on the first example 'pursuing ways'. Elicit the meaning of this phrase and the parts of speech involved. Tell students that the paraphrase can be found in the first paragraph. When students have identified the correct answer (aggressively chasing levels of), ask them to complete the rest of the examples in pairs.

> 1 chasing
> 2 much of this expansion
> 3 explosion in the takeaway trade
> 4 increasing body of evidence

13 Ask students to use the paraphrases from the previous exercises to help them locate the information in the text to complete the sentence completion task.

> 1 growth   2 less developed   3 dietary disaster

14 Ask students to repeat the process in Exercise 12 for the rest of the text.

> 1 the world doesn't want to listen
> 2 taken measures to combat the rise in this trend
> 3 part of our innate behaviour
> 4 changing widespread dietary habits
> 5 stylish

15 Ask students to try the sentence completion task, using the paraphrases to help them locate the relevant information.

> 1 processed food   2 outlets   3 (compulsively) overeat
> 4 aspirational

16 To elicit the idea of quantifiers, draw students' attention to the first parts of the first two sentences from the previous exercise: *Much of the public seems unconvinced… / Many urban councils…*ask students to identify the words that are used to describe quantity and when they would use *much* or *many* (elicit that much is used for uncountable nouns, and many for countable nouns), then ask them whether they think it is important to use quantifiers correctly in sentence completion tasks. Draw their attention to the advice box, then ask them to complete Exercise 16.

> 1 B   2 C   3 A

EXAM SKILLS

Tell students that they are going to try an IELTS reading note completion task. Encourage them to read through the task and to identify the three different types of task (flow chart, table and sentence completion). Before students do this exercise, ask them to read the Bullet boxes that appear in the lesson.

Advice

It is good practice to set a time limit for students to complete the task, as this will train them to manage their time in preparation for the final exam. Tell students that they must pay attention to the maximum number of words for each space, as they will lose marks if they write more. Advise students to skim read the text to get an initial idea before looking at the task.

17 Give students 20 minutes to complete the task individually, then go through the answers as a group.

1	the gut	8	course
2	medical assistance	9	online
3	Local community	10	laboratory capacity
4	treatment	11	new tools
5	slaughter	12	health benefits
6	(the / infected) meat / flesh	13	(worldwide) overuse
7	system/bodies	14	crisis

Alternative

Demonstrate the process of completing exam tasks by getting students to work in pairs and go through the flowchart completion chart together.

- Ask students to look at the title and predict what the text will be about. Students then read through the text quickly and check their predictions.
- Focus student' attention on the flowchart. Ask them to highlight key words and identify the word classes of the missing words.
- Ask students to identify the part of the text where the information from the flowchart can be found, and to identify the missing words. Students check their answers in pairs and then as a group.
- Set a shorter time limit (15 minutes) for students to complete the rest of the task individually.

WRITING

OUTCOMES

- effectively answer 'advantages and disadvantages' questions
- write topic and supporting sentences, developing your ideas in each paragraph
- achieve a higher score in Coherence and Cohesion
- correctly use less common discourse markers.

LEAD-IN

01 Draw 2 columns on the board. Write 'advantages' and 'disadvantages' at the top of each column. Ask students to briefly discuss in pairs any other words they know that have the same meanings. Ask students to complete Exercise 01 and then compare their answers in pairs.

Advantages	Disadvantages
benefits	on the downside
pros	drawbacks
positives	issues
on the plus side	negatives
on the upside	cons
	problems

02 Tell students to close their books and imagine that they have been asked to write an essay on the following title: *What are the advantages and disadvantages of doing contact sports?* Elicit the meaning of contact sports (i.e. sports where players come into contact with each other) and some examples (e.g. hockey, football, rugby). Ask students how they would go about planning to write this essay. Elicit that they would brainstorm ideas of what to write about. Give students 2 minutes to brainstorm ideas for this title, and then elicit ideas from the group. Finally, ask students to open their books and compare their ideas with the examples provided. Ask students to complete the same process with the other 2 topics: *Living in a busy city* and *Increased life expectancy in many societies*.

Alternative

Divide the class into 2 groups. 1 group brainstorms advantages and disadvantages of living in a busy city, while the other does the same for increased life expectancy in many societies. Ask students to work in pairs to brainstorm ideas, and then join larger groups to narrow down their ideas to 3 advantages and 3 disadvantages. Each group then presents their ideas to the rest of the class (or to another group if the class is very large).

Sample answers

1 **Advantages:** more likely to have better access to better facilities (sports clubs, gyms, sports centres, hospitals)

   Disadvantages: stress of city life can affect mental health; pollution can cause health problems such as asthma and eczema; o ice jobs tend to be sedentary (= involving little physical activity)

2 **Advantages:** everybody wants to live longer; older people can lead satisfying lives a er retirement – more time to pursue their dreams; can provide more support and guidance to other family members

   Disadvantages: more strain and costs on health services due to increased numbers of patients; older people o en require more frequent and longer term health care; caring for older family members may be a burden on the family; people are retiring later, which means fewer jobs available

03 Draw students' attention to the advice box on topic sentences. Give them a few minutes to read the information carefully, then ask them to close their books. Elicit from students what a topic sentence is and what it should be followed by in a paragraph. It may be useful to ask some concept check questions (CCQs) e.g. 'Should a topic sentence be short or long?' 'Should it be simple or complex?' etc. Ensure students are familiar with the definitions below:

Ask students to choose one advantage and one disadvantage from their brainstorm, and to try and write a topic sentence for each one. Encourage them to use the language provided for introducing their topic sentences. Ask them to either write their topic sentences on a piece of paper, or on whiteboards of large pieces of paper stuck up on the walls of the classroom.

Feedback

Ask students to peer edit each other's topic sentences. Ask them to use a different colour pen to make any necessary corrections to their partner's sentence. Then choose individual students to read out their topic sentences to the rest of the group.

Alternative

Choose one idea from the brainstorm activity, and ask all students to write a topic sentence for this idea. Ask students to write their topic sentences on the board and then highlight good examples to the rest of the class. Then ask students to choose 2 more ideas from their brainstorm and write a topic sentence for it.

Sample answers

2 The main advantage of doing contact sports is that you can learn to defend yourself.

3 The principle issue with living in a city is the effect of pollution on health.

4 One obvious negative effect of living in a city is the risk of being a victim of violent crime.

5 Another disadvantage of contact sports is that you are at risk of getting hurt or seriously injured.

6 Overall, the benefits of living in a city outweigh the drawbacks because there are many more facilities available than in small towns or in the countryside.

04 Ask students to look again at their two topic sentences and think about what they might include as supporting ideas to their topic sentence. If you used the alternative method for Exercise 03, you could ask students to think of and write down some supporting ideas for one of the example topic sentences. Now turn students' attention to the supporting ideas in Exercise 04. Ask them to work in pairs and identify the two supporting ideas which will not be effective in developing the idea in the topic sentence further.

Idea 3 is illogical because it immediately argues the opposite to the topic sentence, leaving the original idea stated in the topic sentence undeveloped.

Idea 5 is not effective because it does not logically develop the original idea in the topic sentence, which introduces the idea of personal fitness. It does not make sense to expand this into a discussion about the problems caused by a busy doctor's surgery.

Ideas 1, 2, 4 and 6 follow on logically from the topic.

05 Ask students to match the functions of the supporting ideas from Exercise 04 and check their answes in pairs.

a idea 2   b idea 1   c idea 4   d idea 6

06 Draw students' attention to the topic sentence in Exercise 06. Elicit from students the disadvantage of contact sports being described in the topic sentence (i.e. injury or death). Ask them to briefly discuss with a partner the kinds of injury that may result from contact sports and the consequences of such injuries. Then ask students to write down two supporting ideas.

Feedback

Ask students to peer correct each other's supporting ideas, following the same process as they did for the topic sentences. Then show students the sample answers below and ask them to compare these with their own ideas.

Sample answer

(1) There is evidence that some sports, such as boxing, can cause long-term brain damage.

(2) What is more, broken bones and muscle problems are common even in non-violent contact sports like football or cricket.

07 Focus students' attention on the advice box. Elicit from students what 'coherence' and 'cohesion' are and why they are important features to include in an IELTS writing task. Ensure students are familiar with the definitions below:

Ask students to briefly discuss in pairs how they would make sure that their essay has a good level of coherence and cohesion. Ask them to volunteer suggestions and to note down any ideas that they have on the board. Don't worry if they don't come up with many ideas – this question can be reviewed later after they have completed the tasks. Leave any ideas on the board to review later.

Tell students that Exercise 07 focuses on *coherence*. Ask them to look at the notes in pairs and to decide on a logical order for the supporting ideas. Tell students that there may be more than one logical order for the information.

Suggested answers

There are two obvious ways to order these notes:

1 In cities – many gyms

2 250 gyms in my capital city

3 Gyms part of larger chains, people can use any in city

4 Traditional idea – rural life is healthier; not true

OR

> 1 Traditional idea – rural life is healthier; not true
> 2 In cities – many gyms
> 3 250 gyms in my capital city
> 4 Gyms part of larger chains, people can use any in city

08 Focus students' attention on the advice box on discourse markers. Ask them to discuss the meaning of each discourse marker in Exercise 08 (e.g. *On the other hand* is used to introduce a contrasting idea or point). Then ask them to complete the exercise in pairs.

> 1 (example) By way of example, For instance, For example
> 2 (addition of information / an idea) What is more, In addition to this, Moreover
> 3 (cause and effect) Because of this, As a result, Consequently

09 Encourage students to read the advice box and ensure they are aware that they can lose marks for incorrect or unnecessary use of discourse markers. Ask students to close their books and check that they have understood by asking some CCQs (e.g. 'Is it always good to use a lot of discourse markers?' 'What might happen if you use discourse markers incorrectly?'). Ask students to read the example student paragraph and answer the questions.

> 1 Yes. One of the advantages of living in a city is that there are many gym facilities.
> 2 Yes. The writer is clearly arguing the case that the number of gyms in cities is good for the health of citizens.
> 3 Example: *For example*
> Cause and effect: *What this means is that; This is because; because*
> Addition: *Furthermore*
> Contrast: *Despite this*; *However*
> 4 *because*. The obvious alternative here is *so* (*because* gives the cause and *so* gives the effect). If we start a new sentence a er 'chains', we could also use *Therefore, Thus, As a result* to begin the next sentence.
> 5 The following discourse markers could be cut without impeding the flow of ideas: *Furthermore, This is because*. *However* could also be cut as the contrast is implied in the final sentence.

10 Emphasize to students that the examples of paragraphs they have looked at so far have all been main body paragraphs. Tell them that they are now going to focus on how to write an introductory paragraph. Make it clear that there are a number of requirements for how to write a good introduction for a Part 2 IELTS writing task, and that these can be found in the advice box. Ask students to read the advice box and then close their books. Elicit advice for writing a good introduction and / or ask CCQs (e.g. 'Is it okay to just copy the words from the title?', 'Do you need to include your position in the introduction?').

Ask students to work in pairs and discuss the strengths and weaknesses of the three introductions written by students.

Introduction A: This is a good introduction. It paraphrases the question well and leaves the reader in no doubt about what the essay is going to discuss, without revealing the ideas it will cover. However, it does not state the candidate's position and it is a good idea to do so, because candidates can run out of time before writing their conclusion and therefore not manage to state their position.

Introduction B: This is the best of the three introductions. It paraphrases the question well and uses the very useful introduction phrase *In this essay I will discuss …* which clearly tells us what the essay will be about. It also states the candidate's position, as requested in the question.

Introduction C: It is clear what the candidate will talk about in their essay but basically it restates the question without paraphrase. It also doesn't clarify what the candidate's opinion is.

11 Tell students that having focused on introductory and body paragraphs for a Part 2 IELTS writing task, they are now going to find out how to write a good conclusion. Focus their attention on the advice box and elicit what a good conclusion should contain. Ask students to read the 3 conclusions in pairs and complete the tasks.

> Suggested answers
>
> 1 Conclusions B and C are both good as they clearly state the writer's opinion without going into detail. They both paraphrase the original question clearly and briefly state the position of the writer. Conclusion A, on the other hand, simply restates the question and does not give the writer's position on the question in any way.
> 2 In conclusion; Overall; the advantages of … outweigh the disadvantages; In summary; weighing up both sides of the argument, I would say …

EXAM SKILLS

Tell students that they are going to try an IELTS Part 2 writing task. Before students do this exercise, ask them to read the Tips for Exercises 10 and 11 again.

Advice

- Tell students to read the title carefully and ensure that they stay focused on the question.

- Encourage students to brainstorm ideas for their answer, and to decide on a logical order for their ideas before they start writing. This will help them to get a better mark for *Coherence*. Remind students to use discourse markers when appropriate, in order to demonstrate a good level of *Cohesion*.

- Remind students to paraphrase the idea in the title and state their position in the introduction, use topic sentences and supporting ideas in the main body paragraphs and to summarize their main ideas in the conclusion.

- Give students 40 minutes to complete the task.

Refer students to the IELTS criteria specifically for bands 7 and 8 in the introduction to the Teachers' Book. Tell them to firstly determine whether they fully meet the criteria for band 7 and then check if they surpass it and can be judged to meet the grade 8 criteria.

Extension

Ask students to look at the sample answer below and discuss which of the points above the writer has included.

Sample essay

Medical care over the past century has improved dramatically. As a consequence, the world's population is increasingly living long into old age. Is this having a harmful e ect on societies across the globe, or are there more benefits than drawbacks?

One obvious issue with an ageing population is that it can create enormous demands on a nation's health service. As people live longer into their old age, the chances of them suffering from serious illnesses increases. As a result, the likelihood of them requiring medical treatment becomes higher, and it becomes more difficult to provide care for everyone. A further downside is that living longer does not necessarily bring happiness. By this I mean, an older person is unable to do many of the activities that they want to do, leading to the likelihood of depression and a deterioration in their physical health.

Having said that, one obvious benefit to people living longer is that young people can benefit for a longer time from the wisdom handed down to them by older members of their families. In today's fast-paced world, it is o en comforting to seek advice from older generations. Consequently, the physical health of a grandparent is almost irrelevant, as the children and grandchildren will benefit from the experience of an older mind. What is more, retired people today are generally much healthier than they have ever been, and o en enjoy their lives more than they did when they were young. They have the best of both worlds – a family that can care for and look up to them, and better health than at any time in human history.

Weighing up both sides of the argument again, although there are a number of problems that old age brings – predominantly health- related – the benefits that it brings to the family unit and to society as a whole are impossible to ignore. (310 words)

LISTENING

OUTCOMES

- correctly answer table completion and note completion tasks
- use headings and completed cells in tables to help you predict correct answers
- correctly use a variety of determiners and quantifiers.

OUTCOMES

Ask students to focus on the outcomes. The first outcome helps students to complete tables and notes when listening. Tell students that they will need to complete these tasks for the IELTS listening test. The second outcome helps students to use strategies to complete tables when listening. Tell students that for this outcome, they will use clues – headings and completed cells – to help them to predict and identify the correct answers. Ask students to focus on the third outcome. This outcome concerns correct use of determiners and quantifiers and will help students be able to both produce in speaking and writing the accurate expressions when talking about quantities as well as to identify these when listening.

LEAD-IN

01 This exercise tests students' existing knowledge of the specific tasks and details of IELTS listening exam. It also helps students to clarify the contents and structure of each of the parts of the listening exam. Ask students to do this in pairs and monitor. After 2-3 minutes, invite students to give their answers to the whole class. Try to generate a class discussion where many members contribute their opinions and knowledge. Then confirm the answers.

1 everyday, social – 2 speakers
2 everyday, social – 1 speaker (Although it is possible you may hear a second voice at the start, the majority of the audio will be a monologue.)
3 educational or training – 2 or more speakers
4 educational or training – 1 speaker

02 This exercise extends and tests students further. It also acts to check student understanding. Use the procedure outlined in Exercise 01.

You might hear any of the following: 2, 3, 5, 6

03 Again, this exercise extends on the previous two to check and then confirm understanding. Use the procedure outlined in the previous two exercises.

2 Section 4	3 Section 2	5 Section 1	6 Section 3

04 This exercise provides students with practice of table completion as well as strategies to complete this task when listening. Make sure students read the instructions and understand that they need to use the correct spelling, the correct number of words, not repeat words from other parts of the table and not miss out important details such as units of measurement. Before students do this exercise, ask them to read the Bullet box.

Advice

This advice recommends students to consider the context and situation being described. This helps students to predict possible listening content and is a good way to help them to improve their listening effectiveness especially during the listening test.

After students have understood the advice, ask them to complete Exercise 04. After students discuss this in pairs, invite answers and see if other students agree. Confirm the correct answers after doing this.

A   Olympic Records Exhibition
B   Medical Discoveries in History
C   Sports Centre Classes

05 This exercise builds on the previous one by asking students to make specific predictions about content in each table cell. Before students do this exercise, ask them to read the Tip box.

Advice

Make sure students are aware of the value of predicting listening content before the recording starts as well as understanding what specifically they should try to identify (e.g. part of speech etc.). Also, make students aware of the need to look at the instructions to identify how many words are required. This will also help them with this exercise.

Now ask students to complete the exercise in pairs while you monitor. Confirm answers after you invite different students to volunteer. Encourage students to say if they agree or not and to say why. Then confirm answers.

2 Womens 10K (a)		3 penicillin (g)
4 Swiss (c)		5 gene therapy (e)
6 6:30 pm (h)		7 Marco and Victor (b)
8 table tennis (f)		

06 This exercise again encourages students to think about the structure and content of the listening exam Before students do this exercise, ask them to read the Tip box

Advice

Make sure students are aware that this type of task (table completion) usually occurs in Section 1 but that it can appear in other sections.

Now play the recording. Ask students to compare their answers in pairs afterwards and monitor while students do this to see if you need to repeat the recording. Provide confirmation of answers only after inviting students to answer and/or comment on other students' answers.

Table A: Section 2   Table B: Section 4   Table C: Section 1

Transcript 10:

Recording 1

Well, good afternoon, ladies and gentlemen, and welcome to the tour today. It's great to see that so many people out there are as fascinated as I am by the astonishing achievements of our great Olympic athletes. My name is Tom, and I'll be taking you through the exhibition and pointing out particular areas of interest. We'll begin with a bang, with many people's favourite event, the Men's 100m sprint …

Recording 2

Good morning, everyone. Welcome to your introductory science lecture. We'll begin the course by looking at some of the most vital discoveries in medical history. Why would I do this? Why, when so much of science is about looking into the future? Well, if it wasn't for the discovery in 1928 of penicillin …

Recording 3

Man: Good evening, Camgate Sports Centre. How can I help?

Woman: Oh, hello. I'm ringing to enquire about some of the classes

you run. I've just moved into the area and I'd like to find out more. Man: Of course. Is there a particular day or class you're interested in? Woman: Yes, I was wondering if you have any aerobics classes …

07 This exercise gives students practice of prediction skills before listening Before students do this exercise, ask them to read the Tip box.

Advice

Make sure students are aware of the value of looking at table headings to help them predict both listening content and possible answers.

Now ask students to do this exercise in pairs. Follow the feedback procedure outlined in the previous exercise.

1   the name of a society or club, e.g. a game or hobby which could take place in a room indoors
2   the name of a room or place in the university
3   the name of a room or place in the university
4   the name of a society or club, e.g. a game or sport that could take place in the gym
5   a person's name or people's names

08 Students can now practise completing the table. Before playing the recording, make sure students are aware of the word and/or number limit. Now play the recording. Ask students to compare their answers in pairs afterwards and monitor while students do this to see if you need to repeat the recording. Provide confirmation of answers only after inviting students to answer and/or comment on other students' answers.

1 Vegetarian   2 Room A14   3 Room C16   4 Hot Air
5 Siobhan

Transcript 11

Claude:	Hi, I was wondering if you could help me. This is my first week here and I'd like to find out about any societies that could be good for me.
Woman:	Of course. Well, we have literally hundreds of socs here – 'soc' is o en what we call societies. What sort of thing are you interested in joining?
Claude:	I'm really into health and fitness.
Woman:	Oh, there are a number of socs that might suit you. Let's start with the ones closest to where we're standing now. A12, that's where you'll find the <u>Vegetarian</u> Soc, which is run by Paul, and two rooms along you'll be able to find Peter, who's in charge of the Vegan Soc, so that's in <u>A14</u>. Peter and Paul are actually brothers. Both of them are really nice.
Claude:	I don't think either of those socs are for me – I like meat too much, I'm afraid.

Woman:	May be the Healthy Eating Soc then? If you go down the corridor and past the library, then you'll come to room <u>C16</u>, where you'll find Catherine, who can fill you in about their events and activities.
Claude:	Thanks, I may well do that. But you mentioned fitness–that's more like the kind of thing I'm looking for. What about societies for doing some sort of cardiovascular exercise?
Woman:	All of the main types of exercise are covered here. What exactly are you looking for? Cycling, rowing, swimming?
Claude:	Mm,none of those are really my kind of thing – I'm more of a runner.
Woman:	In that case, definitely head for the gym. Go through the main building, and on your way you'll probably see the Push and Pull Soc, but if I were you, I'd steer clear of that. The people in it are all a bit weird. So carry on past them and you'll find Sarah, who runs the <u>Hot Air Soc</u>.
Claude:	Sounds intriguing. What do they do – organise races and running events?
Woman:	They do, yes, and others ports as well, like rowing in the inter-university boat races. That's a lot of fun. The whole university turns out to support them. But if it's only running that you want to do, go and see the Road Running Soc out in the car park. The person running their stall today is Siobhan. I'll spell that for you – it's an old Irish name – <u>S-I-O-B-H-A-N</u>.
Claude:	Never heard that one before. Great. Well that should keep me busy, lots of interesting stands to visit.
Woman:	Yes, there's so much to choose from.

Extension

Ask students to work in pairs to look again at the answers to see if their predictions were correct or not. Give students the audio-script to help them to do this. Students can highlight in the script the clues that helped them.

09 This exercise uses sentences from the previous listening recording in order to analyse them grammatically. Each sentence in this exercise focuses on the use of determiners and quantifiers. This will help students to use these accurately and to be able to correctly identify them when listening. Ask students to complete this exercise in pairs. Monitor while students do this and then encourage class discussion of the answers. Students should say if they agree or disagree with the answers their classmates have given and to provide alternatives and explanations if they disagree. Finally confirm the correct answers.

1	a number of	2	Both of them / Both
3	either of those	4	All of the / All
5	None of those	6	The whole / The whole of the

10 This exercise provides students with further practice of correct use of determiners and quantifiers. Ask students to

complete this in pairs. Monitor and then follow the feedback instructions outlined in the previous exercise.

1	Some people	2	all	3	any	4	no	5	all of us
6	Some of the / Some		7	Many		8	either (correct)	
9	both	10	all						

11 Exercises 11 to 13 link note completion to table completion and help students to understand that similar strategies to table completion can be used here. Before students do this exercise, ask them to read the Bullet box.

Advice

Make sure students are aware that the strategies used for table completion can be used with note completion. Also, highlight to students that note completion usually appears in the later sections of the test.

Ask students to complete this exercise in pairs and invite the class to discuss answers. Then confirm the correct answers.

1 d	2 b	3 c	4 f	5 e	6 a

12 This exercise gives students more practice of predicting correct answers for this type of listening task. To help students, options are given. Ask students to compare their answers together and monitor. Then follow the feedback procedure outlined in previous exercises. Give students explanations and rationales for the correct answers (see below).

1	The President of a Society is likely to be named in full, forename and surname. 'Claire' is a forename, and it would be a little too informal.
2	It is unlikely that a society of keen runners would only complete a distance of 20 km in a whole year.
3	Although some 100km races exist, a team of amateur students would not run this far. And as this society is focused on distance running, not sprinting, 100m is also unlikely.
4	They would be unlikely to run in a sports centre given that the society is for road running (also 'a sports centre' is over the TWO WORD limit).
5	In this case, the answer 'blue dark' will not be correct, but this is for a grammatical reason, i.e. the shade (light, dark, vivid, etc.) goes before the colour.
6	Given the financial situation of the majority of students, a membership fee of £5000 per year would be excessive.

13 This exercise gives students listening practice of note completion and builds on the preparatory work done in exercises 11-12. Play the recording, ask students to compare their answers in pairs afterwards and monitor. Provide the correct answers only after encouraging students to give their answers and/or comment on answers given by classmates

1	Claire Enwark	2	fortnight	3	10K/10km
4	Manchester	5	pale blue	6	50

Transcript 12

Claude: Hi, are you … Fiachra? My name's Claude. I was told to come and talk to you about the Road Running Soc? So you must be the president, I suppose.

Siobhan: Actually no, I'm standing in for her today. I can probably answer any questions you have, but if you need to contact the president you can look her up in the Contacts section of your college email account. Her first name is Claire – C-L-A-I-R-E.

Claude: And her surname?

Siobhan: Her surname's Enwark. E-N-W-A-R-K.

Claude: OK, thanks …. So, first of all, what sort of distance do people usually run each week?

Siobhan: Well, on average, if you take into consideration all of our members, probably 10 kilometres – or, as we say it, 10K – a week, and 20 over a fortnight. That said, it's not unusual for a road runner to cover 20K each week.

Claude: Great. I like to push my self, so hopefully I can keep up with them all. Do you take part in any organised races?

Siobhan: Yes, we do. We've done 10Ks in London, 5Ks in Cambridge, a marathon in Newcastle. The most recent was a 10K in Manchester. The race before that was in Oxford. Both went really well, we got some amazing times.

Claude: And do you have a team kit?

Siobhan: We do, actually. It's white with a dark blue stripe. Well, it has been, but we're changing it for this year. Someone recently pointed out that the university colours are white and pale blue, so this year we're going to keep the same design but have a pale blue stripe instead.

Claude: Well, they're my favourite colours, so I've got to join now. How much does it cost to become a member?

Siobhan: To cover the cost of your vest, there's a one-off signing-on fee of £15. You can begin your annual membership at any point a er that, and once you start, you can either pay monthly or you can pay for the full year in a single payment. That's £50, but if you find that too expensive the monthly fee is £5, which is taken directly out of your bank account.

EXAM SKILLS

14 This exercise brings together all the key components of this unit: table completion, note completion and correct identification of determiners and quantifiers. Students can either complete this exercise individually and compare answers at the end or you can ask them to compare after each set of questions. Monitor to see if students need to listen additional times and provide feedback as described in the previous exercise.

1	vegetarian	2	Wednesford
3	7/seven o'clock / 7.00 / 7 pm	4	covered market
5	Coffee Club	6	free / nothing / £0
7	2/two hours	8	10%
9	(an) email	10	celebrity chefs

Transcript 13

You will hear a student, Claude, asking for information about the Healthy Eating Society. First you have some time to look at questions 1 to 5.

[pause]

Now listen carefully and answer questions 1 to 5.

Claude: Hello, is that the Healthy Eating Soc?

Catherine: Yes, it is, Catherine speaking. How can I help?

Claude: I was give none of your leaflets and am interested in joining. I know you go out for dinner twice a week, but what else do you do?

Catherine: Well, we don't do anything on Sundays, Mondays or Tuesdays, but every Wednesday is our first restaurant visit of each week. It's not always the same place – sometimes we'll go to The Red Tomato, other times we go to Herbs and Flowers – but it's always somewhere that serves vegetarian food. We meet at half past seven on the High Street.

Claude: Sounds good. What about Thursdays?

Catherine: Well, on Thursdays, we usually go off to my aunt's house. She lends us her kitchen and we all prepare a meal together – a big curry, or something. There's a limit of twelve people, so you need to put your name down. We get there for eight o'clock. She lives in Wednesford, so you'll need money for the bus fare.

Claude: Wednesford? That's funny, it's like, 'When's the food?'

Catherine: Ha! No, it's spelt W-E-D-N-E-S-F-O-R-D. It's a village a few miles out of town. Anyway, Friday is our other restaurant evening, not vegetarian this time. We usually meet around 6 o'clock in a juice bar, and once everyone has arrived, we'll head o to a fantastic restaurant that serves European food in town. We always sit down to eat at 7.00.

Claude: And that's in town, is it?

Catherine: It's right in the centre, so you get the bus to Central Square, which is where the juice bar is. It's right next to the little theatre. The restaurant we go to is round the corner in the covered market. It's opposite the cinema.

Claude: OK, I think I've got that. And do you do anything over the weekend?

Catherine: Not a lot. It gets busy in town on a Saturday night, so the only thing we do is meet at midday for what we call Coffee Club, just in the canteen in the Students' Union. They do good pastries.

Before you hear the rest of the conversation you have some time to look at questions 6 to 10.

[pause]

Now listen and answer questions 6 to 10.

Claude: Well, it all sounds lots of fun. How much does it cost to join?

Catherine: It depends. If you go to all of the activities every week–believe me, I know – it can cost you around £40 or more. I originally thought about charging people something like £5 per week as a membership fee, but it takes so much time to collect that it's not worth it. So <u>it's actually free to be a member</u>.

Claude: Mm, £40 is a bit above my budget.

Catherine: Oh, don't worry. You don't have to come to everything, and you don't have to come every week. It's entirely up to you.

Claude: How long do you usually take to have dinner?

Catherine: <u>We're usually in a restaurant for two hours having dinner</u>, so the whole evening lasts about three hours, if you include the drink in the juice bar beforehand.

Claude: And what about service charge at the end of a meal? Do people in this country usually give something extra for the waiters?

Catherine: In general, people often leave a tip of about 12–15% of the total bill. On the other hand, if the service or the food has been bad, they may leave nothing. <u>We always try to make sure we give our waiters 10%</u>. We'd like to give them 15 or 20%, but we're not very rich. We're only students, a er all.

Claude: So how do I book a place on these trips? Shall I give you a call?

Catherine: No, I don't always answer my phone. Some of our members send me a text message, which is fine but I get so many that I might forget yours. The most reliable way to contact me is to send an email.

Claude: Great. So is there anything else I need to know?

Catherine: No, I don't think so. Oh, there is one more thing. It's really important.

Claude: What's that?

Catherine: Well, a lot of the people have very strong opinions about which is the best restaurant in town, which is the best national dish, which country has the best cooks. All of those things are fine, but if you want to fit in with the group, <u>try to avoid talking about celebrity chefs</u>. That's when the arguments really start!

Extension

Students can analyse the listening by reading the script while listening again. This will help students to identify clues in the recording – they can highlight these on the script – and this will help them with future listening tasks of this nature. Ask students to do this in pairs or small groups and then encouraged class discussion.

SPEAKING

> ## OUTCOMES
>
> - improve your score for Fluency and Coherence (FC)
> - extend your Part 1 and Part 3 answers
> - correctly use and pronounce a range of discourse markers.

OUTCOMES

Ask students to focus on the outcomes. Tell students that the first outcome concerns strategies students can use to improve their fluency and coherence scores in the IELTS speaking exam. It's a good idea for students to be aware of the separate criteria and advice in terms of how to improve their scores in each. The next outcome helps students to provide fuller answers when speaking in parts 1 and 3 of the exam. Remind students that these sections are where students have to answer questions. The third outcome helps students to correctly use discourse markers in terms of grammatical accuracy and correct pronunciation. Tell students that this is particularly useful when speaking as it helps students to structure and link together what they are saying.

01 This exercise helps students to improve their speaking scores by learning to use idiomatic language accurately. Students will learn 6 idioms and phrases while being aware of what to avoid doing when speaking. Before students do this exercise, ask them to read the Tip box.

Advice

While students should be encouraged to use idiomatic language, it is important to make sure that students try to only use idioms and phrases that they are comfortable with.

Ask students to now do Exercise 01 in pairs to discuss the idioms' meanings. Monitor to check students are on task and to provide assistance where necessary. Invite students to answer and encourage a class discussion. Confirm answers after this.

1 *going round in circles* = continuing to talk about – or going back to – the same idea without moving the discussion on

2 *losing your thread* = forgetting what you were talking about; bringing irrelevant ideas into the discussion

3 *stumbling over your words* = making mistakes while speaking, often caused by a lack of vocabulary, which can cause hesitation, repetition or mispronunciation

4 *labouring the point* = explaining or discussing something at excessive length

5 *beating about the bush* = trying to avoid talking about the central issue or problem, possibly because you don't know enough about the subject, or because you think it would be impolite to do so

6 *talking at a mile a minute* = speaking so quickly that you cannot be understood

02 This exercise tests students' ability to use the idioms and phrases from Exercise 01. Before students do this, remind them that they may need to change the form of the verbs.

Ask students to complete the exercise and then check their answers in pairs. Monitor as students compare answers. Then follow the feedback procedure outlined in the last exercise.

> 1 stumbling over my words / losing my thread / talking at a mile a minute
> 2 talking at a mile a minute
> 3 beat around the bush
> 4 going round in circles
> 5 labouring the point
> 6 lost her thread

03 This exercise raises students' awareness of the IELTS speaking exam criterion of Fluency and Coherence. It also helps students to understand how to achieve better scores for this criterion. Ask students to read the information about how to avoid losing marks for Fluency and Coherence. As an option, you can ask students to discuss in pairs which of the reasons for losing marks, given in exercise 02, they also worry about doing or not. Alternatively, you can ask pairs to rank the list here in terms of most frequently done by students/ themselves or even most difficult to avoid. Monitor and then encourage class discussion. Clarify where necessary. Before students do this exercise, ask them to read the Bullet box.

Advice

The important message students should take from this us that speaking is marked differently to writing and that students are not expected to speak in perfect sentences. Highlight to students that in natural speech, native speakers use fillers (e.g. um, uh) and can sometimes start sentences with *and* or *but* etc.

Now ask students to complete Exercise 03. Play the recording and ask students to listen individually and make notes if they want about how they rated each candidate's performance in terms of Fluency and Coherence. Then ask students to discuss their thoughts in pairs or small groups. Monitor then invite students to give their opinions. Confirm answers.

Transcript 14

Examiner: How can people be encouraged to do more exercise?

Candidate 1: Well, it's not an easy thing to do. Um, I tend to think that, you know, if people don't want to exercise of their own volition, they're certainly not going to, not really, make a concerted effort simply because the, er, the government or whoever has issued some sort of advertising campaign to get people going. What's more, there's a general, kind of, lack of facilities that makes this possible. It's, it's … Having said that, it's not really an option to simply do nothing. People are getting bigger on average, all over the world, and the health implications for that are, well, extremely serious. So, really, I'm not sure exactly how we could do it … um, but it's something that is getting quite pressing these days.

Examiner: How can people be encouraged to do more exercise?

Candidate 2: It's not an easy thing to do, it's not an easy thing to do, it's genuinely difficult and I tend to think that if people don't want to exercise of their own volition, they're certainly not going to make a concerted effort simply because it's difficult, or if the government or an authority of the government has issued some sort of advertising campaign to get people going. It's not an easy thing to do if you just have the government there insisting, it's really quite difficult and what's more, I have to add something here, furthermore, there's a general lack of facilities that make this possible. So, of course it's not an easy thing to do but having said that, there's not really an option to simply do nothing just because it's a difficult thing to do. People are getting bigger on average all over the world and the health implications for that are extremely serious. Maybe it's too difficult to do, maybe it's not for the government at all, I'm not sure exactly how we could do it, but it's something that's getting quite pressing these days.

> Although it may sound as if the first candidate lacks control of FC, he is speaking in a completely natural way. Saying 'um' or 'er', or pausing slightly, or beginning a sentence and then starting again, are all features of natural speech that are acceptable in the IELTS test. You will only lose credit if you do any or all of these things too often, and it becomes noticeable to the examiner that you are stumbling over your words.
>
> The second candidate is speaking in an unnatural way, talking at a mile a minute, possibly in a misguided attempt to sound 'fluent'. Ultimately, she ends up going round in circles, repeating both vocabulary and ideas, and her turn lacks both fluency and coherence.

Alternative

Instead of confirming answers, you can give the rationale in the box above and delete the word 'first' and 'second' for each candidate. Students can then work in pairs to decide which candidate the rationale is referring to.

04 This exercise gives students more practice of analysing and evaluating IELTS speaking candidates' answers. Ask students to listen and read the answers before working in pairs to evaluate each answer. Monitor as students do this and then provide feedback as outlined in the previous exercise.

Transcript 15

Examiner: How often do you eat healthy meals?

Candidate 1: I'm very much a sociable type of person, so whether I'm eating at a restaurant or at home, as long as there's company around me – could be with friends, could be with family, could be both, personally, I tend not to notice too much where I am and I'll eat pretty much anything.

Candidate 2: Well, there's a lot of pressure these days on people to eat the right sort of things. However, it seems like every day there are new pieces of conflicting advice from the government, or from doctors, about what we should and shouldn't be eating, so who actually knows? For example, one week there's a study telling us chocolate is bad for us and then the next week, there's another which says it's good for us. I try to eat healthy food when I can, but I think it depends on what you mean by 'healthy'.

Candidate 3: It depends what you mean by 'healthy', but I try to keep my intake of junk food down to a minimum. And most days I make sure that I have at least some fruit and vegetables, even if it isn't as much as I should. Also, because I'm young and in relatively good shape, I don't worry about my diet too much at the moment, to be honest.

Although Candidate 1 personalises her response, she has actually failed to answer the question asked of her. She talks about eating, but not in the context she was given. In fact, this is more like an answer to a Part 1 question such as 'What do you like to eat when you go out for dinner?'

Candidate 2 considers the question in a more abstract way, relating it to other people and to the society in which we live, and goes on to question the concept of the word 'healthy'. As such, this answer is far more appropriate to a Part 3 question, not a Part 1 question. Again, it doesn't answer the question that was asked.

Candidate 3 provides the best answer. He personalises response, sticks to what the question is asking, and extends his answer to the appropriate length for Part 1.

Extension

Ask students to work in pairs to provide their own answer to the question asked. Students should listen to each other's response and give constructive feedback. Monitor as students do this. You can then nominate or invite students to give their answers to the whole class for peer evaluation.

05 This exercise analyses the candidates' responses from the previous exercise. Ask students to read about discourse markers first. Highlight to students that there are many discourse markers that they can use and that discourse markers are useful in linking together what they are saying. Tell students that this is particularly important in the speaking exam as it will help them to be more coherent in what they say. Ask students to work together in pairs to complete the exercise. Monitor and provide feedback as outlined in previous exercises.

Adding detail to the previous point: *and, also*
Introducing a contrasting idea: *but, even if, however*
Giving a reason/explanation: *so, because*
Giving an example or clarification: *For example, it depends*
Introducing an opinion: *To be honest, Personally*

06 This exercise helps students to use discourse markers appropriately and accurately within the context of the speaking exam. Ask students to listen and answer individually before comparing in pairs.

Transcript 16

Examiner: How do you like to relax?

Candidate 1: If I had to choose, I'd say that I most like to sink into the sofa, put my feet up and lose myself in a good movie.

The thing is, I've got a lot of pressure on at the moment, as I'm in my final year of study, so I really need time to switch off. Watching a film helps me to forget that pressure for a while.

Examiner: How do you like to relax?

Candidate 2: If I had to choose, I'd say that I most like to sink into the sofa, put my feet up and lose myself in a good movie.

On top of that, in an ideal world, if I wanted to relax completely, I'd switch my phone o, settle down and have something delicious to eat, say a pizza or popcorn. That way I can really start to unwind.

Examiner: How do you like to relax?

Candidate 3: If I had to choose, I'd say that I most like to sink into the sofa, put my feet up and lose myself in a good movie.

In particular, films directed by Ang Lee, whose work I've always admired. So if I could relax in any way I could choose, it would be watching something of his, I'd say.

Examiner: How do you like to relax?

Candidate 4: If I had to choose, I'd say that I most like to sink into the sofa, put my feet up and lose myself in a good movie.

That said, I can only do that at weekends currently. I've got far too much study to do during the week, so I tend to leave the films for the weekend as a reward for finishing everything on time.

1 *The thing is* – A Giving a reason for the previous point
2 *On top of that* – C Adding detail to the previous point
3 *In particular* – B Giving an example related to the previous point
4 *That said* – D Introducing an idea that contrasts with the previous point.

07 This exercise gives students freer practice of using discourse markers within a structured answer to the speaking exam question. Put students into pairs to do this and after monitoring, invite students to give their suggestions for possible answers. Provide feedback and encourage peer feedback before providing sample answers.

Sample answers:

a The thing is, I'm actually really into sports and fitness, but I'm so busy with study that I can barely find time to turn on a microwave, let alone prepare healthy balanced meals on a daily basis.

b For instance, I need to find a way to eat more green vegetables. I'm perfectly happy with tomatoes and carrots, say, but I know that I should force myself to have more greens.

c I would add that I think doing regular exercise is just as important as a healthy diet. In fact, I would say that you have to do both if you want to look after your body.

d Having said that, I don't believe we should be pressurised into eating 5 portions of fruit or vegetables a day, so maybe the stubborn part of me thinks: no, I'm not going to eat this lettuce because the government recommends that I do.

08 This exercise focuses on answering Part 3 of the speaking exam. Highlight to students that the key difference between Part 1 and 3 answers is that Part 1 is more personal while Part 3 focuses on talking about other people, different societies and hypothetical situations – it is more impersonal. To complete this exercise, students can listen and then answer the questions in pairs. Monitor and then provide feedback.

Transcript 17

Examiner: What reasons do people have for becoming vegetarian?

Candidate: What motivates people to stop eating meat? Usually, on the grounds that they object in some way to animals being kept simply as food, o en in really unhealthy surroundings. I think it's a moral decision that people take. They just decide to avoid meat completely. And some people, to build on my point a little more, go even further and become vegan. They don't agree with the idea of animals being killed for food, or for making people's clothes, or even for dairy products. Looking at it from another point of view, other people give up meat purely for the sake of their health. Take red meat as an example. There's a great deal of evidence to suggest that it causes all sorts of health issues, and people in general are increasingly trying to limit how much they eat. Ultimately, I suppose, it's a question of health – either of the animal or of yourself.

1 The candidate 'widens' his answer very well indeed. The only reference to his own views comes in the last sentence. The rest of his turn explores the question in terms of how other people might feel. In other words, this is a very good example of *speculation*.

2 After the rhetorical question at the start, he makes the following four points:

- It is a moral issue for some people.

- Others become vegan, as avoiding meat alone does not satisfy their objections.

- Some people believe eating meat is unhealthy.

- Many people follow the medical evidence that supports this view.

Overall, this answer is very well balanced. The candidate addresses the question from two main angles, providing a number of possible reasons for becoming vegetarian. He also rounds off his turn with a summarising statement which refers back to what he has said – rather like a conclusion in a Task 2 essay.

3 i – b   ii – a   iii – d   iv – c

09 This exercise gives students more opportunity to practise using the correct discourse markers as well as to see an example response to a Part 3 question. Before students do this exercise, ask them to read the Tip box.

Advice

Students need to be aware that even though some discourse markers have the same function, their usage is not always interchangeable. This will depend on the grammar of the sentence. Tell students that they should analyse example sentences in dictionaries and other resources to help them to use discourse markers appropriately and effectively.

Ask students to do this exercise in pairs and monitor as they do this. Then provide feedback.

1 Both *so that* and *on the grounds that* fit grammatically, but the latter would score higher. *Essentially* does not fit grammatically or in terms of meaning; it also tends to appear at the start of a sentence when it is used to introduce a reason.

2 Both *In particular this is true of my country*, and *Take my country by way of example* are grammatically correct and display a good control of less common discourse markers, but the latter would probably score higher. *Such as* cannot be used to begin a sentence.

3 All fit grammatically in spoken English. In terms of what might score more highly, *On the other hand* and *That said* would score more highly than *But*.

4 None would score particularly high but *as well* and *too* are the best because they are used in the correct position; *also* is acceptable here, as we are dealing with spoken English, but is not entirely natural in terms of its position in the sentence.

> 5 *Ultimately* and *At the end of the day* work best here. *Overall* does not work in this context, because the candidate is not summarizing her argument but is concluding her argument with one final point.

10 This exercise builds upon the last one and asks students to consider their own ability and experience before providing students with example discourse markers. Ask students to add to these discourse markers by discussing together in pairs. Monitor then provide feedback.

> 3 Adding detail to the previous point: *Moreover, Furthermore, What's more*
> Introducing a contrasting idea: *Whereas, Conversely*
> Giving a reason/explanation: *For his reason, This is why, As a consequence*
> Giving an example or clarification: *such as, like, say*
> Introducing an opinion: *If you ask me, in my opinion, To my mind*
> Concluding with a final point or summarising an argument: *To sum up, In the end, In a nutshell, What it all comes down to*

EXAM SKILLS

11 This exercise provides students with exam practice of Part 1 questions. Students should listen to their partner's answer and then provide constructive feedback. Then students should swap roles. Monitor as students do this and make notes of any common issues you want to bring up in feedback. You can nominate students to give their answers in front of the whole class for peer feedback or you can allow students to volunteer. Try to encourage constructive feedback from classmates before you provide your own.

Refer students to the IELTS criteria specifically for bands 7 and 8 in the introduction to the Teachers' Book. Tell them to firstly determine whether they fully meet the criteria for band 7 and then check if they surpass it and can be judged to meet the grade 8 criteria.

Extension:

Use any errors you noted down when you monitored. Write a list of these on the board (3-5 is manageable). Also, add 1-2 correct answers. Ask students to identify the correct answers and correct the incorrect ones. This is a good way to recycle what has been learnt in the exercise and to also focus on responding to emerging student errors and needs.

12 Follow the same procedure outlined in Exercise 11.

Alternative and extension:

You can use the same extension as in the previous exercise and/or do the following. Ask students to record their answers on a smart phone or other device. Ask students to listen to their own response and evaluate it. Then ask them to rerecord their answer. This can be done in class or as homework. This can also be done for Exercise 11 responses.

READING

OUTCOMES

- identify main and supporting ideas
- answer true / false / not given and multiple choice questions
- use past tenses correctly.

OUTCOMES

Draw students' attention to the outcomes box. The main aim of the lesson is to focus on true / false / not given and multiple choice questions, which are both common question types in the IELTS reading test. Explain to students that they will learn strategies for answering these questions more accurately. They will also learn how to identify the use of different past tenses which occur frequently in IELTS reading texts.

LEAD-IN

01 Draw students' attention to the discussion questions, and give them five minutes to ask and answer the questions in pairs. Explain that they are going to read some texts about art and architecture, and that discussing these questions will help them to become more familiar with the topic.

> **Alternative**
>
> Provide students with some pictures of well-known works of art. Ask them to discuss the appearance of the work of art, who the artist is and whether or not they like it.

02 Elicit what is meant by a synonym. Remind students that it is important to be able to recognize synonyms, as IELTS reading questions often contain them. Ask students to complete the synonym matching task in pairs. Tell students that they may not know all of the words, but to begin with the words they do know and use a dictionary to check meanings when necessary.

> installations – exhibitions
>
> materials – media
>
> concepts – ideas
>
> cast – mould
>
> abstract – conceptual
>
> groundbreaking – innovative
>
> techniques – methods
>
> experiment – innovate
>
> sculpture – figure

03 Tell students that a common IELTS reading task type is the True / False / Not Given task. Ask students whether they have tried these tasks before and how easy / difficult they found them. This will give you an idea of the students' past experience of this task type and how to pace the remainder

of the lesson. If many of the students have experience of this task type, ask them to briefly discuss in pairs any advice they would give for completing True / False / Not Given tasks. Note any advice that they give on the board to refer to later.

Draw students' attention to the Tip box on True/ False / Not Given tasks. Ask them to read the advice carefully and then close their books. Elicit the difference between 'true' 'false' and 'not given' information. Remind students of the value of skim-reading the text before looking at the questions, in order to get an idea of its structure. Ask students to complete Exercise 03.

> B

04 Ask students to return to the text and complete Exercise 04. Explain that this will help them to become more familiar with the structure of the text, which will help them to locate the answers to questions later.

1 C	**2** F	**3** A	**4** B	**5** D	**6** E

05 Tell students that they are now going to practise identifying information in the text that is true, false or not given. Point out that there is one of each answer type.

Before students do this exercise, ask them to read the Bullet box.

1 NG	2 T	3 F

Advice

When preparing students to answer True / False / Not Given questions, it is a good idea to check how they found the correct answers, in order to ensure that they have not simply guessed the answer correctly. When going through the answers, nominate a student to provide each answer and also to point out which part of the text gave them the correct answer.

06 Ask students to read the Tip box about Not Given statements. Ask students to identify the parts of the text that gave them their answers to the questions in Exercise 05. Elicit possible reasons why students might think that a Not Given statement is true or false.

> **1** We are told Warhol was 'a sickly child' but nothing is said about Rauschenberg's health as a child.
>
> **2** *His* [Rauschenberg's] *mother supported her son as much as she could … Like Rauschenberg, Warhol was close to his mother.*
>
> **3** *Though he was missing a lot of school, he was developing his artistic skills and tastes. … He eventually enrolled in the Carnegie Institute in Pittsburgh.*
>
> The words 'sickly child' might have led some students to choose True for question 1, but this refers to Warhol, not to Rauschenberg.

07 Ask students to look at the possible reasons for getting Not Given statements wrong in Exercise 07 and compare them with their own predictions. Asks students to complete the matching task.

1 b	2 c	3 a

08 Tell students that they are going to practise some more examples of True / False / Not Given questions. Ask them to complete the task individually, then compare their answers with a partner, and to compare which part of the text gave them their answers. Check the answers with the whole group, nominating individual students to provide the answer and where they found it in the text.

1 T	2 NG	3 F	4 T	5 NG

09 Tell students that they are now going to focus on a different type of IELTS reading task – multiple-choice questions. Again, find out students' experience of handling this task type. Draw students' attention to the Tip box and encourage them to read about the strategy of using key words in the question stem to locate the part of the text with the answer. Ask students to read the question stem from the text without looking at the options (N.B. This may work best if you ask students to close their books and then write the question stem on the board). Ask them to scan the text and write down their own answer.

Sample answer: They were both innovators.

Then ask them to open their books and choose the option that most closely matches their answer.

10 Tell students that they are going to practise identifying the correct answer to a multiple-choice question. Make them aware that the ideas in all of the options will be mentioned in some way in the text (this is known as 'distraction', and the 2 incorrect options, 'distractors'), but that only one will completely answer the question. Ask students to complete the task by matching the explanations of why each option is correct or incorrect.

A 3	**B** 4	**C** 2	**D** 1

11 Tell students that they are going to complete a similar task, but that this time they will need to identify the correct part of the text. Elicit how they will do this (i.e. by identifying key words in the question stem and looking for synonyms in the text). Ask them to discuss with a partner why they think the correct answer is correct and the distractors are incorrect. Nominate pairs to feed back their ideas to the group.

> **A** Wrong – The text says *Like Rauschenberg, Warhol was close to his mother* but it does not say that the mothers were the most important influence on them.
>
> **B** Correct
>
> **C** Wrong – The text implies they didn't have family support to go to Art School.
>
> **D** Wrong – The artists themselves, not their families, were pulled (*gravitated*) towards New York.

12 Draw students' attention to the Tip box on multiple-choice questions that ask for the main idea of the paragraph. Ask students to complete the two tasks. Ensure that they highlight the main idea in the paragraph which helped them to find the answers.

> 1 Correct answer D – the whole paragraph goes through Warhol's work in the 60s and uses phrases like *one of the most definitive images of the Pop Art movement* and *which confounded critics and helped cement his credentials as an artist challenging the status quo.*
>
> A Wrong – This is a topic in paragraph F.
>
> B Wrong – The only mention of Rauschenberg is very brief and refers to a similarity between them (*Like Rauschenberg, he didn't limit himself* …)
>
> C Wrong – The text says their work was *equally innovative*, but it makes no comparison about quality.
>
> 2 Correct answer A – *Not content with subverting the conventional art forms of painting and sculpture, both Rauschenberg and Warhol experimented beyond them.*
>
> B Wrong – Warhol *dabbled in* (= experimented with) … *rock music* but did not influence it and this is just one example of working outside of traditional genres.
>
> C Wrong – Warhol *engaged in Performance Art,* and it is suggested that Rauschenberg did too, but this is not the main idea of paragraph E.
>
> D Wrong – This is true, but it is not the main idea of paragraph E.

Explain to students that IELTS reading texts may contain a variety of different verb tenses and that identifying these tenses will help them to follow the main points and may even help them to answer some questions correctly

13 Draw students' attention to the tenses and functions listed. Ask them to complete the matching task.

> 1 past simple   2 past perfect continuous
> 3 past continuous   4 past perfect simple   5 present perfect simple (passive)   6 present perfect continuous

14 Ask students to match the tenses that they identified in the previous exercise with their functions. Check answers as a group.

a past simple		b past continuous	
c present perfect continuous		d past perfect simple	
e present perfect simple		f past perfect continuous	

15 Tell students that they are going to practise using past tenses by choosing the correct form of the verb in some other sentences. Look at the first sentence together as a group. Ask students which tense they think is correct and encourage them to give reasons for their answers, by referring to the functions from Exercise 14. Elicit any language that may help students to identify the tense (i.e. the word *since* indicates the perfect aspect). Give students some time to complete the rest of the exercise and compare answers in pairs.

1 have been	2 married; lasted	3 have now
been developing	4 has had	5 had been living
and working		

EXAM SKILLS

16 / 17 Tell students that they are going to do reading exam practice tasks. Explain that they are going to focus on the two tasks they have looked at in the lesson; true / false / not given and multiple-choice questions. Before students do this exercise, ask them to read the Bullet box.

Advice

- Encourage students to quickly skim read the text to get an idea of its structure. Remind them that it is useful to get an idea of the topic of each paragraph, as this will help them to identify the parts of the text that contain the answers to the questions.

- For the true / false / not given questions, encourage students to identify key words in the question. Make them aware that they may need to look for synonyms of these words in the text. Remind them to be aware of 'not given' answers; those that they may expect to be true, but are actually not referred to in the text.

- For the multiple choice questions, encourage students to identify the part of the text that contains the answer by paying attention to key words in the question stem. Remind them to beware of distraction; all of the information in the multiple choice options will be mentioned in the text, but only one will be completely correct.

- It is good practice to give students a time limit of 20 minutes for completing this task, as this will train them to manage their time when doing reading exams.

Elicit the advice above from the students by asking concept check questions (e.g. 'Will you always find the exact words in the question in the text'? 'Is it better to read the text first or read the questions first?'). Then give students 20 minutes to complete the tasks. When they have finished, check answers as a group.

| 1 F | 2 T | 3 NG | 4 T | 5 T | 6 F |

7 D (*began with Rodin's technique of repeatedly casting the same figure and using multiple casts to create a new piece*)

8 D (the paragraph is essentially a list of innovative forms and the final sentence uses the paraphrase *pioneering forms of sculpture*)

9 C (*Touch, physical participation and social interaction are now common features of the experience of going to see art.*) A is contradicted by *often though not necessarily in mixed media;* B is contradicted by *usually exhibited in an indoor gallery space in an arrangement specified by the artist.* D is not mentioned, although the word 'time' does appear (*Installations are multi-sensory experiences built for a specific time and space*).

WRITING

> ## OUTCOMES
>
> - describe changes on a map, including which tenses to use
> - summarize information with appropriate discourse markers
> - ensure good coherence and cohesion in your answer.

OUTCOMES

The lesson focuses on the IELTS Part 1 writing task which requires students to describe changes over time in response to 2 different diagrams or maps of the same place during 2 different time periods. Explain to students that being able to identify and summarize the most important points is an essential skill for completing this task. They should also provide a cohesive and coherent answer by including a variety of cohesive devices.

LEAD-IN

01 Draw students' attention to the pictures in the book. Ask them to work in pairs and discuss any key differences between the two pictures. Nominate students to share their suggestions with the rest of the group. Note down their ideas on the board. This will help to generate some useful vocabulary that students can use in their writing later.

Tell students that they are going to learn some more useful vocabulary related to the topic of architecture. Tell them to look at the verbs in the box and decide which of the three categories they belong to. Tell students that these words are either synonyms of build / change / remove or words that are closely related. Explain that they may not know every word, but to begin with the words that they do know, and use a dictionary to check the meaning of any new vocabulary. Ask students to check their answers in pairs, then check as a group.

Build	Change	Remove
put up	extend	
develop	enlarge	knock down
erect	alter	tear down
construct	modernize	flatten
	replace	
	relocate	
	expand	
	renovate	
	convert	

02 Tell students that they are going to learn the noun forms of the verbs from Exercise 01. Explain that it is useful to know the different word family members when doing IELTS writing Part 1, as it will be possible to demonstrate a wider range of vocabulary. Elicit the noun forms of a the first few verbs, then ask students to complete the rest of the task in pairs.

put up (v)	putting up (n)
develop (v)	development (n)
erect (v)	erection (n)
construct (v)	construction (n)
enlarge (v)	enlargement (n)
alter (v)	alteration(s) (n)
modernise (v)	modernisation (n)
replace (v)	replacement (n)
relocate (v)	relocation (n)
expand (v)	expansion (n)
renovate (v)	renovation (n)
convert (v)	conversion (n)
knock down (v)	knocking down (n)
tear down (v)	tearing down (n)
flatten (v)	flattening (n)

03 Tell students that they are going to practise asking and answering questions about their home town. Explain that this will help them to generate ideas and vocabulary for the IELTS Part 1 task in which they will need to describe changes to a place over time. Give students 10 minutes to complete this task, and ensure that they swap roles after five minutes. Encourage the student who is listening to write down the key points, so that they can report back later. As students are talking, monitor and make a note of any useful vocabulary / grammatical structures. These can be written up on the board and shared with the group after the task.

04 Draw students' attention to the Bullet box. Explain that when describing changes to plans or maps for IELTS writing Part 1, they will need to follow a specific structure in order to gain good marks for the Task Achievement criterion. Ask them to read the information carefully and then close their books. Elicit what the three sections of an answer to this task type should include.

Tell students that they are going to begin by looking at the first part of the answer; the introductory section. Ask them to look at the diagram in the book and elicit what it shows. Encourage students to first look at the comments and to discuss whether they think they are mainly positive or mainly negative. Elicit what they think may be strong or weak features of introductions based on the comments (e.g. 'a strong introduction should map out what the answer is going to talk about', 'a weak introduction is copied from the question'). Ask concept check questions where appropriate. Then ask students to match the introductions with the comments in pairs.

1	D	**2**	A	**3**	B	**4**	C

05 Draw students' attention to the Tip on summarizing. Point out the example of grouping features into categories, and ask students if they can think of any further examples (e.g. train station, airport, bus station = transport facilities). Then ask students to look again at the map and group features into the categories listed.

children's play area – recreational
Bayley Mansions – residential
café – commercial (recreational)
terraced houses – residential
railway line – industrial
laundry – commercial
Bayley Street Park – recreational
shops – commercial
wasteland – industrial

06 Tell students that they are going to look at the maps again and take some notes on how the area has changed according to the 4 categories listed. Explain that it is good practice to make a brief plan of the key changes before starting to answer the question, as this will provide some structure for the main body paragraphs. Discuss the first category as a group and make a note of any suggestions that students make. Then ask students to complete the rest of the task in pairs.

Sample Answer
- residentially: replacement of terraced housing with flats
- industrially: removal of railway and wasteland
- commercially: relocation and expansion of shops and other facilities
- recreationally: construction of a park and children's play area

07 Ask students to think back to the work they did on coherence and cohesion in Unit 2. Elicit what these words mean and what students will need to do to get good marks for coherence and cohesion in IELTS writing tasks. Elicit that they should use discourse markers in order to improve the cohesion of their response.

Definitions

Coherence: an essay with good *coherence* is easy to follow and understand.

Cohesion: an essay with good *cohesion* flows naturally and logically from one idea to the next.

Ask students to read the information in the advice box carefully and then complete the model answer with the best discourse marker.

1 Overall
2 Whereas
3 Furthermore
4 Another major change to the area
5 On the commercial side
6 To sum up

08 Remind students of the advice they received in Unit 2 regarding accurate use of discourse markers. Elicit how students might use discourse markers inappropriately and the impact that this may have on their mark for coherence and cohesion. Tell students that they are going to check their understanding of discourse markers by matching them to their functions. First give an example of a discourse marker and ask students to explain when it would be used (e.g. *however* is used to indicate a contrast). Then ask students to complete the task.

> a To sum up   b Furthermore   c Whereas
> d Another major change to the area /On the commercial side   e Overall

09 Tell students that there are a number of different discourse markers with the same function, and that it is a good idea to use synonyms in order to demonstrate a wide range of vocabulary. Elicit an example from students (e.g. 'however' and 'in contrast' have similar meanings). Ask students to find synonyms for the rest of the discourse markers from Exercise 08 in pairs.

> *Suggested answers*
>
> Whereas – but, i.e. *In 1990 a railway line ran through the neighbourhood, but by 1935 …* (However, this repeats the structure of the previous sentence, so it would not be a good alternative in this case.)
>
> Furthermore – In addition
>
> Another major change to the area – One other key way in which the area changed
>
> On the commercial side – Turning to the commercial facilities
>
> To sum up – In summary, In conclusion, Overall

10 Tell students that they are going to look up some other methods of cohesion (or 'cohesive devices') besides discourse markers. Elicit any other methods of cohesion that students may know about, then ask them to read the advice box and check their ideas. Ask students to complete the task, matching the examples of cohesion with their descriptions.

> **1** b   **2** e   **3** d   **4** c   **5** a

11 Tell students that they are now going to look at some features of cohesion within paragraphs. Explain that cohesion is not only important at sentence level through the use of cohesive devices; the ideas in the answer need to flow logically too throughout the paragraphs. Draw students' attention to the listed features and then ask them to look back at the model answer from Exercise 07. Ask students to work in pairs and discuss which features are present and which are missing.

> 4 and 6 were not included. The other features are key to the structure of this writing task, which should focus on presenting the facts. Feature 4 is speculation (offering possible reasons for something) and a room 6 is giving an opinion. Candidates should not offer opinions, speculation or commentaries.

12 Tell students that they are going to practise identifying changes that have occurred over a period of time. Ask students to look at the 2 diagrams of a beach hotel in the book and to discuss in pairs what they consider the main changes to be. Encourage students to note down their ideas,

as they did in Exercise 06. Do feedback with the whole group and nominate pairs of students to provide answers.

> *Suggested answer*
> accommodation: more rooms, and a second storey for the hotel
> facilities: have been relocated
> recreation: swimming pool moved and enlarged and made more attractive, access to the beach has been improved by removing fence; water sports facilities have been added

13 Turn students' attention to the example essay describing the main changes over time to the beach hotel. Ask them what cohesive devices they would expect to find in a good answer. Get students to check the cohesive features provided and then complete the task in pairs.

> 1 The most striking alteration is to the hotel's capacity / Recreation had more prominence by 2013.
> 2 Generally speaking, Another significant change, On top of this, To summarise
> 3 show – illustrate
>   facilities – amenities
>   change – alteration
>   relocation – moved
>   during the ten year period – in the ten years between 2003 and 2013 – ten years previously; extend – expand – extension – expansion – increase – enlarged
> 4 second sentence: its final sentence in paragraph 2: its
>   3 paragraph: *This can be seen*; *On top of this* paragraph 4: *its*

14 Elicit from students which verb tenses they think they would use for describing changes over time. Draw students' attention to the Tip box and ask them to read the advice carefully. Emphasize that using verb tenses accurately will help them to get a good mark for the Grammatical Range and Accuracy criterion. Then ask students to complete the task.

> Past simple and past perfect would be the main two tenses. *Used to* is also possible and good to use as a variation on the past simple to demonstrate a good knowledge of grammar.

15 Ask students to look back at the example answers in Exercises 07 and 13 and identify the different tenses that the writer has used. Ask them to discuss why they think these tenses have been used.

> *Sample answer 1*
>
> **Past simple:** In 1900, this area had a combination of residential and industrial features; a railway line ran through the neighbourhood; made room for a spacious park; some new shops were built; the café and laundry were relocated and expanded
>
> **Past perfect:** by 1935 the industrial features <u>had largely disappeared</u>; [terraced houses] <u>had been replaced</u>; the areas of wasteland <u>had gone</u>
>
> *Used to:* the terraced houses which used to dominate the 1900 map

Sample answer 2

Past simple: Recreation <u>had</u> more prominence; the fence which <u>divided</u> the hotel; the hotel <u>underwent</u> an expansion

Past perfect: By 2013, the swimming pool and restaurant <u>had been relocated</u> and its seating area <u>had been enlarged</u>; a water sports centre <u>had been built</u>; [the fence] <u>had been removed</u> by 2013

EXAM SKILLS

16 Tell students that they are going to try an IELTS writing Part 1 task.

Advice

- Encourage students to look carefully at the map and identify what it shows. Remind students that they will be penalized for simply repeating the information in the question in their introduction.
- Remind students to include 3 main sections to their answer: an introduction, 2 paragraphs summarizing the main changes and a concluding paragraph.
- Encourage students to include a range of cohesion devices and to check their use of tenses.
- Give students 20 minutes to complete the task individually.

Refer students to the IELTS criteria specifically for bands 7 and 8 in the introduction to the Teachers' Book. Tell them to firstly determine whether they fully meet the criteria for band 7 and then check if they surpass it and can be judged to meet the grade 8 criteria.

Extension

Ask students to look at the model essay below and to check for the features covered in the lesson.

Sample answer

The two maps show the outskirts of the town of Fosbury in 1980 and 2015. The 35-year period saw changes to the road layout, and to the residential, recreational and commercial facilities.

In terms of the road layout, the main change was the addition of a roundabout in the centre of this area, which necessitated the demolition of a block of flats and a grocer's shop. The residential accommodation underwent further changes with the removal of a street of terraced houses on the right side of the map and the construction of additional housing on the le side. New houses replaced the park, which was relocated to the other side of the road and decreased in size. By 2015 a supermarket with a car park had been erected on the site of the terraced houses.

The area industrialised further during the 35-year period, with warehouses being put up where fields had been earlier. The area's sporting facilities had also been developed, with a new sports centre taking the place of the old tennis courts.

In summary, the area of Fosbury shown on the maps modernised and developed between 1980 and 2015.
(191 words)

LISTENING

OUTCOMES

- use prepositions of place and movement correctly
- label a map or plan
- answer multiple-choice questions
- follow directions
- identify distractors.

OUTCOMES

Ask students to focus on the outcomes. The first outcome helps students to better use prepositions of place and movement and also to correctly identify and understand them when listening. The second outcome helps students to better complete tasks requiring maps and plans to be labelled. The third outcome focuses on helping students to better answer multiple-choice questions. Tell students that for both types of listening tasks above, they will be given strategies to better complete these tasks. The fourth outcome is related to the first and concerns following directions. Tell students that this is particularly useful in the listening exam as well as in a more general setting. Again, students will be given strategies to do this more effectively. The final outcome helps students to identify distractors – incorrect answers in multiple-choice and open questions. Again, this is highly relevant to the listening exam as well as the reading exam.

LEAD-IN

01 This exercise tests students' existing knowledge of prepositions of place and movement. Ask students to work in pairs to use the prepositions in the box to complete the sentences. Monitor as students do this. When you provide feedback, before confirming answers, encourage students to volunteer answers (or you can nominate students to answer) and to comment on whether they agree or not with the answer given by classmates.

1 into / through / across; on	2 in; of
3 between; from/via; from/via	4 to
5 opposite / across from / close to	
6 at; opposite; on	7 up
8 at; behind You cannot use *above* and *below*.	

02 This exercise provides students with vocabulary input and will be useful for the listening task in Exercise 05. Ask students to complete the exercise in pairs, monitor and then provide feedback as outlined in Exercise 01.

2 *the lobby:* an entrance room similar to reception

3 *the drawing room:* a room where guests are entertained (originally called the 'withdrawing room' where guests used to withdraw to from the dining room after a meal)

4 *the cloakroom*; it sometimes has a toilet

5 *the pantry:* a storeroom for food, crockery and other kitchen items

6 *the cellar:* an underground area, usually used for storage

7 *the attic:* a room or area at the top of the house, under the roof, often used for storing things

8 *the ballroom:* a room where balls (dances) and special events would be held

9 *the servants' quarters:* small rooms where the servants lived/slept

10 *the conservatory:* a room with direct sunlight, like an indoor greenhouse, often full of plants

03 This exercise leads into the listening task in Exercise 05 and prepares students for it. Before students complete the exercise, ask them to read the information about labelling maps. Make sure students are aware that this type of task has two variations in the exam (multiple-choice - choosing answers from options - or open answers). Also, explain to students the need to use time between questions to predict the language that may be used in the recording. Ask students to complete the exercise in pairs.

| 1 | C | 2 | B | 3 | A |

04 Students write their own directions here and can use the examples in the previous exercise to help them. Ask students to do this individually and then to compare answers. Monitor and then provide feedback.

Sample answer
Go in the main entrance and turn right. It is right in front of you, next to the library.

05 This exercise provides listening practice of labelling a map. You can point out to students that they need to choose from options here but may not be given options in the exam. Students should listen individually and then compare answers in pairs. Monitor and provide feedback.

B

Transcript 18

Welcome to Westchester Castle, everyone. I know some of you have come a long way today, so I hope you will enjoy your time with us. Westchester Castle dates back to the 11th century and was home to the Westchester family until the 19th century, when it was donated to the National Trust. We are now standing at the main entrance. As you will have seen, the castle is rectangular-shaped, with four turrets, or towers, one at each corner. So, as we enter, you'll see on your left the Grand Hall, where balls were held when the family lived here. If you walk through the Grand Hall you can see one of the four turrets in the corner. You'll see that it's now a gift shop, though it used to be Lord Westchester's bedroom. It has a magnificent view of the aviary, where the birds are kept. You will have plenty of time to purchase your souvenirs there after the tour.

06 This exercise is very similar to Exercise 05 but there are no options to choose from. Before students do this exercise, ask them to read the Tip box.

Advice

Make sure students know that there will be a lot of irrelevant information that they need to ignore and that they need to stay focused on what they are listening for. Also, point out that in listening exams, it is very common that they will hear other places and answers that are incorrect – these are called distractors.

Now ask students to complete this exercise following the procedure outlined in Exercise 05. During feedback, encourage students to say why they think their answer is correct. Then confirm the answer.

Portrait gallery

Transcript 19

Now as we move out of the Grand Hall, notice this wonderful spiral staircase in front of you. It's not in use any more due to health and safety reasons, but at one time that was the only way to get to the upper level. Now we have a lift, situated just down the hallway. If you would like to follow me, we will move straight ahead into the Exhibition Room. At the moment, as you can see, there's a fascinating exhibition of clothes from the 15th and 16th centuries, which you can spend some time looking at later. Now please turn to your left and cross this little anteroom to enter the next turret, which is the portrait gallery. Here you can see portraits of all the Westchester lords and ladies through the ages.

07 This exercise helps students to understand why the answer is correct and why the distractors are incorrect. You can also provide a copy of the script to help students here. Ask students to listen (and read) and then to discuss in pairs the reasons why the distractors given here are incorrect. Monitor and then provide feedback.

Spiral staircase and Exhibition Room are already labelled. Anteroom is not correct because you 'cross this little anteroom to enter the next turret' and room B is in the turret.

08 This exercise provides more extended practice of labelling a map. Asks students to do this individually before comparing in pairs after the recording. Monitor and then provide feedback, encouraging students to say why they think their answer is correct.

| C | sewing room | D | dining room |

Transcript 20

Right, I hope you've had enough time to look at those fantastic portraits. Please follow me back into the Exhibition space. We're going to cross this room and you'll see that this corner of the castle is almost a mirror image of the Portrait gallery, so again we're going to go through a little anteroom into the turret. You can see that this room has been designed to look like a room from the 14th century. All the furniture and even the drapes and tapestries are authentic. Can you guess what this room was used for? A sitting room? No. Well, people did sit in here, but only the ladies. <u>This was the sewing room!</u> It has the best light in the castle. That's why it was used for this purpose.

Next to us is the library, but we can't access it through here. We need to go back through the Exhibition Room and out into the hallway. The library has some ancient manuscripts which are really valuable; that's why you can only look through the door and not enter. But if you keep going, back towards the main entrance, there's a room you *can* enter on your left. This was the <u>dining room, situated next to the kitchens,</u> which I suppose makes sense.

Extension

Give students the script and play the recording again. Once more, ask students to identify why the correct answer is correct and why the distractors given are wrong.

09 Within the same listening context, students are now able to focus on answering multiple-choice questions. Ask students to read the information about multiple-choice questions before students complete the exercise. Make sure students are reminded of the use of distractors in listening tasks. Students should complete the exercise as they listen and then compare their answers in pairs. Monitor and then provide feedback.

> 1 b   2 c   3 a

Transcript 21

OK, so now you've had a look around inside, I'd like to tell you a little about the architecture of the castle building. Westchester Castle has its origins in the 11th century but it was unrecognisable as the castle we see before us. <u>It was not until the 12th century that living quarters were added.</u> The castle was owned by the Westchester family from the 13th to the 19th centuries.

10 Students listen again to answer another multiple-choice question. Follow the procedure outlined above in the previous exercise.

> B (It was not until the 12th century that living quarters were added.)

11 Exercises 11 and 12 are further multiple-choice questions. Before students do this exercise, ask them to read the Tip box.

Advice

It's important for students to be aware that less common vocabulary is often explained in the recording and that they can use context – words around these items of less frequent words and phrases – to help them.

Use the same procedure outlined in Exercise 09.

> drawbridge: the castle needed to be easy to defend and have a secure entry gate and would have had a drawbridge at the main point of entry
> turrets: the round towers at the corners
> moat: vital defence, around the building, is now a dry ditch (implies it once had water)

Transcript 22

As you probably know, the aim of a castle was to provide a secure base against attack. It needed to be easy to defend, while preventing exposure to the attackers. It had to have thick, high walls and a secure entry gate. Westchester, like other medieval castles, would have had a drawbridge at the main point of entry, but sadly, it is no longer standing. <u>The four turrets – the round towers at the corners – remain in a remarkably well-preserved state</u> for such an ancient castle. You can see that there used to be a moat – another vital defence against invaders, but now all you see around the building is a dry ditch.

12 Students listen again to answer another multiple-choice question. Follow the procedure outlined above in Exercise 10.

> C (The drawbridge is no longer standing; the moat is now a dry ditch.)

Extension

For exercises 09 to 12, you can provide students with the script and play the recording again. This will help students identify clues and help them to justify the correct answer.

13 Exercises 13 and 14 give students more practice. This time, students need to fill in the gaps in the sentences. Before students do this, ask them to read the Tip box.

Students should now listen and write their answers. Then ask students to compare their answers in pairs. You can monitor and then provide feedback.

> storerooms, tunnels, dungeons

Transcript 23

The castle would have had <u>storerooms</u> in the basement to store enough food for many months in case of a siege. Unfortunately, we are no longer able to enter the basement area as it's not safe, but we know that there are underground <u>tunnels</u> used for escape and for making sorties, or attacking raids, against the enemy. This castle is unusual in that there has been no evidence found of <u>dungeons</u> – underground prison cells. Perhaps they never took any prisoners!

14 Students can use their answers for Exercise 13 to help them to complete this exercise. Ask students to discuss this in pairs and to look at the script again to identify any clues. Monitor and then provide feedback.

> A

EXAM SKILLS

15 This exercise provides longer listening exam practice of labelling diagrams and answering multiple-choice questions. Students should use the strategies they learnt to try to complete this exercise. After playing the recording, ask students to compare answers. Monitor to see if students need to listen an additional time. Then provide feedback – remember to invite answers and comments from the class before confirming the correct answers.

> | 1 E | 2 G | 3 A | 4 C | 5 B | 6 I |
> |-----|-----|-----|-----|-----|-----|
> | 7 A | 8 B | 9 B | 10 A | | |

Extension

You can provide the script and play the recording again. This time ask students to identify clues and justify the correct answers. Ask students to discuss this in pairs before you provide feedback.

Transcript 24

You will hear a tour guide giving information about a historic house and the organisation that owns it. First you have some time to look at questions 1 to 6.

[pause]

Now listen carefully and answer questions 1 to 6.

As you know, Holloway Estate is one of the few surviving estates in this area that still retains many of the farming features of the past. Let me quickly explain where you can find some of the key attractions.

If you take a look on your map, we are now standing at the foot of the steps to the Manor House. Can everyone see it, marked with an arrow? Don't forget – this is our meeting point for when we leave. So, directly behind us is the fountain. From here, heading left, the path takes you to a gate which leads into the famous Holloway orchards, where for hundreds of years the estate has been growing its highly prized apples, cherries and plums. Incidentally, if you fancy trying them, a range of delicious Holloway jams and preserves are available in the gift shop. Speaking of which, the gift shop is to the right of the main house.

If you go through the gate, the left-hand path takes you to the apiary, that's to say, the bee hives, where Holloway honey has been collected for more than 250 years. And yes, before anyone asks, you can also buy Holloway honey.

If you take the right-hand path, you will come to some old farmer's cottages which have been renovated and are rented out as holiday cottages. Please feel free to admire them from the outside, but as there may be guests staying in them right now, please respect their privacy.

From the back of the main house, crossing the car park and just before you get to the cattle fields, you will find a row of three buildings. The middle one is the old dairy. The dairy is actually working, producing butter and cheeses using traditional methods. Next to that, on the left are the former cattle sheds, where the livestock was kept. Nowadays it's used as a museum, so those of you who are keen to explore Holloway's farming past should pay it a visit. The building furthest from the manor house is the old ice house, which is no longer in use and is due to be restored, hopefully next year.

Last but not least, you may have noticed on the way in that on either side of the main gates are two small houses. This is a traditional feature of country houses of the period. On the right-hand side as you enter the estate is what was known as the gatekeeper's lodge. This has now become the estate office, and the estate manager runs the estate from there. OK, I think that just about covers everything …

Before you hear the rest of the talk you have some time to look at questions 7 to 10.

[pause]

Now listen and answer questions 7 to 10.

OK, everyone, before we begin the tour of the Manor House, I'd like to take a few minutes to tell you about the organisation that now owns the estate, and for which I work – the National Trust. The National Trust is the largest membership organisation in the UK with 4.24 million members. Our annual revenue is £494 million. At the present time, we have 5,899 paid members of staff and an additional 62,000 volunteers. That's an approximate number because new volunteers are joining us all the time.

The Trust owns about 350 heritage properties. Many of these are large country houses that the owners donated to us because they could no longer afford to maintain them. The Trust also owns gardens and industrial monuments. The Trust's sources of income include membership subscriptions, entrance fees, donations and revenue from the gift shops and restaurants within our properties, with much of the money raised being invested back in the preservation of the properties themselves. And of course, this is the principal purpose of the National Trust: the conservation and protection of historical places and spaces, with a view to making them available to the public.

As well as owning stately homes and houses associated with famous people, the National Trust has gradually extended its collection of art, and it also owns valuable books, clothing, furniture, ceramics and all kinds of unusual objects.

Now if you would like to join the National Trust, I have the forms here, or you can visit our website, and join online. You will get unlimited access to hundreds of wonderful days out across the country. Lifetime membership costs £1,555, but most members join for a year at a time. Individual membership is currently £64 annually but it's cheaper to join with your partner or another family member as it'll be £108 for two people living at the same address. For a family of four (two adults and two children) a year's membership costs £114. It's a great gift for a birthday or other special event. There are lots of benefits to being a member. As well as free parking at all our locations, you receive a National Trust handbook full of information to help you plan your visits, and if you pay by direct debit, you will receive a free pair of binoculars. Oh, I almost forgot, all members receive a free copy of the National Trust magazine sent to you by post three times a year.

SPEAKING

OUTCOMES

- make notes for your long turn in Part 2
- structure your long turn
- use a range of spoken discourse markers.

OUTCOMES

Ask students to focus on the outcomes. The first two outcomes help students with Part 2 of the IELTS speaking exam. Tell students that it is important to use the one minute available for making notes to help them structure what they going to say.

The third outcome concerns the use of spoken discourse markers and builds upon phrases already learnt in previous units. Students will be better able to use a greater range of discourse markers and identify specific functions for each. This will help students to produce better structured and longer turns for Part 2 of the exam.

LEAD-IN

01 This exercise tests students' knowledge of phrases used to describe pieces of art. It also builds students' vocabulary and these phrases can then be used for other topics during the speaking exam. Ask students to complete this exercise in pairs or small groups. Monitor as students do this. During feedback, invite students to answer and try to encourage a class discussion by asking other students to say if they agree or not with the answer given by their classmate. Then confirm answers.

1 NS	2 Y	3 Y	4 NS	5 Y
6 N	7 NS	8 Y	9 N	10 N

02 This exercise gives students the opportunity to talk about pieces of art and to use the phrases learnt in Exercise 01. Ask students to complete this exercise in pairs and monitor as students do this. Encourage students to use the phrases from Exercise 01 as you do this. Invite students to give their comments about each piece of art to the whole class. If students use phrases from Exercise 01, you may want to ask the following questions to the whole class to check they understand:

Does he/she like it?

Does he/she dislike it?

Is he/she not sure about it?

03 Exercises 03-10 focus on making notes effectively for Part 2 of the speaking exam. In this exercise, students evaluate example notes. Before students do this exercise, ask them to read the Bullet box.

Advice

Make sure students are aware of what they need to do for Part 2 of the exam. Point out that they should cover all four points on the card and that they should make notes. It's a good idea to ensure students know to only write down key words as this will save time.

Ask students to evaluate the example notes in pairs and monitor to check students are on task. Encourage class discussion and then confirm the answer.

Suggested answer

The notes are not complete (no mention of how her work makes her feel) perhaps because she has wasted time on unnecessary words and writing words out in full. Notes should be key words only.

04 This exercise gives students the opportunity to revise the example notes by listening to the recording. Ask students to listen and make notes individually. As answers will differ, it's a good idea to show students the example answer below. Ask students to look at the example notes and say what changes have been made (e.g. only key words used, short forms used and all points covered). Alternatively, you can show the example notes only after Exercise 06.

Suggested answer

Sal. Dali

Born 1904? Catalunya, Spain

Died – 1980s?

Type: Surrealist, used symbolism e.g. Persistence of Memory – about time

Why like?

– interested in Maths, Sci like me

– unconventional, eccentric – interesting character

– later in life – sculpture / film sets – innovative

– colours

Feel? – proud

Transcript 25

The creative person I have chosen is Salvador Dali. I visited the Dali Foundation in Figueres last year, and it made a great impression on me. He was born in Catalonia in Spain. I'm not sure of the exact year but I think maybe around 1904 and he died in about the late 1980s, when he was in his 80s. He was a surrealist painter, so he used symbolism a lot. What that means is in his paintings things don't look like what they are. One of his most famous paintings is called The Persistence of Memory and it shows watches or clocks that are very soft, which is supposed to show that time is not as most people understand it. He was fascinated by Maths and Science, and so am I, so that is one reason why I like him. Another reason is that he was quite unconventional – and even eccentric in his behaviour, so that makes him an interesting character, who was not like other people. The same is true of his art. And what's more he didn't just stick with painting. Later in his life he did sculpture and worked on film sets. So, to put it in a nutshell, I like the fact that he was innovative and totally different from others. Oh, and one more thing, the colours in his work are amazing, so they're good to hang on your walls – not the originals of course! His work makes me feel proud because he's from my country – from my region, actually, and he brought fame to Catalunya.

05 This exercise asks students to compare notes in pairs and to evaluate each other's notes using the three questions. Monitor as students discuss their answers.

06 In this exercise, students work in pairs to improve the notes they have made. As answers will differ, you can ask pairs what changes they made.

07 Students have the opportunity to improve their notes now based on the feedback given by peers. Before students do this exercise, ask them to read the Tip box.

Advice

Tell students that specialist knowledge is not expected in Part 2 and that the answer is not restricted to more conventional definitions of artists.

Now ask students to complete the exercise individually.

08 This exercise gives an opportunity for further peer feedback. Encourage students to look at each other's notes and say what they think their partner will talk about. Ask students to also evaluate the notes based on the three questions from Exercise 05.

09 This exercise introduces the idea of using mind maps rather than linear text notes. Ask students to complete the exercise together in pairs and monitor. Encourage class discussion before suggesting the possible answers below.

> *Advantages of mind maps:* easy to add to, easy to access at a glance, can show relationships between ideas.
>
> *Possible disadvantages:* notes like these don't put the points in order, so you need to make sure your talk follows a logical order; you also need to be sure you don't omit any of the points on the card.

10 Students can try to apply this system of note-taking to their own notes. As preferences of note-making style can be personal, encourage students to show their mind maps to partners and to share their opinions about whether they think they will use this style or not.

11 Exercises 11 to 16 focus on improving the structure of long turns by using discourse markers. Before students do this exercise, ask them to read the Tip box. Focus again on the marking criteria in the introduction.

Advice

Make sure students are aware that they should structure their talk according to the bullet points given on the instruction card for Part 2 of the speaking exam.

Exercise 11 gives students the opportunity to analyse the written form of an example Part 2 answer. Ask students to complete the exercise individually and then to compare their answers in pairs. Monitor as students do this and then invite students to volunteer answers. Before confirming correct answers, encourage other students to say if they agree or disagree with answers suggested by their classmates.

> Yes, she talked about the four points in order.
>
> *what you know about the life of this person*
> The creative person I have chosen is Salvador Dali. I visited the Dali Foundation in Figueres last year, and it made a great impression on me. He was born in Catalonia in Spain. I'm not sure of the exact year but I think maybe around 1904 and he died in about the late 1980s, when he was in his 80s.
>
> *what kind of creative work this person does/did*
> He was a surrealist painter, so he used symbolism a lot. What that means is in his paintings things don't look like what they are. One of his most famous paintings is called *The Persistence of Memory* and it shows watches or clocks that are very soft, which is supposed to show that time is not as most people understand it.
>
> *why you like his/her work*
> He was fascinated by Maths and Science, and so am I, so that is one reason why I like him. Another reason is that he was quite unconventional – and even eccentric in his behaviour, so that makes him an interesting character, who was not like other people. The same is true of his art.

> And what's more, he didn't just stick with painting. Later in his life he did sculpture and worked on film sets. So, to put it in a nutshell, I like the fact that he was innovative and totally different from others. Oh, and one more thing, the colours in his work are amazing, so they're good to hang on your walls – not the originals of course.
>
> *describe the way his/her work makes you feel*
> His work makes me feel proud because he's from my country – from my region, actually, and he brought fame to Catalunya.

12 This exercise gives the opportunity for further analysis of the example answer to Part 2 of the speaking exam in Exercise 11. Follow the guidelines outlined above for Exercise 11.

> 1 d 2 b 3 h 4 g 5 f 6 c 7 i 8 e
> 9 a

13 Students can now listen to the example Part 2 answer given by Yaz. Ask students to look again at the notes in Exercise 09 as they listen. Students should listen individually and discuss their answers together in pairs. Monitor as students do this and follow the feedback guidelines outlined in Exercise 11.

> I'll start by   possibly   I'm not 100% sure about that.
> OK, so moving on   As well as   so   for some
> reason   So why do I like him?   Primarily
> because of   yet   Finally,   I suppose
> So, that's about it.

Transcript 26

For my creative person, I'm going to talk about the British artist David Hockney. So, I'll start by saying that he was born somewhere in the North of England, possibly Yorkshire, but I'm not 100% sure about that. I'd say he was born in about the 1930s as he's still alive today but he's getting on a bit. OK, so moving on to talk about his art. He's a modern artist and he was part of the Pop Art movement. As well as a painter, he's a photographer and printmaker, so he's pretty versatile. He paints country scenes and for some reason he used to love painting swimming pools. So why do I like him? Primarily, it's because of the colours he uses. His paintings are so bright and cheerful. They show real things you can recognise; yet they have a modern feel. Lots of modern art is so abstract, you have no idea what it's supposed to be, but Hockney is different. Finally, when I see Hockney's paintings, I feel happy and relaxed. I feel as if it's warm and sunny. I suppose it's that feel-good factor that makes me like him so much. So, that's about it.

14 Students now have a second opportunity to listen and focus specifically on the discourse markers used. Before students listen, they can work in pairs to try to predict the missing words. Then ask students to listen and complete the exercise individually before comparing answers in pairs. Complete the feedback procedure outlined in Exercise 11.

1	I'll start by	2	so, moving on	3	As well as
4	Primarily	5	yet	6	Finally
7	that's about it				

15 Students now have the opportunity to practise their long turn for the Part 2 task question in Exercise 03. Ask students to follow the instructions given for this exercise. Ask students to do this in pairs and monitor as they do this. Make notes of any common issues you want to bring up in feedback. You can nominate students to give their answers in front of the whole class for peer feedback or you can allow students to volunteer. Try to encourage constructive feedback from classmates before you provide your own.

Refer students to the IELTS criteria specifically for bands 7 and 8 in the introduction to the Teachers' Book. Tell them to firstly determine whether they fully meet the criteria for band 7 and then check if they surpass it and can be judged to meet the grade 8 criteria.

Extension

Use any errors you noted down when you monitored. Write a list of these on the board (3-5 is manageable). Also, add 1-2 correct answers. Ask students to identify the correct answers and correct the incorrect ones. This is a good way to recycle what has been learnt in the exercise and to also focus on responding to emerging student errors and needs.

16 This exercise gives students the opportunity to use the feedback given to them to improve their answers. Follow the same procedure as outlined in Exercise 15.

Alternative and extension

You can use the same extension as in the previous exercise and/or do the following. Ask students to record their answers on a smart phone or other device. Ask students to listen to their own response and evaluate it. Then ask them to rerecord their answer. This can be done in class or as homework.

EXAM SKILLS

17 This exercise gives students exam practice of a full IELTS speaking exam based on the topic of the unit. Before students do this exercise, ask them to read the Tip box.

Advice

Make sure students are aware that in the real exam, the topic for Part 1 will be different from Parts 2 and 3. However, tell students that in this book, they are sometimes the same.

Ask students to complete Exercise 17 in pairs and to take turns doing the practice test. Students can either swap roles after each part of the test or at the end of the complete test. Encourage students to give constructive feedback to each other. Monitor and make notes of any common issues you want to bring up in feedback. You can then nominate students to give their answers in front of the whole class for peer feedback or you can allow students to volunteer. Try to encourage constructive feedback from classmates before you provide your own.

Alternative and extension

Extensions and alternative suggestions outlined in Exercises 15 and 16 can also be used here.

READING

OUTCOMES

- successfully answer 'matching feature' questions.
- develop whole-text understanding to enable you to answer global multiple-choice questions.
- consider the meaning and use of modals of obligation, past and present.

OUTCOMES

In this unit, students will focus on two IELTS reading task types: matching features tasks and global multiple-choice questions. Matching features tasks are used with Reading passages that contain theories or comments about different people, places years and things. In Unit 4, students will practise identifying the views of several different people in a text. In order to do this, they will need to be able to scan the text for information and recognise paraphrasing. Global multiple-choice tasks are multiple-choice questions that involve identifying a purpose or aim of the writer. In order to answer these questions successfully, students will need to develop strategies for gaining a good understanding of the whole text.

LEAD-IN

01 Ask students to close their books. Write the word 'Finance' on the board. Elicit the part of speech and other word family members (i.e. 'financial', 'financially', 'to finance'). Get students to work in groups and give them three minutes to brainstorm words they associate with the topic of finance. Encourage students to share their ideas as a class and write down their suggestions, checking meaning where necessary. Then turn their attention to Exercise 01, and ask them to complete the task in pairs.

> **2** A *loan* is an amount of money borrowed for any purpose. A *mortgage* is an amount of money borrowed specifically to buy a property.
>
> **3** Regulations are the procedures or rules set by any authority or person in charge in order for an organisation/business to function properly. *Laws* are instructions that are put in place by the government and apply to everyone in the country, and regulations can be part of them.
>
> **4** There is little effective difference in meaning. *Go bust* is more informal and used in spoken communication rather than written.
>
> **5** A *lender* provides a *borrower* with the money that they have asked for. In other words, a borrower receives a loan and a *lender* gives a loan.

> **6** *Savings* are money that is put into a safe place so that it cannot easily be spent, and may even make some profit in interest. *Investments* are money that is put into a less safe place, such as shares in a company, in the hope that it will make a profit.
>
> **7** *Taxes* are a certain percentage of someone's income or the cost of things that is taken by the government to help pay for public services and infrastructure. A *pension* is an amount of money that someone receives a er they have retired from work, possibly from the government, possibly from a private pension company.
>
> **8** Broadly speaking, a *businessperson* is someone who takes over an existing business/position, while an *entrepreneur* is someone who starts new businesses and/or companies.

02 Ask students to close their books. Write '2008' on the board. Ask students if they know what significant financial event happened during this year. It may be useful to show them some pictures related to the 2008 global financial crisis to elicit the answer (e.g. workers at Lehman Brothers leaving their office, houses with repossession signs etc.). Then give students five minutes to discuss the causes and effects of the 2008 financial crisis in pairs.

Alternative

If you think that your students will not have a lot of knowledge of this topic, you could write a small number of causes taken from the reading passage on the board as sentence halves or prepare a PPT slide containing this information. Ask students to work in pairs and identify causes.

e.g.

Investment bankers tried to make big profits	by buying packages of debt from commercial banks and mortgage lenders.
People in low paid employment	were offered mortgages.
Credit rating agencies	gave the debt packages AAA ratings.
Investment banks	paid the credit rating agencies.

Having discovered this information, students can then discuss what they think happened as a result of these factors.

Matching features tasks are used with Reading passages that contain theories or comments about different people, places years and things. For these tasks, the different options are listed in a box and students will need to match them to sentences that paraphrase the information in the passage.

Begin by asking students whether they are familiar with this question type and elicit what it involves. Then turn students' attention to the Bullet box on matching features. Tell them to read the information carefully, and concept check them on the key points (e.g. 'What kinds of information might you be asked to match?', 'Will you find the information in order?'). Emphasize that in matching features tasks the information will not be in order, which means that students will need to use their scanning skills in particular to locate the correct information.

The answers are in the reading passage.

03 Tell students that they are going to practise identifying some features in a text, and looking at specific language to help them identify these features. Look at the first example together and ask students how they think they would identify a writer being mentioned for the first time. Encourage them to read the tip box, and then ask them to read through the text and check their predictions.

1 Their full name is given.
2 Usually just a surname is given.
3 It is in italics. Sometimes titles may appear in 'quotation marks'.
4 The exact words written appear in 'quotation marks'.

04 Tell students that they are going to practise matching people mentioned in the text with their views about the 2008 financial crisis. Explain that matching writers with their views is a common example of a feature matching task in the IELTS reading exam. Ask students to read through the text and to draw boxes around the names mentioned in the text and explain that this will help them to quickly identify the writers, and will help them to match their views more quickly.

Advice

Tell students that in the IELTS Reading exam, the people mentioned may appear in several different sections, and that they will need to scan the whole passage carefully. Some of the people in the list may be distractors, and they may not need to use all the letters. Explain that in the tasks that follow, they will focus on smaller sections of the text, in order to become more familiar with the task type and to practise using strategies for completing these tasks successfully.

05 Tell students that they are going to match the names with details in the text for the first three paragraphs only. Ask students to go through the task individually, and then to compare their answers in pairs. It is important that students are able to explain their reasons for their chosen answers by referring to the part of the text where they found them.

1 A (Alicia Pillory) paragraph 2: 'The grand, misguided theory was that any repayments would have to be made to the companies or people who now owned the mortgages, and everyone would get rich.'
2 C (Charles Vane) paragraph 3: 'The main purpose of these organisations is to evaluate in a neutral way the amount of risk an individual or company might face in a potential investment. […] the credit rating agencies were actually paid by the investment banks themselves, […] 'which is actually very far from being neutral'.'
3 C (Charles Vane) paragraph 3: 'We have to take that into consideration before isolating and criticising the investment banks too harshly.'

06 Instruct students go through the same process for paragraphs 4, 5 and 6.

4 A (Alicia Pillory) paragraph 4: 'So many people were *taken advantage of* (= exploited),' writes Pillory, and 'this *irresponsible lending behaviour* (= careless way of working) was never made to stop, with no ultimate consequences for the bankers, who simply *became very, very rich* (= got more wealthy)'.
5 B (Dr Alfred Moran) paragraph 5: 'The AAA ratings gave everyone a *dishonest guarantee* (= false assurance) that the system could not collapse. Unfortunately for the *world's economy* (= global economy), the insurance companies *followed those ratings blindly* (= accepted [those ratings] without question).'
6 A (Alicia Pillory) paragraph 4: She maintains that the *authorities* (= government) could, and should, have *put a stop to it* (= brought [the problem] to an end) earlier. Instead, 'at this point, *another industry saw the potential for profit* (= a new profit-driven industry) and greedily *stepped in* (= became involved)'.

07 Tell students that they are going to look at one view taken from paragraph 6 and match it with the person who expresses it. This will help students to focus on the specific sections of text containing views, and will discourage them from simply guessing.

It is the view of Charles Vane, who is mentioned several lines earlier in the paragraph. Although it may appear that the opinion belongs to the writer of the passage, it is actually the case that the writer is reporting, rather than quoting, Vane's words. The phrase 'By extension' also helps you to understand that this is not the view of the writer, but that it follows logically from what Charles Vane said.

08 This task introduces the global multiple-choice question in which students choose the option that best summarizes a main idea in the text.

Advice

In order to select the correct answer, students need to choose the option that is entirely true, and that applies to the whole text, rather than a specific paragraph or section. The distractor options may be only partially true, or may to refer to an idea in one paragraph or section, rather than one that is expressed throughout the text.

Explain to students that there are some 'hints' to help them to choose the right answer. Encourage them to scan the text to find the answers to the questions in each hint first, and then to decide which option best summarizes the writer's main idea. Encourage students to read the advice in the tip box.

C – The global financial crisis was created by a number of groups and has had only negative effects.
A incorrect: The writer only mentions debtors' prisons in the first and final paragraphs to show how attitudes to debt have changed. However, there is no mention of them in the rest of the text, so this is not the main idea.

B incorrect: In paragraph 6, Charles Vane compares the 'unwise' way in which people in the West save, compared to Chinese people. This is the opinion of Charles Vane, not the writer, and it only appears in this section, not the whole passage.

C correct: Three (= 'a number of') main groups are focused on – commercial banks, investment banks, insurance companies (and, arguably, 'investors'). There are no positive effects mentioned throughout the passage.

D incorrect: It is true that widespread attitudes to financial responsibility are heavily criticised throughout the passage. However, the word 'worldwide' makes this the incorrect option because the writer does not suggest that everyone has the wrong attitudes.

09 In this exercise, students do some further supported practice of global multiple-choice questions. This time both parts of the statement are placed in boxes. Use this task to make students aware of distractor options that may be only partially true. Ensure that they check whether or not both parts convey correct information.

> A – *incorrect*. There is no comparison made between the two eras. The 19th century is mentioned but not how they approached saving their money.
> B – *correct*. Three differing views from three writers are brought together in a summary of the topic.
> C – *incorrect*. The writer's tone is critical, but not just of investment banks. Also the writer is specifically evaluating the causes of the financial crash, rather than the more abstract 'unhealthy concept of debt'.
> D – *incorrect*. The writer does list some of the failing processes, such as the mishandling of the AAA credit rating. However, the writer has chosen to include various interpretations of what brought about the crisis and in the final paragraph says 'Whatever the root causes of this highly devastating period in our history', which tells us that the writer is not committing to one interpretation or another.

10 This task focuses on the 'choose a title' question type for global multiple-choice questions. For this task type, students will need to ensure that the information in the options is fully correct, and that the correct 'title' refers to an idea that is expressed throughout the text, and not just in one section.

Ask students to read through the tip box carefully, and then complete Exercise 10.

> The best title is D.
> A – *incorrect*: The passage is not a historical account of debt, as it focuses on a short period of time from 2008 until the present. This is not enough time to be considered 'the modern era'. Furthermore, although there is reference to another point in history (the 19th century), there is no description of what happened between then and now.
> C – *incorrect*: The text focuses on a specific disaster, not many disasters, and one which resulted from the actions of specific groups of people working in specific industries. 'Finance and investment' is too broad a term to fit.

D – correct: The writer may not state conclusively who they think is to blame, but the text presents different perspectives about where the responsibility for the crash lies.

Write the first example from Exercise 11 on the board: 'We have to take that into consideration'. Check students' comprehension by asking them to identify the main verb and modal verb in the sentence (i.e. 'take' and 'have to'). Ask students to identify the function of the modal verb in this case. Elicit that it is a modal verb of obligation. Explain that modals of obligation may be commonly found in texts that contain a number of different arguments, which are often included on the IELTS reading exam.

11 Ask students to look at the words in italics in the sentence and discuss whether they refer to the past or present. Explain that being able to identify tense use in text can help them to select the correct answers.

1 present	2 past	3 past
4 present	5 present	6 present

12 Tell students that they are going to do some further work in identifying the correct use of modal verbs. Do the first task in Exercise 12 as a group, reminding students to pay attention to verb tenses, then let them complete the rest of the task in pairs.

1 have to	2 should not have / shouldn't have	
3 must	4 ought to have got	5 are supposed to sign in

EXAM SKILLS

13 Tell students that they are now going to practise completing some matching feature and global multiple-choice questions under timed conditions.

Advice

- Remind students to search for specific information, such as the names of people in the text and to draw boxes around them, so that they can be identified quickly.
- Remind students that their answers will not always appear in the text in the same order as the questions.
- For global multiple-choice questions, encourage students to identify both parts of the question and to check whether both are correct.
- For 'choose a title' questions, ask students to consider how 'general' titles sound in the options, and not to choose titles that only concern one paragraph or section of the text.
- Set a time limit of about 20 minutes for students to complete this task.

> 1 C – paragraph 5: *Furthermore, although younger people are traditionally thought to be more willing to try any number of routes into work before deciding on an industry in which they want to develop, such an approach to employment no longer excludes workers of a more advanced age.*

2 B – paragraph 3: *'Older people are taking opportunities away from their grandchildren. Post-education, those new to the world of work are not able to earn any sort of living wage, nor are they getting the opportunity to develop the 'soft skills', e.g. social intelligence, that will enable them to flourish in the job market.'*

3 B – paragraph 4: *The 'zero-hours' worker ... can be instantly dismissed without any hope of recourse. Employment laws [...] do not protect the new breed of worker from being unfairly dismissed at a moment's notice by their manager.*

4 A – paragraph 2: *This has a number of debilitating long-term effects, not least because this assurance of a growing economy is based more in myth than fact. Thomas explains, 'Without tax income, the economy cannot grow; if the economy stays weak, new jobs will not be created.'*

5 A – paragraph 3: *... created a problem for a huge number of retired workers, who are starting to find that the sum of money they have saved for their retirement does not stretch far enough to provide the financial security that they had expected.[...] there has been a widespread return of these workers to the job market*

6 A – paragraph 5: *Thomas agrees: 'Most of today's self-starters believe that the job market offers a vast array of potential opportunities from which they can learn and gain experience. Whether they have a wide range of existing experience, or none at all, is irrelevant to them.'*

7 C – paragraph 5: *A 2015 study by William Haroldson, How the Market Adjusts to Opportunity, advocated a definition of a new type of multi-skilled worker: the model employee who not only refuses to age, but also does not want to work in the same office every day, or even to be an employee in the first place. In such a progressive, forward-looking environment ...*

8 C – *The Changing Face of Working Life*
A is incorrect because the conflict between younger and older people looking for the same work is used as an example to support Lawrence's point that younger people are becoming worse off because of older people's return to the workplace. Furthermore, in paragraph 5 the writer quotes Haroldson, who actively encourages cooperation between young and old.
B is incorrect because, although modern workers' adaptability is praised, it is also suggested that exploitation in the workplace is widespread, and even the most adaptable could suffer.
D is incorrect because, if anything, the passage discusses the type of qualities that today's workforce *needs*, rather than wants.

Extension

Go through the answers to the tasks as a group. Nominate students to provide the correct answer and ask them to identify how they know it is correct (i.e. the part of the text that gave them the answer). After each answer has been discussed, project a copy of the text on a screen with the parts of the text that give the answers highlighted.

WRITING

OUTCOMES

- produce a balanced 'agree/disagree' essay
- write an introduction and conclusion for this type of essay
- use a range of discourse markers to help sequence your ideas logically
- understand exactly what the essay question is asking you to write.

OUTCOMES

In this unit, students will learn how to write a balanced 'agree/disagree' essay. Students are asked to consider a range of structures for this essay type and will practice using discourse markers to logically sequence their ideas. In order to get a high score for the Task Achievement criterion, students will need to demonstrate that they have fully understood the question, and that they are aware of both sides of the argument, even if they adopt a position that favours one side. Students can additionally increase their score for Cohesion and Coherence by including a range of discourse markers to clearly sequence their ideas.

LEAD-IN

01 Write the phrase 'financial responsibility' on the board. Ask students to work in pairs and discuss what financial responsibility means to them. Explain that this unit will prepare them to write an IELTS Task 2 response to a question on the topic of finance, and that this exercise will help them to come up with vocabulary and ideas.

Sample answer

There is no clear definition of this term. Some would argue that meeting your minimum credit card repayment every month is being financially responsible, while others would disagree, saying that being in any kind of debt, however small, is irresponsible.

Broadly speaking, being financially responsible might include:

- not spending more than you earn
- knowing the difference between luxuries and essentials, and adjusting your spending on each according to your earnings
- saving for old age
- paying for things upfront, rather than on a credit card.

Alternative

Draw a mind map diagram on the board with 'financial responsibility' in the centre. Give students a few minutes to discuss what this means to them and then invite them to add their own idea to the mind map.

02 Ask students to close their books. Write the first statement on the board. Check any necessary vocabulary, then ask students to raise their hands if they (a) agree, (b) disagree

or (c) don't know. Ask students to give reasons to support their choices and make a note of these on the board (or ask students to write them up). Explain that when they are writing an 'agree/disagree' essay, they will need to decide on their view quickly and give reasons to support it.

Ask students to open their books and compare their ideas with the examples given. Divide them into smaller groups and give each group one of the other three statements. Give the groups five minutes to come up with reasons why they agree / disagree, then get each group to present their ideas to the group.

Sample answers – these issues and arguments will form the basis of essay questions in later exercises

1   Today's world places a high value on consumer spending and having the most up-to-date versions of technology. Human nature is competitive, and people want to possess more and have better products.
    Technological developments, such as social media and new electronic devices, mean that people spend less time communicating face to face and more time online. However, it can be argued that social media make it easier for people to communicate with friends and family wherever they are in the world.
    It is a generalisation to say that everybody puts possessions before relationships.

2   The consumer nature of society encourages people to spend money on things that they cannot necessarily afford, and young adults are less experienced when it comes to making financial decisions.
    Most teenagers leave school without a basic understanding of personal finance, such as how credit cards work or what is involved when getting a mortgage, so they don't necessarily realise how to make sure they avoid getting into serious debt.
    Banks and moneylenders encourage debt because this is how they make their money.
    On the other hand, people are free to choose what they want to buy and everybody has to take responsibility for how they manage their own personal finances.

Focus students' attention on the bullet box and ask them to read it carefully. When they have done this, tell them to close their books and ask concept check questions about the content (e.g. 'Is it okay to present a balanced argument in your essay?', 'Should you mention both sides of the argument').

03 Look at the first statement with the whole class as an example. Ask students to read both statements and identify the italicized words in the second. Elicit how these words change the meaning of the statement (i.e. 'should always' is stronger or more absolute than 'should aim to', 'a large percentage' might be more difficult to save than 'a certain percentage'). Ask students to discuss whether they have different opinions about the two statements. Then ask them to work in pairs to complete the rest of the task.

1   The A statement asks you to evaluate if, how much, and why people in today's society value their possessions over their friendships.
    The B statement is more confrontational, with a more pessimistic slant; it asks you to consider if people value their possessions so much that they are willing to sacrifice their relationships with family and friends. While the first question asks you to weigh up this statement, the second requires you to discuss whether the issue is *black-and-white*.

2   There is a greater sense of urgency in the B statement – 'increasing *dramatically*' – and a suggestion that we have little choice but to force students all over the world to learn how to be financially responsible – 'a new *compulsory* subject *must* be introduced in *all* secondary schools'. The first statement allows you more room to consider when and how the matter should be addressed. Again, the B statement is less equivocal than the A statement.

04 Ask students to close their books. Write the word 'Introduction' on the board and ask students to discuss what they think they would include in an introduction to an IELTS Task 2 essay question. Ask what they could do in the introduction to score higher overall. Then ask students to open their books and compare their ideas with the information in the bullet box.

Next focus students' attention on the essay title in Exercise 04. It is important that they understand the title, as they will need to decide whether it is reflected in the sample introductions. Before students do this exercise, ask them to read the Bullet box.

Advice

It is worth turning students' attention to the tip box, and pointing out the advantage of stating their position in the introduction. Point that making their position clear in the introduction can help them to improve their score for Task Achievement, but that they will need to refer to this position throughout the essay. Ask students to work in pairs to match the introductions with the comments.

1 D   2 B   3 A   4 C

05 Focus students' attention on the three essays plans, and ask them to discuss in pairs how they differ.

Advice

It is important to point out to students that all three plans would be effective for answering IELTS Task 2 Agree/Disagree essays. Point out that in spite of the different positions demonstrated, the student considers both sides of the argument in each plan, indicating that they have thought carefully about their position. Remind students that considering both sides of the argument will contribute to a high score for Task Achievement.

Sample answers

Essay Type 1 is a more conventional, balanced essay. The first paragraph presents arguments that agree, the second – arguments that disagree. In a balanced essay like this, candidates often write an introduction that presents the topic, but do not state their opinion until the conclusion. However, it is also good practice to state your opinion in the introduction in case you run out of time in the exam.

Essay Type 2 is a plan for an essay that agrees more than it disagrees. Over the first two paragraphs, the writer intends to make three main points to express this agreement. The third paragraph discusses two opposing arguments. It is likely that the conclusion – and the introduction – will both express the fact that the writer is broadly in agreement with the statement given.

Essay Type 3 the writer intends to show their strong disagreement with the statement. In the first paragraph, they plan to provide two strong main points to support their disagreement. In the second paragraph, they plan to discuss two possible arguments that do agree with the statement but with the explicit intention of *arguing that they are incorrect*, rather than simply *presenting* them and expressing disagreement in the conclusion.

06 Focus students' attention on the essay question. You could ask them to close their books and discuss their own feelings about the question before comparing their ideas with those in Exercise 06. Ask students to complete the task individually, and then compare their answers with a partner.

> 1 ✓   2 ✓   3 ✗   4 ✗   5 ✓

07 Ask students to discuss the questions in pairs. When going through the answers, it may be useful to make students' aware of the Cohesion and Coherence criterion. Explain that logically ordering their arguments may help them to improve their score for Cohesion and Coherence.

> 1 Three agree: 1, 2, and 5; two disagree: 3 and 4.
> 2 They are in a logical order.
> 3 *Suggested answer*: Arguments 1 and 2 could form one paragraph and arguments 3–5 another.
> 4 This is a type 3 essay.
> 5 *Suggested answer*: The candidate seems to agree strongly – see how the strength of their opinion is presented when they disagree with the counterarguments: 'in my experience, neither of these points are particularly valid' – so the likeliest option is a.

Explain to students that in addition to the logical organization of arguments within paragraphs, the appropriate use of discourse markers may also contribute to a higher score for coherence and cohesion. Encourage students to carefully read the information in the bullet box.

08 Turn students' attention back to the arguments from Exercise 06 and tell them this time to focus on the blank numbered spaces. Go through the first example with students, and ask them to volunteer which discourse marker

would not fit in the space. Encourage students to discuss the meanings and functions of the discourse markers (i.e. 'Primarily' means 'most importantly', whereas 'First' and 'To begin with' are used to introduce a first point), as well as the context in which they are used. Emphasize using incorrect or inappropriate discourse markers may have a negative impact on their score for Coherence and Cohesion. Ask students to complete the rest of the task in pairs.

> 1 *First* and *To begin* with announce the writer's first argument of a series. *Primarily* is incorrect, as this is an adverb which highlights or emphasises a point in comparison with (an)other(s).
>
> 2 *Secondly* introduces the second point, *Next* introduce a subsequent point. Following is lexically/grammatically incorrect. *Following (on from)* this would work in its place.
>
> 3 *That said* and *On the other hand* both introduce a contrasting or opposing argument. *Alternatively* is incorrect, as this is an adverb which offers the reader another option or possibility.
>
> 5 *Despite of this* is grammatically incorrect; the other two options are correct.

09 This exercise returns to the issue of forming a logical argument. Ask students to predict the kinds of problems that may stop them from getting good marks when forming arguments. Then focus their attention on the two paragraphs and ask them to identify any potential problems.

> **Paragraph A**: The topic sentence has established the main idea of the paragraph: that the considerable financial rewards are not worth the problems that are caused in these professionals' lives as a result. The candidate then introduces a contrasting idea with the discourse marker *That said*, but their counter-argument does not follow on clearly or logically from the previous two sentences. The examiner would struggle to establish what argument the candidate is making.
>
> **Paragraph B**: There is no real consideration or evaluation of the opposing idea, just a statement of belief from the writer that their opinion is correct.

10 Focus students' attention on paragraph A. Tell them that they are going to write an improved ending to the paragraph. Ensure that students understand the meaning of a 'counter argument' (i.e. one that is different from their main argument). Encourage students to use the key words in italics to form their counter argument. Elicit the discourse marker used to introduce the counter argument in this instance (i.e. 'That said, there is an argument that…')

> *Sample answer*
>
> That said, there is an argument that those at the very top of their profession were aware of these potential outcomes when they began their careers, and so any sympathy for their problems should be limited.

Ask students to close their books. Ask them what they would expect to see in a good conclusion to an Agree / Disagree, and note any of their ideas on the board. Then get students to open their books and compare their ideas with the information in the tip box. Emphasize that restating their position in the conclusion will help them to score points for Task Achievement.

11 Ask students to look carefully at the notes and structure of the conclusion. Ask them to identify a discourse marker used to connect ideas (i.e. 'Granted') and check the meaning and function if necessary (i.e. it is used to make a concession to a counter argument – similar to 'even though'). Then ask students to complete the task in pairs.

> **a** sentence 2
>
> **b** sentence 4
>
> **c** sentence 1
>
> In conclusion, I can see no reason why people in high profile positions should not be paid as well as they usually are. Granted, others in society often earn too little for the important work they do, but it shouldn't mean that these talented individuals are paid less. These high-earners create happiness and act as role models for younger people, often while their own privacy and well-being suffers.
>
> Sentence 3 does not fit, as it introduces a new idea that the candidate didn't previously discuss in their essay.

12 Emphasize again the importance of using correct and appropriate discourse markers in order to avoid losing marks for Coherence and Cohesion. Also bring levels of formality to their attention, emphasizing that appropriate formal language should be used in all IELTS writing tasks. Ask students to complete the task, thinking carefully about the meaning and function of each discourse markers.

> **Appropriate**: To conclude; To sum up; On the whole; In summary,
>
> **Inappropriate**: CONCLUSION (*Headings cannot be included in IELTS essays*); Summarising, (*lexically/ grammatically incorrect*); The point is /Basically (*acceptable in the Speaking test, but too informal for a written essay*)

13 Encourage students to read the whole essay, emphasizing that they have already seen the main body paragraphs in previous exercises. Ask students to look back at the conclusion template from Exercise 11, and to use it to write a conclusion to the essay topic that the paragraphs in Exercise 06 were based on. Encourage students to look at the introduction and skim the main body paragraphs to get a clear idea of the writer's position.

Feedback

Ask students to swap their conclusions with a partner. You could supply them with the band descriptors for Coherence and Cohesion and ask them to comment on how logically the ideas are organized, and whether appropriate discourse markers have been used in their partner's conclusion.

Sample conclusion

> In conclusion, financial responsibility should absolutely be taught as a genuine subject at school. Granted, there are concerns over some students' level of maturity or mathematical ability, but young people should not be denied the chance to become financially independent. It would help to ensure that current levels of debt are managed better in the future.

EXAM SKILLS

Tell students that having looked at different sections of an essay, they are now going to practise writing a response to an IELTS Task 2 'agree/disagree' essay. Before students do this exercise, ask them to read the Tip boxes and Bullet boxes in this lesson again.

Advice

- Encourage students to focus carefully on the title, taking into account any words in the rubric that may influence what the title is asking them to do.
- Emphasize that it is a good idea for students to express their stance in the introduction, in order to ensure that they fulfil this aspect of the Task Achievement criterion.
- Encourage students to brainstorm ideas and make a brief plan before they start writing. Remind them that referring to both sides of the argument will show that they have thought carefully about their position and will help them to get a higher score for Task Achievement.
- Remind students that they should try to organize their arguments logically and use discourse markers appropriately to improve their mark for Coherence and Cohesion.

Sample answer

> It is widely accepted that, for most people, their daily working lives will not be spent in their dream jobs. Despite this, I do not feel that people should instead prioritise becoming a high earner above all other concerns.
>
> To begin with, I strongly believe that people need stimulation in their daily working lives in order to feel a sense of reward. Very few of us can go through an entire career staying in a position or an industry that we find boring purely for the financial incentive. Secondly, there are so many people who see their working life as a search for fulfilment and contentment in helping others, rather than a search for wealth. It seems unlikely that the priority for, say, every nurse or teacher in the world is to become well-o , and jobs such as these are rarely extremely well-paid.
>
> Despite this, some would argue that those people who have families to support should always prioritise earning a high income; a er all, it means securing their children's future. Others point out that, as the job market becomes increasingly unstable across the globe, it is vital to earn more and therefore save more. However, I do not agree that a good salary should necessarily be the number one concern for everyone. Too many people become preoccupied with the next pay rise or career move, and eventually become unhappy or even depressed, neither of which help them to save or to provide for their family.

> In summary, earning as much money as is humanly possible should not be anyone's main concern. Granted, it arguably brings financial stability, for individuals and for their families, but it is simply not worth tolerating a lifetime of unhappiness at work purely for the money. (*291 words*)

Extension

After students have written their essays, ask them to swap essays with other students and provide some peer feedback on Task Achievement and Coherence and Cohesion.

Refer students to the IELTS criteria specifically for bands 7 and 8 in the introduction to the Teachers' Book. Tell them to firstly determine whether they fully meet the criteria for band 7 and then check if they surpass it and can be judged to meet the grade 8 criteria.

LISTENING

OUTCOMES

- use the questions to help you follow a talk
- successfully complete short-answer questions
- correctly answer diagram-labelling tasks.

OUTCOMES

Ask students to focus on the outcomes. The first outcome helps students follow the listening task by using the questions. The second outcome concerns questions which require short answers. The third outcome refers to diagram labelling tasks.

Using the questions to help follow the listening task is particularly useful during the IELTS listening exam as it helps students to understand the structure of the listening and also helps students to predict the content of the listening. Remind students that they will only hear the recording once during the IELTS listening exam and so this skill can be very beneficial to them. In the listening exam, students will often have a word limit of up to three words for their answers. In this unit, students will be able to use clues in the question to help them to answer.

Students may need to label diagrams during the IELTS listening exam and this unit helps students to complete these types of tasks effectively.

LEAD-IN

01 This exercise introduces the topic of finance and business and encourages students to use ideas and vocabulary that may appear in the subsequent listening tasks. Students should discuss these questions in pairs or small groups. Monitor to check students are on task. Then encourage class discussion by allowing students to volunteer their answers and then for other students to comment on whether they agree or to offer alternative answers.

02 Exercises 02 to 08 concern short-answer questions. This specific exercise focuses on using clues in the questions to help students to follow the listening. Before students do this exercise, ask them to read the Bullet box and Tip box for this exercise.

Advice

Make sure students are aware that they need to typically answer *Wh-* questions but that they are given a word limit. Remind students that generally for the IELTS listening exam, the questions will be in the order they come up in the recording. Also, tell students that they need to use the exact words from the recording.

Also, tell students that they should read the questions before listening. In addition to helping students predict content, it's a good idea to do this as it helps students understand the structure of the recording.

Ask students to complete the exercise individually before comparing with a partner. Monitor as students discuss their ideas. For feedback, encourage class discussion of the answers before giving the suggested answer below.

> *Suggested answer*
>
> The questions suggest that the talk will feature some detailed discussion of early coins and how they are made, and have been made, in different parts of the world. Around the middle of the talk, there appears to be a section in which the lecturer will focus in more detail on Chinese coins.

03 This exercise focuses specifically on key words in the question and how students can use these clues to help them better answer the questions. Ask students to complete this exercise in pairs and after monitoring, try to encourage class discussion. Then provide the answers below.

> 1 You will need to listen out for a plural rather than a singular noun for your answer. It is likely that this will either be a plural noun, an adjective + plural noun, or a compound plural noun.
>
> 2 The word *natural* suggests that the lecturer will say that these coins are made of a material that is found in the physical world rather than one that is artificially created.
>
> 3 You will need to listen for a single material or substance of some sort.
>
> 4 As is often the case in IELTS questions, the adverb that is used in the question is very important. This one tells you that you will probably need to listen out for a paraphrase of *most*, and also that you may hear a distractor – in this case, another quantifier.

04 This exercise encourages students to use the questions to predict possible answers. Before students complete the exercise, ask them to read the advice box.

Before students do this exercise, ask them to read the Tip box.

Advice

Students are encouraged to use the questions to make predictions of the possible answers. This is a good way for students to be active listeners and helps them to answer the questions. However, remind students that they need to use exactly the same words from the recording.

Ask students to complete the exercise in pairs. Monitor and then complete feedback using the guidelines outlined in Exercise 02.

05 This exercise encourages students to think about how the answer may be paraphrased in the recording. This is a good habit to get students into doing. Ask students to look at the advice box before they complete the task.

Advice

Tell students that by thinking about how the recording may use words paraphrased from the question, they may be able to predict what words are used in the recording. This will help students to identify the correct answers and to follow the recording better.

Ask students to complete the exercise in pairs. Monitor and then complete feedback using the guidelines outlined in Exercise 02.

06 Students can now practise using their predictions, paraphrases and clues in the questions to listen and answer the questions. Ask students to answer the questions individually and to compare answers in pairs after the recording finishes. Make sure students remember to follow the word limit. Monitor as students do this to see if the recording needs to be played additional times. Then invite students to answer or you can nominate. Before confirming answers, encourage other students to say if they agree with the answers provided by their classmates or to suggest alternatives.

1	sea shells	2	gold and silver
3	bronze	4	knife blades

Transcript 27

Good afternoon, everyone. Today, the next in our series of lectures on the development of currency, we are going to focus on how and why there was such growth in ancient trade and commerce: the arrival of a physical, portable means of payment. I'm going to give you a brief overview of what type of currency was first used, and describe how it developed later in the form of coins.

Now, going back thousands of years, you might imagine that precious stones were the first form of currency, but these were not found in sufficient numbers at that time. We do though have firm evidence of <u>sea shells being used</u> <u>as a primitive form of money</u>. They were very much valued items at the time, and <u>were perfect for trade</u>. They were taken in vast quantities along the great trade routes, and I'm sure you can imagine how significantly they enabled these civilisations to grow as a result.

For now, let's move on to a time when we first find precious metals and minerals being used in the form of coins. Now, there's some debate as to when and where this happened, but it seems to have taken place at some point around the 7th century BC in and around Greece and the Middle East. In the past, archaeologists believed that the first coins were made from pure gold, or artificial mixtures or alloys, but we can now be sure that they were actually produced from a substance known as electrum, <u>an alloy that occurs naturally, and is a blend of gold and silver</u>.

Meanwhile, thousands of miles away to the east, the Chinese appear to have had the same idea at the same time. While those in Greece and the Middle East were busy forging coins from electrum, their contemporaries in China had the same idea of creating coins to use as currency, but with a completely different manufacturing process. For years prior to this, the Chinese had used paper money made from white deerskin, but <u>now they turned to casts and moulds, into which they poured liquid bronze and left it to set, eventually forming coins</u>. If we were to look at examples of these coins, we would see that there was some variety in their shape – some looked like little spades, <u>but the vast majority resembled knife blades</u>. There is intricate decoration on each surface, demonstrating magnificent workmanship.

07 This exercise provides further practice of paraphrasing. Follow the guidelines outlined in Exercise 04 here.

08 Students now listen and answer the questions. Follow the procedure outlined in Exercise 06.

5 square hole	6 (royal) gifts	7 elaborate design
8 mass production		

Transcript 28

Moving forward from the 7th century, and 400 years later, we meet <u>Shi Huangdi</u>, one of the first emperors of China. Sometime around the year 220 BC he took these early forms of currency and simplified them into more basic coins <u>of a circular shape with a distinctive square hole in the middle</u>. Its design reflected a number of Chinese beliefs. For example, the round shape symbolised heavenly commandment, while the square symbolised the authority of the emperor. Some historians suggest that these types of coin had been invented hundreds of years before and that Shi Huangdi's coins were derived from ring-shaped jade discs from the Zhou dynasty, which are believed to have been used as gifts for dignitaries. Whatever the case, we do know that Shi Huangdi decreed his new coins as the only legal currency in his empire and perhaps this is the secret of their longevity; they survived for over two thousand years. The coins themselves were fashioned of gold and bronze and weighed around 8 grams, though this varied as time went by. Sadly, one thing these coins did not retain was the elaborate design of earlier coins. Instead Shi Huangdi's coin was more functional and could be made in a short space of time. In fact, it can be argued that in order to do this, Shi Huangdi created an early model of what eventually became mass production, though of course a cruder and less efficient version of what we see today.

But an interesting thought nonetheless.

Extension

It's a good idea to offer students an opportunity to reflect on the strategies they used to help them with these types of questions. You can ask students to work in pairs or small groups to reflect on which strategies they think were most effective. Encourage class discussion and highlight the strategies that were used.

09 This exercise focuses on helping students to complete diagram labelling tasks. Ask them to work together to try to predict the type of information missing in each box. Tell students that they should do this before completing this type of task. Monitor as students do this. Invite them to give answers or you can nominate. Confirm answers only after asking other students if they agree with an answer give an alternative.

> 1 a number or a quantifier such as much   2 a noun (phrase)   3 a noun (phrase)   4 a noun (phrase)
> 5 an adjective to describe light

10 In this exercise students need to listen to the third part of the recording in order to label the diagram. Before they do this, ask them to read the Tip box.

Advice

It's important that students are able to use different ways to correctly express numbers. If you feel students need more help with this, you can create an activity where students say or spell out how numbers are said (e.g. *120,105 = one hundred and twenty thousand, one hundred and five*). This can be done for large numbers, dates, fractions, decimals etc. Also, make sure students know that words connected by a hyphen (-) count as one word and that spelling is important. Remind students that they will lose marks for spelling errors.

Now ask students to complete the exercise individually and then compare in pairs after the recording. Monitor as students compare to see if the recording needs to be played additional times. Conduct feedback as outlined in Exercise 09.

> 1   15 percent   2   (see-through) window
> 3   silver patch   4   rainbow effect
> 5   UV/ultra-violet

Transcript 29

In your previous talks, you have looked at coins and then the rise of bank notes as the form of currency. Now today I'd like to briefly cover the idea of bank note security. I thought that the 2017 introduction of a new £5 note in the UK would provide a great example of how banks are fighting against fake or counterfeit money.

Now you may already know that the newer note is not as large as the previous one, 15 % less to be exact, and is made of a durable polymer, sometimes referred to as 'plastic', which will give the note a longer life and make the note harder to copy. On the left-hand part of the note there are three security elements of particular interest: a small portrait of the Queen, … the Elizabeth Tower, with Big Ben, … and lastly a pound sign which changes from purple to green depending on the angle you look at it. All these are incorporated on a see-through window.

In addition, the image of the Elizabeth Tower shows as gold coloured on the front of the note, but on the back of the note it is silver.

Directly below this is a kind of hologram. It's a silver patch which shows either the word 'five' or the word 'pounds' depending on how you look at it.

And above the Elizabeth Tower is a similar feature, but this one shows the coronation crown in three dimensions, and produces a rainbow effect when viewed at certain angles.

Interestingly, on the back of the note this patch shows the word 'Blenheim', but the metal foil here, that's to say, the metal that forms the patch, is green.

Last but not least, is something you cannot see, well, at least not under normal conditions. In the top-middle section of the note, the number 5 will appear in the white triangular shape underneath the words "Bank of England", but only when viewed under UV or ultra-violet light.

Most bank notes these days have similar features and …

11 This exercise highlights how to avoid losing marks when answering these types of question. Ask students to do this in pairs and monitor. Encourage them to volunteer answers in the feedback session and confirm only after giving other students the opportunity to say if they agree or not with answers given by classmates.

> 1   Incomplete answer: without *percent* 15 does not make sense.
> 2   Word limit: written in this way, the answer is three words long, not two.
> 3   Spelling mistake: silver
> 4   Incomplete answer: we don't know what kind of effect.
> 5   Word limit: UV and ultra-violet are the same thing and repetition of light exceeds word limit.

EXAM SKILLS

12 This exercise gives students practice of the skills and strategies developed during the unit within an IELTS exam-style context Remind students that completing short answer questions and labelling diagrams are tasks that can feature in the IELTS Listening exam. Students can do this individually and then compare their answers after completing the exercise. Monitor as students compare to see if the recording needs to be repeated additional times and then conduct feedback as outlined in Exercise 11.

1 thieves 2 locking device 3 4,000 BC	
4 steel springs 5 precise construction 6 brass	
7 strong/steel bar 8 pushed down 9 pins	
10 (combination) dial(s)	

Extension

A good way for students to remember to use the strategies outlined here is to ask students to reflect on which strategies they used to answer the questions and what they found more effective. Ask students to discuss this in pairs or small groups. Then encourage class discussion to make sure all students are aware of the strategies recommended for these type of tasks.

Transcript 30

You will hear part of a lecture about the history of locks. First you have some time to look at questions 1 to 10.

[pause]

Now listen carefully and answer questions 1 to 10.

Good afternoon, ladies and gentlemen, and welcome back, as we continue our lecture series on currency, from ancient times to the modern day. For today's talk, we are going to discuss a need that emerged from an age-old, negative side to human nature. When wealth is portable – particularly when it can be easily compressed into thousands of individual items of coinage – it inevitably becomes more attractive to a certain group of people. Even in ancient times, the wealthy, people of status, traders and so on, realised that, to discourage thieves, their money would need to be either hidden or protected. And to do that, they had a choice. They could either keep their riches safe by keeping them in temples which were guarded twenty-four hours a day, or they could find a way to store their assets somewhere closer to home, where access was more convenient. And so the ancient Egyptians came up with a locking device. This was a mechanism similar to what is known today as a dead bolt that required the insertion of a key. The key operated a series of pins, and allowed a long metal bolt to be withdrawn from its locking position, which in turn gave the owner access to their valuables. How long ago did this happen? We're a little vague on this, but definitely at some point later than 4,000 BC. Since the Egyptians wanted their locks to be very strong, these locks suffered from one notable problem – their size. Some of the bigger examples we have found are over half a metre long, and weigh around 30 kilos.

The Romans later adapted these Egyptian locks to make them more functional and available for use in regular homes. They took the Egyptians' designs, made them smaller, and added their own inspired invention, one that enabled them to create a more sophisticated locking system: steel springs. One negative side-effect they did suffer from was that, by using a spring instead of a bolt, it was relatively easy for a particularly dedicated and powerful thief to damage or remove the lock using brute force. However, the Roman locking mechanisms made it difficult to actually force the lock open, thanks to their precise construction. For their time, it is hard not to be impressed by such technology.

[short pause]

The examples we have talked about so far are key-based locks, but next I would like to look at a variation on this – the combination lock. The combination lock is the basis of many modern safes. As we will see, the combination lock shares many features of those used by the Egyptians and Romans.

For the purposes of this explanation I'll begin by looking at a combination padlock, which is easy to grasp.

One of the most important aspects of any locking system is protecting the lock itself. In the case of the padlock, there's a secure outer casing to protect the delicate lock mechanism inside. This casing is usually constructed from a hard metal, such as brass. Having this strong outer casing prevents a potential thief from simply breaking the padlock with a tool, such as a hammer.

The main moveable part of the lock, the part which opens and closes, is a strong bar, often made of reinforced or galvanised steel. As you can see, the bar is curved, almost u-shaped, but much longer on one side. At the end of this longer side is a metal spring, which is pushed down when the padlock is locked.

So how is a combination lock unlocked? The metal bar has four pins on it, which prevent it from being opened. However, each of the pins can be released by moving a combination dial. These are circular and numbered from 0 – 9. Move all the dials into the correct position, and the spring is released, forcing the lock to open.

Now that is a very simple combination lock. The lock of a safe, on the other hand …

SPEAKING

OUTCOMES

- improve your score for Lexical Resource
- use a range of expressions for introducing opinions
- correctly use discourse markers to help justify your arguments
- review correct grammar and pronunciation of modals of obligation.

OUTCOMES

Tell students to focus on the outcomes. The first outcome helps students to receive a higher score for the criterion of Lexical Resource in the IELTS speaking exam. Tell students that Lexical Resource concerns accurate and effective use of a wide range of vocabulary. In this unit, students will learn how to use more challenging and varied phrases when speaking in the exam. The second outcome helps students add variety in terms of the language used when giving opinions. Again, this is useful for the criterion of Lexical Resource. In addition, the third outcome focuses on the use of discourse markers – this time when helping to support arguments. Discourse markers help students structure their talk and help to increase scores for the criterion of Fluency and Coherence. Finally, the fourth outcome focuses on helping students to use models of obligation accurately in terms of grammar and pronunciation. This outcome helps students perform better specifically in the criteria of Grammatical Range and Accuracy as well as Pronunciation.

LEAD-IN

01 This exercise tests students on their existing knowledge of collocations related to business. This also helps students to build their business-related vocabulary. Before students do this exercise, ask them to read the Tip box.

Advice

Highlight to students the importance of using collocations so that students can obtain higher scores in the speaking test. Explain to students that collocations are word partnerships and that they should use these accurately when speaking in the exam and try to use less frequent ones where possible to improve their Lexical Resource score.

Ask students to do this in pairs and monitor as students do this to check students are on task and to assess how much of the vocabulary students already know. As answers are given in the next exercise, you can invite students to volunteer answers and see if other students agree with the answer given but do not provide confirmation of answers yet.

Students' own answers. Answers checked in exercise 2.

02 This exercise gives students the opportunity to check their answers and also provides them with a model of the pronunciation of these phrases. Make sure students are aware that this is Part 3 of the speaking exam. Ask students to listen individually and then to check in pairs after the recording has finished. Monitor as students discuss answers to see if the recording needs to be played more than once. Students can volunteer answers or you can nominate. Before confirming answers, give students the opportunity to comment on answers given by classmates. Also, focus on pronunciation. As this is something students are graded on in the IELTS exam, it is important that students are encouraged to use the correct pronunciation. If there are mispronunciations, invite students to try again or ask other students to help and provide a correct model.

1	market research	2	product development
3	launch a new product	4	business opportunity
5	make a profit	6	target market
7	customer satisfaction	8	time management
9	sales figures	10	close the deal
11	apply for a loan	12	file for bankruptcy

Transcript 31

Examiner: What qualities would you say are needed to become a successful businessperson?

Candidate: I'm not sure there's an easy answer to that one. There's so much to being successful. For example, you can't just come up with an idea for a new product and then sell it. You have to be sure that people will actually want it, so it's vital to do good deal of <u>market research</u> and spend time on <u>product development</u>,

so you can correct all the potential problems first. Then you can devise a plan to <u>launch the product</u> into the market place. But I suppose, yes, some people are just naturally gifted in seeing new <u>business opportunities</u>, and will always <u>make a profit</u> because they understand their <u>target market</u> – you know, the people who the product is aimed at – because, after all, <u>customer satisfaction</u> is key in anything like that. Having said that, it's not just the creative qualities that are enough; the other stuff is also necessary, like having good <u>time management</u> skills, keeping a close eye on <u>sales figures</u>, being able to <u>close the deal</u>, knowing when to <u>apply for a loan</u> or even, if things go badly, how to avoid having to <u>file for bankruptcy</u> because you owe too much money to too many other companies.

03 This exercise helps you to make sure students fully understand the meaning of the phrases. Ask students to complete this exercise in pairs. Monitor and conduct feedback as outlined in Exercise 02.

Suggested answers

2   the stages or steps in the process of creating a product, including design, testing, marketing

3   to release or present a new product to the public/ markets

4   a situation with the potential to be beneficial for a business

5   to make more money than you spend / have spent

6   the intended customers of a product

7   how well a product meets the expectations of the people it is intended for

8   the effective and productive use of your time, particularly at work

9   figures which show how much money you make, or how many products you sell

10   to finalise a business agreement with a customer or client

11   to complete the paperwork requesting a bank to lend you money

12   When a business is no longer able to pay its costs or debts, it must do this legal process.

04 This exercise uses the transcript from the listening in Exercise 02 to help students further develop their vocabulary. Before students do this exercise, ask them to read the Bullet box.

ADVICE:

Highlight the criterion of Lexical Resource. Students should understand that wide and varied vocabulary is rewarded and that students should avoid overusing the same phrases. Tell students that more complex and less frequent phrases are likely to receive higher marks. Tell students that it is sometimes better to take risks by demonstrating a wider range of vocabulary than to worry so much about accuracy that they only use more simple words and phrases.

Now ask students to complete the exercise in pairs. Monitor as students do this. Then play the recording and ask students to check their answers. Complete feedback using the guidelines outlined in Exercise 02.

1 e	2 g	3 b	4 d	5 h	6 c	7 f	8 a

Transcript 32

Examiner: Why has online shopping become so popular with so many people?

Candidate: To be honest, I understand why people like it, but I'm not sure why it holds so much appeal. I suppose the main reason must be that it's so easy and convenient. You can just relax at home, at work, wherever you are, and do your shopping. Plus, there's very little you can't buy on the internet – and, above all else, once you've paid, it quickly gets delivered to your door without having to deal with the hassle of going to a busy high street. So there are plenty of real plus points to online shopping. But, for me, there's no substitute for heading to the store itself and having a look at whatever it is you're thinking of buying. Also, you have the sales assistants to talk to, and they can point you in the right direction.

05 This exercise provides freer practice of making changes to a Part 3 answer in order to improve Lexical Resource scores. Ask students to do this in pairs. Monitor as students do this. As answers will be given in the next exercise, invite answers from students and ask other students to comment on whether they agree with answers given or to suggest alternatives.

Students' own answers

06 Ask students to listen individually to check their answer and then to compare their answers in pairs. Monitor as students do this and then provide feedback as outlined in Exercise 02.

I suspect it might be because it has become so easy to get credit from banks: credit cards, overdrafts, **whatever it is you might need**. Of course, there are a number of **real plus points** to this – you can buy whatever you want more quickly, and you don't have to pay the loan off until later, so I do see why **it holds so much appeal**. And online banking has actually made it easier to do this **without having to deal with the hassle of going into the branch** and standing in a queue for ever. **There's very little you can't do** through your online account. For example, you can apply for a loan **wherever you might be**, and most of the time you'll be given the money. But, for me, there's no substitute for speaking face-to-face, where a bank advisor can **point you in the right direction**, as far as savings or debt is concerned. **Above all else**, they won't allow you to get into debt that you can't pay back.

Transcript 33

Examiner: Why do some people have problems managing their personal finances?

Candidate: I suspect it might be because it has become so easy to get credit from banks: credit cards, overdrafts, whatever it is you might need. Of course, there are a number of real plus points to this – you can buy whatever you want more quickly, and you don't have to pay the loan off until later, so I do see why it holds so much appeal. And online banking has actually made it easier to do this without having to deal with the hassle of going into the branch and standing in a queue for ever. There's very little you can't do through your online account. For example, you can apply for a loan wherever you might be, and most of the time you'll be given the money. But, for me, there's no substitute for speaking face-to-face, where a bank advisor can point you in the right direction, as far as savings or debt is concerned. Above all else, they won't allow you to get into debt that you can't pay back.

07 Exercises 07 to 10 help students to express and justify opinions and use discourse markers to help students do so effectively. Exercise 07 provides students with phrases with which to express and justify their opinions. Before students do this exercise, ask them to read the Tip box.

Advice

Make students aware that in Part 3 of the speaking exam, they may need to evaluate how important something is. Highlight the importance of using a variety of phrases to do this.

Now ask students to complete the exercise in pairs and monitor as they do this. Students can then volunteer answers or you can nominate. Confirm answers only after inviting other students to say if they agree with their classmates' answers or to suggest alternatives.

1 N	2 N	3 I	4 N	5 I	6 N	7 I

08 This exercise gives students freer practice of giving and justifying opinions. Ask students to work in pairs to do this. Students in each pair should take it in turns asking and answering the questions. Monitor as students do this and note down anything that you want to go through in feedback. This can be typical mistakes many of your class are making or examples of good practice. For feedback, you can invite students to provide their answers for classmates to comment on. Provide your feedback after other students have given their opinions. You can also then show the suggested answer below for students to evaluate.

Extension

Use any errors you noted down when you monitored. Write a list of these on the board (3-5 is manageable). Also, add 1-2 correct answers. Ask students to identify the correct answers and correct the incorrect ones. This is a good way to recycle what has been learnt in the exercise and to also focus on responding to emerging student errors and needs.

Suggested answers:

1 For me, it's a must. Too many people spend more than they can afford and go into debt as a result. They spend their lives paying even more money on interest payments and can become trapped in debt their whole lives.

   For an increasing number of people these days, it's not a matter of life or death. After all, most people can't afford to buy a house and so they take on a mortgage and buy their house gradually. Most people use credit cards to buy essential things they don't have the money for at that moment, but knowing they can pay the money back.

2 I'm not sure. It's pretty inconsequential to my life, but I know I'm in the minority. Society is obsessed with having the latest versions of smartphones or tablets and it can be argued that buying new products is good for the economy.

   Perhaps they just think that it's an absolute necessity, and that if they don't have the most up-to-date products, they'll be left behind. So many people depend on technology for their everyday lives and feel that having it will improve their quality of life.

3 It's hard to say. Personally, I don't really think it matters, but the world we live in seems to be built on the idea of accumulating wealth. Perhaps it's just human nature to want to have more than the next person.

   For some people, it's absolutely essential because they or perhaps their society lacks the resources that other societies have and, as a result, they prioritise money and wealth in order to look after themselves and their families.

09 Exercise 09 focuses on discourse markers students can be encouraged to use to help them express and justify their opinions. Before students do this exercise, ask them to read the Tip box.

Advice

Make sure students are aware that they will need to say why they think something is true or to show how certain they are in Part 3 of the exam.

Now ask students to complete the exercise in pairs and monitor as students do this. Then conduct feedback as outlined in Exercise 07.

1 apparently, supposedly   2 clearly, undoubtedly
3 arguably, conceivably, feasibly   4 for the most part, by and large   5 as far as I'm concerned, from where I stand

10 This exercise provides students with freer practice of using the discourse markers from Exercise 09. Ask students to do this in pairs and to take turns. Monitor as students do this. Monitor as students do this and note down anything that you want to go through in feedback. For feedback, you can invite students to provide their answers for classmates to comment on. Provide your feedback after other students have given their opinions.

You can also then show the suggested answer below for students to evaluate.

Extension

Use any errors you noted down when you monitored. Write a list of these on the board (3-5 is manageable). Also, add 1-2 correct answers. Ask students to identify the correct answers and correct the incorrect ones.

Sample answers

2 I can understand why some people might think this. *Supposedly* young people are highly irresponsible with money, and so having the ability to spend money they don't have is risky.

3 *Arguably* this is the case for many people, *but from where I stand*, people need to take responsibility for their own debt and not blame technology.

4 *By and large*, having a degree in Business Studies would benefit a businessperson, but *clearly* it is not absolutely necessary. Many of the most successful business people in my country don't have higher qualifications in this subject.

5 *Clearly* this is a ridiculous idea. Businesses are about profits, not about human beings. Politicians may not be perfect, but they have a far better understanding of the importance of society and community than business people.

6 *Conceivably* people would manage their finances better if they saved more and didn't get into *debt. But as far as I'm concerned*, I don't think it really matters. It's an individual choice.

11 Exercise 11 focuses on improving grammatical accuracy for modals of obligation. This exercise tests students on what they already know in terms of these language structures. Remind students that higher levels of grammatical accuracy and range are rewarded in the exam. Ask them to complete this exercise in pairs. Monitor as students do this. Conduct feedback as outlined in

1 **had to**: the grammar is incorrect, as the speaker is referring to how they see the general situation in the present, not referring to a particular time in the past.

   have to / have got to: both correct and acceptable in the Speaking test. However, *have got to* is a little too informal for the Writing part of the IELTS test.

2 **mustn't**: incorrect. The speaker is saying that there was no obligation to be 'ultra-qualified' at that time; *mustn't* is used when a speaker wants to suggest that there IS an obligation NOT to do something. Also, *mustn't* refers to the present, not the past.

   don't have to / didn't have to: both correct, but *don't have to* suggests that the speaker is again generalising, while *didn't have to* is referring to the situation at the time when his/her father left school.

3 **had to / would have to / needed to:** all correct. *Had to* again refers to the particular time at which his/her father started in business, and what the father felt he knew. *Would have to* has essentially the same meaning, but the grammar is slightly different, i.e. the father said at the time, 'I will have to use my natural business acumen to get ahead'; this then changes into reported speech as the father is quoted in the present time.

4 **must:** incorrect (see explanation for question 2)

    should have: incorrect, as the grammar here – *should + have* + past participle – is used to express regret or blame (i.e. he should have worked long hours, but he didn't). When referring to a present time, *should* can be used to suggest 'I think there is an obligation to …'; e.g. 'You should work long hours every day, if you want to become successful.'

    had to: correct, again this refers to a past obligation.

5 **didn't have to** + *made* is incorrect grammatically.

    shouldn't have / needn't have: suggest slightly different meanings. Consider: 'He shouldn't have made such a risky investment!' = It's his fault we have no money. Whereas 'He needn't have made such a risky investment!' = Although it worked out OK in the end, there was no need to take such a big risk. Therefore, in this context, *shouldn't have* seems to fit better.

6 **didn't have to:** correct; there was no obligation, need or requirement to wait long before the money returned.

    mustn't have to / hadn't to: both grammatically incorrect.

12 This exercise focuses specifically on the pronunciation of the modal of obligation: *have to*.

Advice

Make sure students understand that the word *have* has a strong and weak form and that they are pronounced differently. Check that students know when they should be using each form. Tell students that the strong form is often used when *have* is the main verb and that the weaker pronunciation is when *have* has a more grammatical function (e.g. when part of the present perfect).

Now ask students to complete the exercise in pairs. Ask students to then listen individually and then compare their answers together. During feedback, ask students to explain their answers before inviting other students to comment. Then confirm answers.

1 strong	2 strong	3 weak	4 weak	5 weak

Transcript 34

Examiner: Should school children have /hæv/ lessons on financial responsibility?

Candidate: Yes, for me, it is absolutely essential. I didn't have /hæv/ lessons like these at school but I think they would have /əv/ benefitted me a great deal. For example, when I got my first credit card, I now know I should have /əv/ paid more attention to the implications of using it.

I found I was spending too much, and often forgot to make the repayments, so I got into debt very quickly. Perhaps if I'd understood them better, I might have /əv/ avoided this.

EXAM SKILLS

13 Exercises 13 and 14 provide exam practice of the skills learnt in this unit. For exercise 13, tell students to complete this in pairs. Tell students to take it in turns to speak. Ask the non-speaking partners to provide constructive feedback.

Refer students to the IELTS criteria specifically for bands 7 and 8 in the introduction to the Teachers' Book. Tell them to firstly determine whether they fully meet the criteria for band 7 and then check if they surpass it and can be judged to meet the grade 8 criteria.

Monitor as students do this and make notes of anything you want to bring up in feedback. For feedback, you can invite students to provide their answers for classmates to comment on.

Extension

Use any errors you noted down when you monitored. Write a list of these on the board (3-5 is manageable). Also, add 1-2 correct answers. Ask students to identify the correct answers and correct the incorrect ones.

Alternative

Students can create an audio recording of their answers on a smartphone or another device. Students can then listen to their recordings in class or for homework and then record an improved version. You can use these new versions in class or provide individual feedback.

14 This exercise provides students with exam practice of Part 3 style questions. Ask them to work in pairs and take turns asking and answering the questions. Monitor as students do this. Use the feedback guidelines outlined in Exercise 13. The extension and alternative activities can also be used here too.

READING

> ### OUTCOMES
>
> - **identify a writer's claims or views**
> - **deal with 'selecting from a list' and 'Yes / No / Not Given' task types**
> - **use second, third and mixed conditionals**

OUTCOMES

In this unit students will focus on two common IELTS reading task types typically found in argumentative texts which involve identifying a writer's claims or views. In order to answer both question types correctly, students need to be able to differentiate between a writer's claims and views, and to use skimming and scanning skills to identify these in a text.

In this unit, students will learn step-by-step strategies for completing Selecting from a List and Yes, No, Not Given task types. They will also be familiarized with the use of 2nd, 3rd and mixed conditionals, which often occur in more complex, argumentative texts.

LEAD-IN

01 Encourage students to think about the topic of monarchy by providing them with some visual aids. If your students come from a country/countries that have a royal family, provide some pictures of them. If they do not, provide some pictures of the royal family in a country that they are likely to be familiar with. Ask them what they know about this royal family. Then give them several minutes to discuss the questions in Exercise 01.

> ### Sample answers
>
> Bahrain – King Hamad bin Isa; Belgium – King Philippe; Denmark – Queen Margrethe; Morocco – King Mohammed VI; Saudi Arabia – King Salman bin Abdulaziz al-Saud; Spain – King Felipe; Sweden – King Carl XVI Gustaf; UK – Queen Elizabeth II

02 Encourage students to look at the words in the box. Explain that all these words can be used in relation to royalty. Some are used specifically to discuss this subject, while others are used in other contexts. Ask students to discuss in pairs which of the words could relate to other contexts (not just royalty).

> rule, era, heir, dynasty

> ### Extension
>
> Ask students to write down example sentences which include the words in a different context.

03 Ask students to close their books. Write the four words in the example exercise on the board and ask students to identify which word is the 'odd one out' (i.e. does not follow the same pattern as the others). Encourage them to give a reason for their answer. Then ask them to open their books and check the example exercise. Ask students to complete the rest of the task in pairs.

> ### Suggested answers
>
> 1 *dynasty*: it is a period of time, or a series of rulers from the same family; the others are synonyms for the lands ruled by a king or emperor
> 2 *regent*: a person acting for a monarch – the others are actual monarchs or rulers
> 3 *abdicate*: it means to give up the role of monarch; the others mean to lead as the monarch
> 4 *crown*: it is an object; the others are events

Ask students to close their books. Elicit the reading strategies that they might use to identify what a writer generally thinks about a particular topic. If students appear unsure, ask them whether they think they would skim or scan the text. Then ask them to open their books and check by reading the advice box.

04 Explain to students that identifying the purpose of the text is a useful skill that will help them both to answer specific IELTS reading questions, and to gain an overall understanding of the text. Ask them to skim the text and complete the exercises.

> 1 A
> 2 C (Someone who is pro-royalty would be unlikely to write a text that focuses on the eccentricity of royalty and someone who is anti-royalty is unlikely to defend rulers and royalty, which this text does at times.)

05 This task encourages students to differentiate between claims and views. Ask students to explain the difference between a 'claim' and a 'view', then ask them to check their ideas by reading the tip box. Then ask students to complete the exercise.

> | 1 claim | 2 claim | 3 claim | 4 view |
> |---|---|---|---|

Ask students to carefully read the advice box. Then ask them to close their books and ask them come concept check questions to check their understanding (e.g. 'do you need to read the whole text to complete these tasks?', 'Can you use each option more than once?' etc.).

06 Ask students to look at the four statements carefully and to identify the paragraph in the text in which they are mentioned. Tell them not to match them with the list of people yet; explain that locating the correct part of the text is the first step to answering this task type, and that they are then going to practise some strategies for successfully completing this task type.

> Caligula – paragraph E
> George III – paragraph D
> Charles VI – paragraph B
> Fyodor I – paragraph C

07 This exercise encourages students to focus on the paraphrasing of information in statements from the texts. Ask students to carefully read the section about Caligula again, and to identify the correct paraphrase.

> C (= It is claimed he talked to celestial bodies.)

Ask students to specify which words they identified as synonyms (i.e. 'the moon and Jupiter = celestial bodies). Draw students' attention to the tip box and explain that identifying paraphrased information is an important skill for this and many other IELTS reading task types.

08 Tell students that they are going to return to the paragraph on Charles VI and complete some missing information about him. Explain that they will not have to do this as part of the exam task, but that they will do it now as a strategy for matching the correct person with the correct information. Ask students to complete the missing information and then to select the correct statement about Charles VI from Exercise 06.

> He forgot that he had a wife and children / that he was king.
> He believed that he was made of glass.
> His son-in-law had to take over as regent.
> He ran around the palace grounds, howling like a wolf.
> Statement 1 in exercise 6 relates to Charles VI.

09 Tell students that now they have practised some strategies for completing the 'selecting from a list' task type, including recognizing paraphrases and summarizing information from the text, they are going to apply these strategies to complete the remaining tasks. Ask students to complete the tasks and discuss their answers, and how they found them, with a partner.

> Fyodor I – statement 2
> George III – statement 4

By this stage in the book, students will have already learnt about and practised True, False, Not Given questions. Ask students to read the information in the box, and then ask them how this question type is different from True, False, Not Given questions. Elicit that Yes, No, Not Given questions are more likely to be used to interpret the writer's claims or arguments. Ask concept-check questions (e.g. 'Are Yes, No, Not Given questions usually about factual information?', 'Are they usually asked about argumentative texts?' etc.). This will emphasize to students that Yes, No, Not Given questions are generally associated with argumentative texts.

10 Tell students that they are going to practise identifying statements where the answer is 'Yes'. Elicit whether in the exam they are likely to find the exact words from the statement in the text or whether the information will be paraphrased. Ask students to look at the information taken from the text and to match it with the paraphrased information in the statements. Encourage them to identify synonyms for words and ideas in the statements, but also other 'clues' such as pronouns (e.g. Joanna of Castile = 'her'). These clues will also help students to locate the information in the text.

> **1** b   **2** d   **3** a   **4** c

11 Tell students that they are now going to practise identifying statements to which the answer is 'No'. Explain that this time the information in the statements contradicts the information in the text. Ask students to first locate the part of the text where the information is found and then to identify the information that contradicts the statement.

> **1** *Happily for him, his subjects saw his childlike simplicity as being divinely inspired.*
>
> **2** *On the other hand, by many accounts she was a gifted and intelligent woman with a talent for diplomacy.*
>
> **3** *However, it should be pointed out that many of these 'reports' about Caligula were written more than 80 years after his death, so their accuracy is open to question.*

12 It is common for students to have difficulties identifying the difference between 'No' and 'Not given' questions. This exercise gives students the opportunity to identify the difference. While in a 'No' statement, the information in the statement clearly contradicts the information in the text, a 'Not Given' statement contains information that cannot be found in the text. The latter is, however, closely related to the topic, and we may therefore expect to find it in the text. Encourage students to read the tip box, then ask them to read the 'Not Given' statement in Exercise 12. Ask students to re-read paragraphs A and G and to explain why the statement is 'Not Given' in the text.

> We might expect this to be true, given the title and subject of the text, but the writer never claims that the majority are eccentric. The closest it comes to this is when the text says 'there have also been a number of bizarre, frankly eccentric, rulers', which is not a confirmation, and the text also carries the message that we should not believe everything we read about eccentric monarchs.

13 Tell students that now they have practised using these strategies when they knew the statement type, they are now going to look at three statements and identify which one is Yes, No, and Not Given. Encourage them to use the strategies practised in the previous exercises of identifying information in the text that supports or contradicts the information in the statement, or information that is related to the topic but is not mentioned directly in the text. Ask students to complete the exercise and then check their answers with a partner.

Advice

Encourage students to do the following when they are completing the questions and checking their answers:

YES statements: give supporting evidence from the passage

NO statements: correct the statements so that they match the views of the writer

NOT GIVEN statements: say what you **do** know about the passage and say what part of the passage gave you your answer

<table>
<tr><td>

1 No (... for one thing we should celebrate royal eccentricity. It certainly makes reading history much more interesting.)

2 Not Given (the text only mentions this in the case of Charles VI, Fyodor and Joanna)

3 Yes *(Had he left an heir, Russian history might well have gone in a different direction.)*

</td><td>

1 Yes (*the pharaoh's chief responsibility was to maintain Ma'at or Universal Harmony, and warfare was an essential part of this*)

2 Yes (*many women held considerable power as the 'great wife', the first wife of the reigning pharaoh*)

3 Yes (*Hatshepsut, the first female pharaoh, ... made her mark on history. ... history remembers her as a great leader*)

4 No (*In ancient Egypt kingship usually passed from father to son. ... Some, like Hatshepsut, seized power illegally*)

5 Not Given

6 No (*the team from Pennsylvania managed to piece together most of King Senebkay's skeleton*)

7 B

8 D

9 C

10 A

</td></tr>
</table>

2nd, 3rd and mixed conditionals are grammatical structures that occur relatively frequently in more complex, argumentative texts. It is therefore useful for students to be familiar with these structures in preparation for the IELTS reading exam. Have students close their books and then write the following sentences on the board.

If I were king, I would reduce taxes.

If I had been king, I would have reduced taxes.

Ask students whether these are real or imaginary (hypothetical) situations. Ask them to discuss the difference between the two examples, and then open their books and compare their ideas with the advice box.

14 Ask students to complete the table with the correct structures.

1 D   **2** A   **3** C   **4** B

Extension

Give students some further conditional stems and ask them to complete them using their own ideas and the correct conditional structures. e.g. If I were King / Queen. If Fyodor hadn't been mad etc.

15 Tell students to practise identifying different types of conditional. Draw their attention to the first example in the exercise. Elicit which type of conditional it is and how they know (i.e. from the tenses used in each clause). Then ask them to complete the rest of the exercise. Encourage students to read the tip box for examples of further variations to conditional structures.

1 second   **2** third   **3** third   **4** mixed

EXAM SKILLS

Tell students that they are now going to a reading exam practice task which will include the two main task types that they have looked at in this unit (Selecting information from a list and Yes, No, Not Given questions. Before students do this exercise, ask them to read the Bullet boxes and Tip boxes that appear in this lesson.

Advice

Remind students of the following information:

- For Selecting Information questions, remember to locate the information in the text that matches with the statement before attempting to answer the questions.
- For Yes, No, Not Given questions, locate the information from the question in the text and confirm whether the text confirms, contradicts or does not mention the information in the statement.
- It is good practice to set a time limit for exam practice tasks. Set 20 minutes for this task, then go through the answers as a class.

WRITING

OUTCOMES

- describe information in a table or bar chart
- use linkers and cohesive language to improve your Coherence and Cohesion score for Task 1
- avoid repetition of language to improve your Coherence and Cohesion score for Task 1.

OUTCOMES

In this unit, students will practise describing information in a table or bar chart; a common IELTS Task 1 writing task type. They will practise identifying the most important information in table or chart and deciding from the task whether they will need to describe changes over time or make comparisons between two or more sets of information. They will particularly focus on how to improve their score for the Coherence and Cohesion criterion by learning how to use discourse markers appropriately to organize their ideas, and how to avoid repetition using paraphrasing, synonyms and pronouns.

LEAD-IN

01 These questions will get students thinking about the topic that will be used in the sample answers for describing information in a table or chart. It may be useful to find a few pictures to serve as visual aids to get students thinking about the topic and to check vocabulary that they may encounter or use later in the unit (e.g. the inside of a factory, a port with shipping containers etc.). Give students five minutes to discuss the questions and compare their answers together.

02 Explain to students that these terms will be used in a sample task that they will look at later in the unit. Ask students to match the terms with their definitions.

1 c   **2** a   **3** d   **4** b

In Task 1 of the IELTS reading test, students may be asked to describe information in a chart or table. Candidates will be asked to describe visual information in the form of a chart or table. They will usually either be asked to describe changes over time, or to compare two or more sets of information. As they will only have 20 minutes to answer the question, they will need to be able to read and understand the information in the chart or table quickly in order to be able to write about it.

03 Focus students' attention on the sample IELTS Writing Task 1. Ask them to read through the task instructions and the information in the table quickly in order to answer the questions. It is important to ensure that students understand what is meant by a 'general trend', as they will need to describe this in the first part of the task. Elicit or feed the following definition:

Definition

General Trend: Important changes that have taken place either over a period of time or between several different set of information.

> **1** The general trend is a decline in the number of mines
>
> **2** 1913–1943 – the number of mines almost halved
> 1963–1983 – about 80% of mines closed
> 2003–2015 – very few mines left

04 Ask students to close their books. Write the four different IELTS marking criteria on the board and ask students what they think they would need to do when describing information in a chart or table in order to get a good mark for each marking criterion. Once the group has discussed this, ask students to open their books and check their ideas with the description of the criterion.

Next, ask students to work in small groups of three or four and look at the sample answer to the task in Exercise 03. Ask them to use the marking criteria to identify strength and weaknesses in the sample answer.

Alternative

Divide the class into four groups. Each group takes a different marking criterion and applies it to the essay. Each group discusses their main comments for each criterion and then feeds back to the rest of the class.

Suggested answers
Strengths of the essay
TA: The description is accurate and there is data to support the description.
CC: Overall structure makes sense, with logical paragraphing
LR: A fairly good range of vocabulary is used to avoid repetition: *decline, disappeared, decrease, fell sharply, dropped, only 5 left.*
GRA: Past tenses are generally used correctly

Weaknesses
CC: Some of the cohesion is faulty: *nevertheless, surprisingly, obviously* and *at last* are used incorrectly.
CC: A wider range of linkers / cohesive language could be used. For example, when referring to time periods, the writer almost always uses *In* + year to introduce the information.

Tell students that since Coherence and Cohesion were identified as weaknesses in the sample answer, they will now focus on this criterion in more detail, so that they will know how to improve their score in this area. Ask students to close their books and briefly discuss what features may contribute to a high score for Coherence and Cohesion. Make a note of students' suggestions on the board, then ask them to open their books and check their ideas with those mentioned in the advice box.

05 Focus students' attention on the written feedback from a teacher on Coherence and Cohesion in the sample answer. Ask students to choose linking words and phrases from the box to replace the inappropriate ones used by the student.

> **1** The clear trend in the figures is that
> **2** For example
> **3** It is striking that
> **4** By the end of the period shown, in 2015

06 Tell students to look at a sample answer to the same question with much better coherence and cohesion. Ask students to read the sample answer and identify discourse markers which fulfil the functions specified in the exercise.

> **2** The overall trend is clearly
> **3** However
> **4** in the 100-year period between 1913 and 2015; by the end of the given time frame; In the early decades of the twentieth century; By the middle of the century; by the turn of the twenty-first century

07 Tell students to read another example of an IELTS Task 1. Elicit the type of graphic used in the example and then encourage students to read the task and identify the general trend as they did with the previous example.

Sample answers
1 China/Europe have the highest proportion of car manufacture.
Between them, countries in South East Asia (China, Japan/Korea, South Asia) produce more cars than the rest of the world put together (approximately 51%)
Few cars are made in the Middle East/Africa
2 Greater China manufactures slightly more cars than Europe.
North America produces nearly 5 times as many cars as South America.

08 Tell students to look at another sample answer and complete the gaps with appropriate discourse markers. Stress that they should choose discourse markers which have appropriate functions and which fit grammatically with the structure of the sentence.

> 1 For the purposes of this data set
> 2 What stands out is
> 3 in terms of
> 4 respectively
> 5 By contrast
> 6 Turning next to
> 7 Whereas
> 8 moving on to
> 9 although

09 Emphasize to students that in order to obtain a high score for Coherence and Cohesion it is important to use not only discourse markers with the correct function, but also a range of different discourse markers to avoid repetition. Ask students to match each discourse marker from the previous exercise with the correct function.

> 1 Showing contrast: *whereas, although, by contrast*
> 2 Introducing a new point/idea/section: *in terms of, moving on to, turning next to*
> 3 To emphasize or exemplify an idea or point that you are making: *What stands out is*
> 4 To introduce a statement which clarifies the data: *For the purposes of this data set*
> 5 To indicate that some information is in the same order as connected information mentioned in a previous statement: *respectively*

10 Explain to students that their score for Cohesion and Coherence will not only be based on their use of discourse markers, but also the ability to avoid unnecessary repetition. Such repetition can be avoided by using synonyms, paraphrase and some pronouns to refer back to something mentioned previously. Focus students' attention on the Tip box and encourage them to identify these ways of avoiding repetition. Ask them to complete the exercise by identifying what the underlined word or phrase refers to. Ask them to also specify the type of repetition avoidance (e.g. 'one' = synonym')

> 2 *the given time frame* is a paraphrase of *the 100-year period between 1913 and 2015* to avoid repetition
> 3 *of them* replaces *coal mines* to avoid repetition
> 4 *the number* is short for *the number of coal mines* to avoid repetition
> 5 *this type of vehicle* is a paraphrase of *passenger car* to avoid repetition

EXAM SKILLS

11 Tell students that they are going to practise completing an IELTS Task 1 question in which they will need to describe a chart. Before students do this exercise, ask them to read the Bullet boxes and Tip boxes that appear in this lesson.

Advice

- Encourage students to read the information quickly but carefully in order to identify the most important information. Ask them to consider whether they think they will describe changes over time or make comparisons between different pieces of information.
- Refer students to the IELTS criteria specifically for bands 7 and 8 in the introduction to the Teachers' Book. Tell them to firstly determine whether they fully meet the criteria for band 7 and then check if they surpass it and can be judged to meet the grade 8 criteria.
- As students have focused on Coherence and Cohesion in this unit, encourage them to think carefully about paragraphing, use of cohesive devices and avoiding repetition.
- Give students a time limit of 20 minutes to answer the question, as they would have in the exam.

Sample answer

The bar charts divide the UK workforce into five categories based on the type of industry they work in for the years 1841 and 2011.

The overall trend shown in the data is a steep rise in the proportion of employees engaged in the service industry, coupled with a decline in manufacturing. The most salient feature is that in 2011 81% of the workforce were involved in providing services, which contrasts sharply with the figure of 33% in 1841. In contrast, we observe a huge drop in the manufacturing industry from over a third in the mid nineteenth century to just 9% by the early twenty-first century.

Furthermore, the 170-year period saw a marked fall in the agriculture and fishing sectors, leaving food production with a tiny 1% of UK workers. Similarly, workers in energy and water companies decreased by two thirds. On the other hand, the construction industry experienced significant growth from 5% to 8% over the period.

In conclusion, the job profile of the UK workforce changed radically between 1841 and 2011, with the increases coming in the construction and service industry but all other areas seeing a decline.

Extension

When students have finished the task, get them to work in pairs or small groups and discuss the chart together. Ask them to compare what they identified as the most important information and how they described this in their answers. Tell them to look again at the description of the criteria for Coherence and Cohesion and to check each other's answers for use of paragraphing, discourse markers and avoidance of repetition. Then get students to look at the sample essay and apply the four criteria, discussing their ideas first in a small group and then with the rest of the class.

LISTENING

OUTCOMES

Ask students to look at the outcomes. The first outcome focuses on helping students when listening to monologues – either in Section 2 or 4 of the IELTS Listening exam – to understand and describe trends and periods in history. Students will need to be familiar with time phrases including accurate understanding and use of prepositions of time (final outcome) in order to do this more effectively. The second outcome helps students with the common IELTS exam task of identifying a speaker's attitude or opinion. Tell students that in this unit, they learn to use clues to help them identify attitudes and opinions. The third outcome concerns two different task types: selecting answers from a list and matching from a list. Advice about strategies for each task type is given to help students perform better when completing these tasks.

LEAD-IN

01 This activity tests students' existing knowledge of time phrases including use of prepositions of time. Ask students to complete it in pairs and monitor as they do this to check that they are on task. For feedback, you can invite students to give answers or nominate individual students. Only confirm correct answers after encouraging other class members to comment on whether they agree with answers classmates have given or to suggest alternatives.

a on	**b** end	**c** season	**d** from	**e** in
f between, in	**g** on	**h** era	**i** recent	

02 The first part of this exercise acts as preparation for the listening in the second part. Students should match the events as a way of predicting listening content. Ask students to do this in pairs. You can invite students to give their answers and elicit from others if they agree or disagree. Then play the recording and ask students to listen individually before comparing their answers in pairs. Monitor as students do this to see if they need to listen more than once. Finally, complete feedback as outlined in Exercise 01.

> 1 g – since the ninth century AD
> 2 b – in the mid-twentieth century
> 3 d – between 1642 and 1649
> 4 i – in the last 200 years
> 5 a – during the 1070s

> 6 f – from 1914 to 1918
> 7 e – a er the restoration of the monarchy
> 8 c – during the Victorian era
> 9 h – in the first decade of the twenty-first century

Transcript 35

1 The monarchy has existed in England since the ninth century AD.
2 Elizabeth II became Queen of England in the mid-twentieth century.
3 There was a Civil War in England between 1642 and 1649.
4 The Tower of London has had many functions in the last 200 years.
5 The Tower of London was built by William the Conqueror during the 1070s.
6 The First World War lasted from 1914 to 1918.
7 King Charles II gained control of the Tower of London after the restoration of the monarchy.
8 The Tower of London became a tourist destination during the Victorian era.
9 The number of visitors to the Tower of London rose to 2 million per year in the first decade of the twenty-first century.

03 Exercises 03 to 06 focus on the IELTS listening task type of selecting answers from a list of options. Before students complete Exercise 03, ask them to read the Bullet box.

Advice

Tell students that when choosing answers from a list of options they should read the question and options carefully. Make sure students are aware that they need to focus on key words to help them to do this. Also, remind students that the recording is likely to use different words compared to the questions and options.

Exercise 03 helps students to identify synonyms for words in the box. These synonyms may feature in the recording. Ask students to do this in pairs. Monitor as they do this and then provide feedback as outlined in Exercise 01.

> **A** home – residence; king or queen – royalty
> **B** arms – weapons
> **C** place of worship – church
> **D** destination – attraction; sightseers – tourists
> **E** currency – money; manufactured – made

04 This exercise gives students practice of the listening task. Ask them to do this individually and then to compare answers after the recording. Monitor and then provide feedback.

> C

Transcript 36

Welcome to the Tower of London. Before the tour starts, I would like to give you some background information about the Tower.

The Tower of London is one of the UK's most popular tourist attractions with over 2 million visitors per year. It was during the Victorian era – that is when Queen Victoria was on the throne – that it became a tourist attraction. Before that, the Tower had many other functions. It was a royal residence, a menagerie – that's a kind of zoo – it even had lions. And it used to house the Royal Mint – that's where money is printed and coins made. It also served as a storehouse for weapons, a fortress and most famously of all, a prison!

05 This exercise again gives students practice of identifying synonyms they are likely to hear in the recording. In this exercise, students need to provide synonymous phrases and think of different ways to express a phrase. Before students do this exercise, ask them to read the tip box.

Advice

Make sure students know that in addition to the use of synonyms, the recording may use words and ideas expressed using different parts of speech or grammatical structures.

Now ask students to complete Exercise 05 in pairs. Monitor and then provide feedback.

Suggested answers
B controlled – ran, managed
C enemies – opponents; lost their lives – died, were killed
D zoo – wild animals; six centuries – six hundred years
E got back – regained, recovered, recaptured

06 Students can now practise answering this type of listening question. Before they do this, ask them to read the Tip box.

Advice

Make sure students are aware that the order in which the options in this type of task appear will be different to that of the recording.

Ask students to do this exercise individually and then to compare answers in pairs after the recording. Monitor and provide feedback as outlined in Exercise 02.

C, D

Transcript 37

The Tower of London was built in the 1070s by William the Conqueror, who had invaded England and defeated the English king, Harold. He wanted a strong fortress to consolidate his rule over the English people. The Tower was then extended by later kings, including William II, Henry VIII and Edward I, the last two being chiefly responsible for creating the form in which the Tower exists today.

It has a long and interesting past which places it at the heart of many key events in British history. During the reign of Henry VIII, the Tower housed a large number of political and religious prisoners. Many of them were executed. When Henry VIII broke away from the Church of Rome, many of those who opposed this move ended up in the Tower, including the second of his six wives, Anne Boleyn, who was also executed here.

The Tower also played a key part during the English Civil War from 1642 to 1649, when it was fought over by the armies of the King, Charles I, and his opponents, the Parliamentarians. The enemies of the King gained control of

the Tower and the Crown Jewels – the ceremonial jewellery of the royal family were destroyed and melted down so the gold and jewels could be sold and the money used for the good of the people. However, after the restoration of the monarchy in 1660, the new king, Charles II, regained control of the Tower and it became the home of the new Crown Jewels which he had specially made.

And here's another fact which may surprise you – it was once home to lions and tigers! As long ago as the 1200s, King John founded the Royal Menagerie for the entertainment of the court. The first creatures were lions, an elephant and even a polar bear, a gift from the King of Norway. Attached on a lead, the polar bear was allowed to swim and catch fish in the River Thames! The Menagerie survived for 600 years, until the mid 1800s, when it was closed and the animals moved to Regent's Park and became the basis of London Zoo, which you can visit today.

07 Exercise 07 brings together the processes of identifying key words, synonyms and listening to answer this type of listening task. Students should do this individually and compare answers in pairs afterwards. Monitor and then provide feedback.

A, E

Extension

It may be useful for students to read the tapescript and listen again. As they do so, students analyse where the answers are in the text and what synonyms or different grammatical structures were used. This can also be done for Exercises 04 and 06. To do this give students a copy of the tapescript (below) and ask them to listen individually and compare in pairs. Encourage a class discussion of the possible answers before confirming.

Transcript 38

Most visitors to the Tower ask about the ravens – the big, black birds who live within the walls of the Tower. They are known as the Guardians of the Tower and there are always at least six of them. They are fed on raw meat by a Raven Master and visitors are asked not to feed them as they can attack. Legend has it that if the ravens ever leave the Tower of London, the kingdom will fall.

Another famous sight at the Tower is the Beefeaters, or as they are correctly called, the Yeoman Warders. They were first appointed in 1485 by Henry VIII as the ceremonial guards of the Tower and the Crown Jewels. Nowadays they entertain visitors from all over the world with their colourful stories of the Tower's history. However, it's not a position many of us can aspire to. To become a Beefeater, you need 22 years' military service with a medal of good conduct.

08 Exercises 08 to 10 focus on helping students identify speakers' attitudes and opinions when listening. Ask students to read the Bullet box.

Advice

Tell students that to do this effectively they should listen carefully for opinion verbs, adjectives, adverbs and expressions as well as pay attention to how a speaker responds and reacts to a situation.

Exercise 08 tests students' existing knowledge of words and expressions which show an opinion or attitude. Ask students to complete this exercise in pairs. Monitor as students do this. Provide feedback by inviting answers from students (or nominating students to answer). Elicit from other class members if they agree with an answer given or suggest an alternative. Then confirm answers.

1 sub-standard	2 dazzling	3 phenomenal
4 My favourite part was	5 frightening	6 apprehensive
7 famous	8 challenging	

09 This exercise helps students to identify opinions and attitudes when reading a sentence. You can use the same procedure as for Exercise 08 here.

1 B	2 C	3 A	4 B	5 A

10 This exercise brings together the identification of opinions with the listening task of selecting answers from a list. Ask students to do this individually and to compare their answers in pairs after the recording ends. Monitor and provide feedback as outlined in previous exercises.

C, D

Extension

The extension process outlined in Exercise 07 can also be used here.

Transcript 39

Student 1: So, what are we going to focus on for our Tower of London presentation?

Student 2: There are lots of aspects we could talk about, but we've only got eight minutes, remember. Our topic needs to be simple and attention-grabbing. What about a time line? I mean a brief history of the Tower, you know, covering all the major events.

Student 1: Do you think we can really cover nearly a thousand years of history in eight minutes? I don't. We need to be specific and focus on one aspect of the Tower only. We could, say, talk about the history of the Beefeaters and the ravens. For example, I don't think many people realise that it is actually the ravens who are the ones that eat the beef, not the guards.

Student 2: That's worth considering, though I'm not sure there's enough for an eight-minute talk. Surely there isn't that much to say about them?

Student 1: OK, I take your point… I'm also interested in military history, so the Fusilier Museum fascinated me. We could actually do a whole presentation on the weapons in there.

Student 2: Not *everyone's* interested in weapons and war. We need to think of a topic with broader appeal.

Student 1: All right… um… Well, don't they conduct special ceremonies in the Tower, like the Ceremony of the Keys, every evening, when they close up the Tower for the night? It's a bit like the Changing of the Guard at Buckingham Palace, only better. That should have more general appeal.

Student 2: I guess that might be more appealing to the rest of the group. We want our presentation to have a wow factor, right. Oh wait. Speaking of wow factor, we haven't mentioned the Crown Jewels.

Student 1: Yes! There's so much history associated with them and they still get used for state occasions like coronations and royal weddings. I can't see anyone being bored by that topic.

Student 2: Hey! We could ask the other students to guess the value of some of the jewels as part of the presentation? We could give a prize for the closest guess!

Student 1: But the jewels are priceless really, so it would be impossible to put an accurate value on them. Not one of you best ideas!

Student 2: OK, so summing up based on what we've talked about then, it should be either the Beefeaters, the Ceremony of the Keys or the Crown Jewels. I would go for the last one myself.

Student 1: I'd still like to do the Fusilier Museum personally speaking, but OK, let's settle on the Crown Jewels. It would probably have the most universal appeal. Shall we meet after lunch and start planning the presentation?

11 Exercises 11 and 12 focus on the listening exam task of multiple matching. To help students to fully understand this task, ask them to read the Bullet box.

Advice

The key point for students to understand here is that they need to match numbered questions with lettered answers. Tell students that sometimes there are more answers than questions. Therefor some of the possible answers are not needed as they are distractors. Sometimes there are more questions than answers and so some answers can be used more than once.

Exercise 11 prepares students for the listening task in Exercise 12. Ask students to do this in pairs. Monitor as students do this. Provide feedback by inviting students to answer or nominating and then encouraging other students to comment on the answer given by saying if they agree or to suggest alternatives. Then confirm answers.

A display – exhibition; clothes – costumes, outfits
B artists – painters; buried – in tombs
C updates – renews, changes; exhibits – displays, objects; from time to time – occasionally, regularly
D lived up to its reputation – was as good as you hoped/ expected it would be
E queues – lines, standing in line
F flower displays – floral exhibits
G hosted royal weddings – been the venue for royal weddings, royal weddings took place there, royalty was married there

12 This exercise gives students listening practice of this type of listening task. Ask them to do this individually before comparing answers in pairs after the recording. Monitor and then provide feedback as outlined in Exercise 11.

1 C	**2** A	**3** G	**4** E	**5** D

Transcript 40

Harry: So Olga, how did your visit to London go? Did you get to see everything on your list?

Olga: Well, on the whole pretty well, though I didn't get to do everything I wanted. I'd love to go back and do it again.

Harry: Did you manage to get into Madame Tussauds this time? I know you didn't last time you were in London.

Olga: Oh, yes. No problems with long queues or exhibits being closed this time around. I loved seeing the waxworks of the Royal Family again. Did you know that they change the waxwork of the Queen every few years, as she gets older? And it's the same with Prince William and Kate, and Prince Harry. It's scary how life-like they look. They even recreate their clothes.

Harry: Well, you've always been fascinated by the British Royal Family so you were bound to enjoy that. Speaking of which, did you get on that tour of Buckingham Palace? I know it was top of your list of places to see.

Olga: Oh, yes, I did, and I wasn't disappointed. My favourite part was the State Rooms. They were so impressive. I loved the interior design. There are so many masterpieces there from some of the world's most famous painters: Rubens, Van Dyck …

Harry: When I went, they had an exhibition to celebrate the Queen's 90th birthday. It was called 'Fashioning a Reign' and it showed outfits the Queen has worn from the 1930s right up to the present. And after Buckingham Palace, where was next?

Olga: Westminster Abbey. I had to see that. So many famous people are buried there. Kings, queens, prime ministers, the list is endless. And let's not forget Prince William and Kate got married there, like many royals before them.

Harry: I can tell from your voice that you loved it there. How about the Tower of London? Now there's a place full of royal history. Think of all the executions that took place there. They say it's a terrifying place.

Olga: I wouldn't know. On the day we went there, there was some kind of event going on to do with poppies – red flowers – and we couldn't even get close to the entrance. It felt like the whole of London was there, standing in line.

Harry: Oh yes, I read about that. Hundreds of thousands of ceramic poppies decorating the building. I saw photos online – it looked very impressive.

Olga: It was. The flowers looked amazing from the outside, but I didn't have the patience to wait for hours and hours. Instead we went to a newer attraction called the London Bridge Experience. It's supposed to be 'The UK's scariest year-round attraction,' so I thought it would be fun. It didn't disappoint. I can't remember how many times I screamed.

Harry: Doesn't sound very historical to me.

Olga: Maybe not, but certainly worth a visit.

EXAM SKILLS

13 This exercise provides students with exam practice of the two listening task types discussed in this unit. You can either ask students to do this individually and to reflect on what they did and how they felt they performed after completing the exercise or alternatively you can ask students to compare predictions, synonyms and answers after each stage. Monitor when students discuss answers and experiences and provide feedback as outlined in previous exercises. It is important that students reflect on the process they undertook and how it helped them. Try to reinforce good practice.

1 C	**2** E	**3** B	**4** D	**5** G	**6/7** C, E

Extension

The extension process outlined in Exercises 07 and 10 are appropriate here but also incorporate the opportunity for students to reflect and discuss on their experiences as this can help inform better practice in future.

Transcript 41

You will hear a student discussing his dissertation with his tutor. First you have some time to look at questions 1 to 5.

[pause]

Now listen carefully and answer questions 1 to 5.

Adrian: So, I'd like to talk to you about my dissertation. I have to do something about the city of Petra, you know, in Jordan. But I'm not sure which aspect to look at.

Jayne: Oh, OK, yes, there's plenty to write about there. What topics have you thought about?

Adrian: Well, there's the historical angle. Petra dates back to prehistoric times, but there's a lot of information available from about 2,000 years ago.

Jayne: OK, so you'd have to concentrate on sometime in the last 2,000 years. But that's still a long time with a huge number of changes happening. That's really too wide a focus. You need to narrow it down. Why did Petra become well known at that time, do you think?

Adrian: Well, because of the trading routes mainly. Its location made it an ideal place for traders to stop when they were travelling between East and West.

Jayne: True, and the trade route is interesting. But … you wouldn't really be talking just about Petra itself, as it was only one of many places on the trade route. I would rule that one out because your topic needs to concentrate on one place.

Adrian: OK. I'm also interested in the various *conflicts* that took place as people started to travel and mix with very different cultures.

Jayne: Right, but to be honest, that's going to be a lot of research. For such a small sub-topic, there's a surprisingly large amount of material to read on this. I think it might take too long.

Adrian: Yes, I had noticed that. So, I guess that leaves Petra's architecture, though it might be seen as rather an obvious choice.

Jayne: Well, there's a lot of potential there. You could talk about the unique style of half building and half carving into the rocks.

Adrian: That is really fascinating, but I'm worried that it might require some specialist knowledge of building techniques and so on. I'm *interested* in architecture, but my background is more history and social studies.

Jayne: Understood. So any other thoughts?

Adrian: Actually I'm very interested in the buildings in the context of the present day community of Petra. Apparently, people go and sleep in the cave dwellings, even though they've been given modern houses to live in. Living in caves is very much part of their culture.

Jayne: Well, I agree it's interesting, but I think you would get drawn into talking about tourism and that's not really suitable for your degree. I think some kind of focus on the past would be more relevant for a dissertation.

Before you hear the rest of the discussion you have some time to look at questions 6 and 7.

[pause]

Now listen and answer questions 6 and 7.

Jayne: OK, Adrian, so you've finally decided to focus on one aspect of Petra, which is the water management systems. What have you found out so far?

Adrian: Well, mainly that the people of Petra had a really good understanding of how to make use of every bit of groundwater and rainwater they had access to.

Jayne: Can you give me some examples of that?

Adrian: Well, agriculture was one of the most important uses of water. Petra is located in the middle of the desert, so keeping their plants well irrigated was essential and they developed systems to do that.

Jayne: You mentioned that you haven't studied much science. Do you think this area is going to be too technical for you?

Adrian: Well, actually the water supply process is fairly simple to grasp. They used clay pipes and thought about the height of different areas so they could make use of gravity. You don't need a degree in engineering to understand it.

Jayne: OK, that's good. And what about the storage of water?

Adrian: They built huge reservoirs – as simple as that.

Jayne: And is there anything else that's particularly noteworthy?

Adrian: There's an aqueduct in Petra which is around 2,000 years old. That's a bridge which carries water. It was unbelievably ahead of its time. Other similar regions were uninhabitable at that time because of the lack of water management.

Jayne: OK, and what other aspects do you want to focus on?

Adrian: Well… the social history angle – apart from the benefits of irrigation, initially it was the elite – that is the rich – who gained from all this technology. Ordinary people didn't have the luxury of baths and running water, for example.

Jayne: Hmm, and that's still the case with any new technology, isn't it?

SPEAKING

OUTCOMES

- use a range of past time phrases
- use expressions for agreeing and disagreeing
- improve your score for grammatical range and accuracy
- develop your answers in Part 3.

OUTCOMES

Ask students to focus on the outcomes. The first outcome concerns helping students to accurately talk about past events by building students' vocabulary of past time phrases. Accurate use of a wide range of vocabulary is rewarded in the IELTS Speaking exam under the criterion of lexical resource. The second outcome is similarly geared towards this criterion but focuses more on expressions for agreeing and disagreeing. This is particularly useful for Part three of the speaking exam. The third outcome provides students with recommended strategies to improve scores for grammatical range and accuracy. A key point here is to encourage students not simply to be accurate when they speak but also to incorporate more complex grammatical structures. The last outcome focuses on Part three of the speaking exam and looks at strategies for students to follow in order to provide more well-developed answers.

LEAD-IN

01 This exercise tests students on their knowledge of past time phrases within the context of famous historical periods. Ask students to complete this exercise in pairs and monitor as they do this and provide any assistance as some historical periods may be unfamiliar. For feedback, invite students to give their answers and encourage other students to comment on whether they agree or not with answers given by classmates. Then confirm correct answers.

Sample answers

2 between the 5th and the 15th century

3 after the Middle Ages, 14th to 17th century, the rebirth of classical learning

4 in 1999–2000

5 between 1900 and 1920

6 in 2000

7 before recorded history

8 three thousand one hundred years before the birth of Jesus Christ

02 This exercise helps to prepare students before they speak about important events in the past for their country. Ask students to complete this exercise in pairs and monitor. Conduct feedback as outlined in Exercise 01.

a 7 **b** 5 **c** 2 **d** 1 **e** 8 **f** 4, 6 (Y2K = the Year 2000) **g** 3

03 Students can now practise using the past time phrases identified in Exercise 01 and those in the box. Students should spend 1-2 minutes preparing individually before talking with their partner. Monitor as students do this and make notes of anything you wish to discuss in feedback. This could be typical mistakes made by a number of class members but could also be examples of good practice you might want to highlight. Use any errors you noted down when you monitored. Write a list of these on the board (3-5 is manageable). Also, add 1-2 correct answers. Ask students to identify the correct answers and correct the incorrect ones. This is a good way to recycle what has been learnt in the exercise and to also focus on responding to emerging student errors and needs.

Students' own answers

04 This exercise is a more formal IELTS Speaking Part two style task concerning the same topic as in the previous exercise. Before students do this exercise, ask them to read the Bullet box.

Advice

Students should be encouraged not simply just to avoid mistakes but also to try to use more complex grammatical structures in order to obtain higher scores. You may want to show examples of simpler and more complex grammatical structures to help illustrate this.

Refer students to the IELTS criteria specifically for bands 7 and 8 in the introduction to the Teachers' Book. Tell them to firstly determine whether they fully meet the criteria for band 7 and then check if they surpass it and can be judged to meet the grade 8 criteria.

Now ask students to listen to the example individually before answering the questions in pairs after the recording finishes. Ask students to look at the IELTS descriptor for bands 7 and 8 above to help them evaluate the language used. Monitor as students do this and then complete feedback as highlighted in Exercise 01.

1 He mentions all the points.

2 He mentions them in order.

3 Yes. He covers all the points, uses correct grammar and vocabulary, he speaks for the correct amount of time and has excellent pronunciation.

Transcript 42

Dan: Actually, I can talk about a historical event that I witnessed in person in my country. It happened in November 1989, when I was just a young boy, about 10 years old. All my life there had been a wall dividing our city – and our country – into East and West. I often saw the wall when I went around town with my family or friends. It was a fact of life. I never expected it to come down in my lifetime, but I often wondered what it would have been like to live on the other side. As I lived on the Western side, I had been on the other side several times, but I knew that my aunt and cousins, who lived in the East, were not allowed to come over to our side. But that winter's night it all changed. We could hear people running through the streets shouting 'Tor auf' – 'Open the gate!' Even though it was past midnight, my parents took my sisters and I to the wall. It was like a huge street party. People were dancing and shouting, everyone was excited. At midnight they opened the checkpoints and people from the East flooded through. We bought a huge bunch of flowers from a stand. My sisters and I handed them out to people coming across from the East to welcome them. At the time I didn't know what caused the event, but later I found out it was the end of the Cold War. People still think of this event as a symbol of peace. I was very fortunate to be present to see history being made. Those of us who live in Berlin often think what life would be like today if the wall hadn't come down on that fateful night in 1989.

05 This exercise helps students to analyse the language used in the speaking example from Exercise 04. Ask students to complete this exercise in pairs and monitor. Feedback can be given as outlined previously.

1 j   2 h   3 a   4 i   5 e   6 g   7 f   8 b
9 d   10 c

06 This exercise also helps students to analyse language used during a speaking exam. Ask them to complete this exercise in pairs and monitor as they do this. As previously, invite answers from students but do not confirm correct answers until other students have had a chance to comment to say if they agree or to suggest alternative answers.

1 past perfect tense needed – I <u>had</u> never <u>been</u> to Beijing before.

2 present participle needed – … costumes <u>flying</u> across the stage.

3 third conditional error – If one <u>had made</u> a mistake, the whole show <u>would have been ruined</u>.

4 unnecessary article – ~~the~~ Beijing

07 As with the previous exercises, this exercise aims to help students analyse the language used by the candidate in the speaking exam in order for students to be aware of how to score more highly when they do this task themselves. This time, students listen rather than read. Before students do this exercise, ask them to read the Tip box.

Advice

Make sure students are aware that they will be asked one or two follow-up questions at the end of their talk for part 2 of the exam. It is important that they are aware that they shouldn't introduce new ideas and to use one or two full sentences to answer.

Now ask students to complete the exercise individually and then to compare answers in pairs. Monitor as students do this. Conduct feedback as outlined in the previous exercise.

> Answer 3 is the best. This answer is the optimal length and does not introduce new ideas. Answer 1 is impressive but too long and introduces new ideas. Answer 2 is clearly too short.

Extension

If you feel students need more support, you can play the recording again and give students the tapescript below. Students can then work in pairs to analyse the words and content used.

Transcript 43

A. Yes, this is something children all over the world learn about because it represents the end of the 'Cold War'. The Cold War is the name given to the relationship between the USSR and the USA after World War two and Germany was caught up in middle and became a divided country. The wall was erected in 1961 and separated East and West Germany for the next 28 years, probably the key period of the Cold War so yes, it is something that is taught in schools.

B. Yes, they do.

C. Yes, I think this is a significant event in history that children all over the world learn about. Certainly, back home in Germany, it is considered extremely important especially since the reunification of Germany.

08 Exercises 08 to 13 focus on the function of agreeing and disagreeing. Ask students to read the Bullet box.

Advice

Tell students that in Part three of the exam they may need to agree or disagree with something that the examiner says when they answer questions. In order to do well, it

is advisable for students to use a range of phrases and to provide extended answers using reasons, explanations and examples.

This exercise helps students to identify phrases used to show agreement or disagreement. Ask students to listen individually and then to compare their answers in pairs. Monitor as students do this and then provide feedback.

> **1** c   **2** a   **3** d   **4** b

Transcript 44

Examiner: So, Atsuko, we've been talking about a historical event and I'd like to discuss with you one or two more general questions related to this. Do you think it is important for children to learn history at school?

Minji: Yes, definitely. At primary school they <u>should be taught</u> the history of their own country and community. It is way of helping them understand who they are and their place in the world and also the relationships between different countries.

Examiner: You said children should learn the history of their own country. What about world history?

Minji: I'm not so sure about that. I think in the history of their own country of people's <u>should</u> definitely come first. I <u>remember learning</u> about Romans and Egyptians when I was quite a young child without <u>knowing</u> anything about my own country or even my own continent – I mean Asian history. I <u>think learning</u> about world history should come later, say at high school or secondary school.

Examiner: Yes, that's a good point. Do you think most children are interested in learning history these days?

Minji: To be honest, I'd say probably not, which is quite sad, as it's a really important subject. Even though kids are obsessed by their smart phones and computers nowadays, they <u>could</u> still use the technology to learn about history. I think the problem is how history <u>is taught</u>. It <u>needs to be made</u> more fun and attractive to children.

Examiner: Right. You mentioned technology. I was going to ask you about that. Can technology help us learn about history?

Minji: Absolutely! We have the technology to really bring history alive. Lots of museums now have interactive exhibits with holograms and so on. Websites are also becoming more exciting, with videos of re-enactments of historical events, interactive quizzes and things like that. But, for me personally, <u>the best way</u> to learn about history will always be to go to the place <u>where the event took place</u>. For example, I'll never forget the trip we made to Berlin when I did a tour of Europe with my family. Seeing where the Berlin Wall used to stand and the visiting the museums. That really brought history alive for me.

09 This exercise focuses on identifying how the speaker expands on her answers. Follow the procedure identified in the previous exercise.

Sample answers

Do you think it's important for children to learn history at school?

primary school – should learn about own community/ country – help them understand own identity

You said children should learn the history of their own country. What about world history?

national history should come first, world history later, possibly at secondary school

Do you think most children are interested in learning history these days?

more interested in technology – could use it to learn about history

Can technology help us learn about history?

examples of how technology can be used in learning history – going to place where the event took place is best way to learn

10 In this exercise, students can build on existing knowledge of vocabulary for agreeing and disagreeing. Ask students to do this in pairs and monitor as they do this. As before, only confirm correct answers after inviting students to answer and comment on whether they agree or not with answers given by classmates.

Agree: Certainly. Of course. Sure. Without doubt.

Neither agree nor disagree: Well, there are two ways to look at this. Possibly. To some extent. It's hard to say.

Disagree: Not really. Definitely not! No, not at all. To be frank. It's not very …

11 For this exercise, provide a copy of the tapescript. Students can analyse the language used by the speaker. The focus here is on identifying grammatical structures used and this is a good way to raise awareness amongst students that they should use more complex grammar when speaking in the exam. Ask students to complete this exercise in pairs and monitor as they do this. Follow feedback instructions outlined in the previous exercise.

1 I think learning, I remember learning

2 without knowing

3 should be taught, how history is taught, needs to be made

4 the best way

5 should, could

6 where the event took place

12 Students have the opportunity to look closely at exam-style questions in order to identify what type of typical functions are being asked of them to produce. Before students do this exercise, ask them to read the Tip box.

Advice

Make sure students are aware that they should not talk about personal experiences in Part three of the exam. Instead they need to explain or give reasons for something. Tell students that these questions are designed to test students' ability to use complex language structures and vocabulary. Remind students that they should try to show high levels of range and accuracy in terms of grammar and vocabulary here.

Ask students to complete the exercise in pairs and monitor as they do this. Provide feedback as outlined in previous exercises.

1 d	2 b	3 a	4 c, b

13 This exercise helps students to plan their answers for Part three of the speaking exam. Make sure students follow the instructions. Students should do this individually.

Students' own answers

Extension

Ask students to ask and answer the questions from Exercise 13. Tell students to listen to their partner's answers and evaluate them using the following criteria which can be put on the board or in a handout:

Does your partner:

Answer the question asked?

Use words of agreement or disagreement where necessary?

Give an extended answer?

Use advanced grammar structures and vocabulary?

Monitor as students do this. This time, make notes of anything you wish to discuss in feedback. This could be typical mistakes made by a number of class members but could also be examples of good practice you wish to highlight. Use any errors you noted down when you monitored. Write a list of these on the board (3-5 is manageable). Also, add 1-2 correct answers. Ask students to identify the correct answers and correct the incorrect ones.

EXAM SKILLS

14 This exercise provides students with exam practice of Part 2 and 3 of the exam. Students should be reminded to follow the advice given in this unit when preparing and completing this task. Ask students to provide constructive feedback using the criteria outlined in Exercises 04 and 13. Monitor as students complete this and make notes of anything you wish to discuss in feedback. Ask students to identify examples of good and bad practice that you have noted down when you deliver feedback.

Students' own answers

Extension

After feedback, if you want to give students more practice, you can do the following open-pair practice. This is where pairs are selected from different parts of the classroom and they do the pair work in front of the class. This allows students and you to hear the discussion or role-play and students can get a model of good practice or, where errors occur, they can help to correct their peers. This encourages greater student participation and peer learning.

1. Select a student from one side of the classroom.
2. Select a second student from the other side of the classroom.
3. Ask the selected students to complete the activity so that everyone can hear.
4. Thank the two students and if correct, confirm this to the class– this provides a good model.
5. If a student is incorrect, give him or her an opportunity to self-correct. You can gently ask students to do this by repeating the incorrect word(s) with a questioning intonation.
6. If that student can't self-correct, ask other students to help and confirm to all students what the correct answer was.
7. Repeat as desired.

Alternative

Students can create an audio recording of their answers on a smartphone or another device. Students can then listen to their recordings in class or for homework and then record an improved version. You can use these new versions in class or provide individual feedback.

READING

OUTCOMES

- do summary completion tasks with and without boxes of options
- label a diagram
- check your understanding of future tenses.

OUTCOMES

In this unit students will learn how to complete summary tasks, with and without options and diagram labelling tasks. These tasks involve locating the parts of a text that contain specific pieces of information and completing either a summary or a diagram with relevant information from the text. This task often involves paraphrasing information by using a different part of speech to that used in the text. Students will also consider future tense use in IELTS reading texts and how the different use of tenses may affect the meaning of a question in a summary or diagram-labelling task.

LEAD-IN

01 You could begin with some brief discussion of questions about Science and Technology based on the text to get students thinking about the topic. (e.g. How often do you use social media? What positive and negative effects has social media had on society?). Give students about five minutes to briefly discuss these questions, then ask them to compare their ideas with the text. Finally, ask them to read through the text and identify ten places where the writer has used the incorrect part of speech. Explain that using the correct part of speech is important when completing summaries and diagrams, which students will practise later on in the unit.

> Technology has greatly improved the <u>life</u> of many people around the world, according to a considerable amount of <u>researches</u> that has been conducted over the past century. The use of the internet in <u>particularly</u> has become so widespread in so many countries that our daily existence would now be <u>imaginable</u> without it. This is not necessarily a positive <u>developed</u>. As the work of Guillerme Vínculos concludes, when social media first started to become <u>popularly</u>, it was an <u>innocence</u> extension of the standard types of interaction between friends and new acquaintances. These days, however, there are two <u>noticeably</u> extremes; both negative. One, where the platform is used as a <u>substituted</u> for human-to-human contact. The second is where it is <u>employment</u> as a way to bully or aggressively intimidate other people.

02 Once students have identified the words with the incorrect part of speech, ask them to complete the table with the correct version.

Incorrect	Correct
2 researches (noun, countable)	research (noun, uncountable)
3 in particularly (adverb)	in particular (adjective)
4 imaginable (noun, positive)	unimaginable (noun, negative)
5 developed (verb, past or adjective)	development (noun)
6 popularly (adverb)	popular (adjective)
7 innocence (noun)	innocent (adjective)
8 noticeably (adverb)	noticeable (adjective)
9 substituted (verb, past or adjective)	substitute (noun)
10 employment (noun)	(is) employed (verb, past participle to form the passive)

Explain to students that there are two types of summary completion tasks; one that has a box containing possible answers and one that does not. Explain to students that they will be looking at both types of summary, but that they will begin by looking at the type with a box of answers.

03 Ask students to read the text carefully and answer the questions about it. Tell them not to complete the summary yet, as they are going to first learn some strategies for completing summaries with options more effectively. Explain that it is important to notice features of the text, such as the parts of speech, acronyms, whether there are more options than answers, and so on.

> **1** All the words are adjectives. There are more options than gaps, so there are distractors.
>
> **2 a** It is about the future of VR.
>
> **b** The acronyms 'HMDs', 'CDs' and 'PDAs', plus the date '2030', are all useful when scanning the passage to locate the correct places in the text where the answers will be found. Although the acronym 'VR' is mentioned twice, it is the topic of the whole passage and is included in this form throughout and so is not very helpful for locating the right paragraphs to scan.
>
> **c** paragraph A (To what extent VR establishes itself as an integral part of our lives…)
>
> **d** 'Paragraph H'

04 Before asking students to complete the summary task, ensure that they read the tip box, which explains how to enter their answers (using letters, not numbers). Ask students to begin by identifying the parts of the text which contain the information in the summary, and then try to select the correct letter for each space. Before students do this exercise, ask them to read the Tip box.

Advice

A summary task differs from a note completion task in that it consists of complete sentences that are connected grammatically. Students therefore need to do the following to complete the task:

- carefully read and understand the summary.
- decide what type of word is needed to complete each gap in the summary.
- locate and carefully read the relevant part of the passage.
- choose the word or phrase (either from a box of answers or from the passage) that accurately fills each gap.

> **1** A   **2** I   **3** E   **4** G   **5** D

05 Draw students' attention to the Tip box, which explains that some answers can be found directly in the text, while others may require synonyms or paraphrases to be used. Tell students that they, therefore, need to be careful not to include words in the summary just because they appear in the text. Ask students to check their answers to Exercise 4 in the text, writing S next to words that are the same and P next to ideas that have been paraphrased or use synonyms.

> **1** mainstream = P (integral part of our lives; move from niche technology to common usage)   **2** conceivable = P (possible)   **3** outmoded = P (consigned to history)   **4** incapable = P (the vast majority of computers and consoles available for the home market lack the required processing power)   **5** reluctant = P (unwilling)

Tell students that they are now going to look at the summary type that does not have a box of possible answers. For this task type, students will again need to look at the spaces in the summary and identify the correct type of word to go in them. It is also possible that the answer may consist of more than one word. Draw students' attention to the advice box before they complete the next exercise.

06 Ask students to read the summary and answer the questions, but not to complete the task yet.

> **1** paragraphs D–G
>
> **2** Not necessarily. The rubric says no more than two words so it is likely that some answers are more than one word.

07 Ask students to focus on a candidate's answers for questions 1 and 2 in the summary task, and to discuss why they are grammatically incorrect. Elicit that the candidate has used the incorrect part of speech, and then ask students to correct it.

> **1** The gap requires an adjective (phrase), not an adverb (phrase).
>
> **2** The gap requires a singular noun, not a plural.

08 Encourage students to focus on the remaining gaps in the summary and discuss the word type that will probably need to go in the space. Remind them that the information in the text often needs to be paraphrased in order to make it fit grammatically into the summary, and that by doing this they will be prepared to use the correct part of speech.

> **3** noun (phrase)   **4** adjective (phrase)   **5** noun (phrase) beginning with a vowel   **6** noun (phrase)   **7** adjective (phrase)   **8** noun (phrase), probably plural nouns for a group of people

09 Tell students to complete the summary writing no more than 2 words from the passage for each answer.

Advice

- Make students aware that the answers to the questions will not necessarily appear in order in the text
- Tell students that if a word in hyphenated (e.g. long-term) it will only count as one word)

> **1** far-reaching   **2** field / industry   **3** creativity
> **4** secondary   **5** immersive world   **6** composition
> **7** interconnected   **8** (avid) travellers

In diagram labelling tasks, candidates will see a diagram and a description of a process. They will need to carefully read the part of the passage that describes the process and complete the diagram with the words from the passage.

10 Ask students to scan the text and identify the part of the text most likely to contain the description of the process.

> Paragraphs B and C

11 Ask students to label the diagram using no more than 3 words for each answer. Draw their attention to the tip boxes and emphasize that they will not necessarily find the information in the same order in the text.

> **1** computer   **2** natural differences
> **3** tailored picture   **4** aircraft flight

Tell students that different texts in the IELTS reading exam are likely to use a range of different tenses depending on their topic or theme. Explain that because this text is related to future technology, it is likely to contain a variety of future tenses. Explain that when completing summaries and diagrams, there may be some questions which involve selecting the correct tense.

12 In this task, students will discuss how meanings may differ depending on which future tense is used. Do the first example together as a group, and then ask the students to discuss the remaining examples in pairs.

> *Suggested answers*
> **1** In A, the suggestion is that the development of this new form of non-physical communication will begin and end in 2030.
> In B, the verb form changes the meaning completely, so the writer is suggesting that this new form will already be in use by 2030. The completion date of the development is unclear, but we know it takes place at some point between now and 2030. More often, with this grammatical form, *in* + year/month/etc. is replaced with *by* + year/month/etc.
> In C the active, rather than passive, verb form suggests something different again, and something rather strange. In this case, the writer is stating their belief that this new

form communication will inevitably begin in 2030, but as a natural process, apparently without human involvement. As such, it does not really make logical sense.

2 **A** This sentence suggests that the inventor has a fully tested and functional product ready to launch – or recently launched – into the marketplace. They are entirely confident in its potential to sell from the moment it is available to buy. They are expressing their confidence as a given fact, rather than a prediction.

B This example is similar to A in terms of the inventor's confidence in the product. However, this time, the verb form reflects a prediction. The prediction is that the product will work once the inventor has finished developing it.

C In this example, the inventor still feels positive about the outcome – i.e. that he/she is going to be rich – but the use of the word *could* throw a little more doubt onto the product. Maybe it is still in development; maybe the market research they have conducted suggests that its success is far from guaranteed. In fact, to make more sense, the sentence should read, 'I *might* be rich soon because I know this *could* work.'

3 **A** The writer is making a 'so ' prediction. The popularity or importance of Coding as a subject is not guaranteed, neither does the writer over any timescale as to when it can be expected to become 'the most important and popular subject'.

B The writer is more confident in their prediction, and they are suggesting that its future importance and popularity is much more likely to happen than not. This effect is achieved by the addition of the word well after the modal verb. A similar meaning is expressed by *might/may/could* + *well* + bare infinitive.

C Here, the writer is suggesting that Coding is, in the eyes of educators, very soon to become the most important and popular subject in schools, etc. This is not a prediction based on any form of subjectivity or guesswork; perhaps educators all over the world have produced overwhelming evidence to support their claim. Using 'about to' allows the writer to produce a more objective statement than with options A and B, which are more speculative/hypothetical.

EXAM SKILLS

13 Tell students that they are going to practise under exam conditions the IELTS reading task types they have learned about in this unit. Ask them to look at the summary task and elicit which type of summary task it is (i.e. a summary *with* options).

Advice

Remind students of the following:

- Look at the spaces in the summary and work out which part of speech is needed.
- Scan the text for the section that contains each piece of information in the summary. Be aware that the information in text may contain some of the same words as the summary,

but may also be paraphrased. Be careful not to use the same words just because you have seen them in the text.

- Remember to use letters to complete summaries with options. You will not get any marks if you use words instead of letters.
- For diagram-labelling tasks, begin by locating the part of the text containing the process.
- It is good practice to set a time limit for exam-practice tasks.

Give students 20 minutes to complete the tasks, then go through the answers as a group.

| 1 G | 2 D | 3 F | 4 J | 5 A | 6 lighting rig |
| 7 beam | 8 mirrored surface | | 9 transparent (foil) | | |

WRITING

OUTCOMES

- write a 'two questions in one' essay
- increase your chances of a high score in Grammatical Range and Accuracy (GRA)
- write complex sentences with *despite* / *although* concession clauses and participle clauses.

OUTCOMES

In this unit, students will focus on 'two questions in one' essay type in IELTS Part 2. In order to increase their chances of getting a good score for Task Achievement, they will need to ensure that they address both parts of the question in their answer. They will also learn how to write two types of complex sentence; those containing concession clauses and participle clauses, in order to help them to improve their score for the Grammatical Range and Accuracy criterion for Writing Task 2.

LEAD-IN

01 Ask students to work in pairs and give them five minutes to discuss the questions about social media use. Explain to them that they will be looking at some sample answers to IELTS Writing Task 2, and that this will prepare them for this topic.

02 Tell students that they are going to look at some verbs that are commonly used in IELTS Task 2 essays. Explain that sometimes these verbs can be used to mean the same thing, but sometimes they have different meanings. This is important because if students use these verbs incorrectly for writing Task 2, they could lose marks for the Lexical Resource criterion. They could also lose marks in Grammatical Range and Accuracy if they use the incorrect grammatical form associated with these verbs. Ask students to complete the exercise and then have them check their answers in pairs.

| 1 all correct | 2 all correct | 3 advise |
| 4 suggested | 5 recommended | |

03 Following on from Exercise 02, this exercise focuses on using the correct grammatical structure for the verbs 'advise' and 'recommend/suggest'. Do the first example or two as a whole

class and ask students to suggest example sentences. Then ask them to work in pairs and select the grammatical structures that can be used with each verb and write an example sentence.

Suggested answers
to advise (i) *advise* + (*that*)* + clause
*I (would**) advise that you record yourself practising a Part 2 Speaking task.*
(ii) *advise* + someone + *to* infinitive
I advised him to record a Part 2 test and listen back to it.
(iii) *advise* + *-ing*
*I don't/wouldn't** advise turning up to the IELTS test without ID – they won't let you sit the test.*
(iv) advise + *against* + ing
My teacher advises against learning answers off by heart.
to suggest
(i)   suggest + (*that*)*+ clause
I suggest (that) you spend more time working on your pronunciation.
(ii)   suggest + *-ing*
I suggest spending more time working on your pronunciation.
(iii)   suggest + *to* + someone + *that* + clause
I suggested to him that he watch an online video of the Speaking test to help him improve.
* optional
** *would* is more polite/formal

This Writing Task 2 type involves a question containing two parts. Draw students' attention to the Bullet box and the suggested structure for two questions in one essays.

04 Tell students that they are going to look at an example of a Two Questions in One essay title and a candidate's sample answer. Ask students to focus on the two questions in the title and to briefly discuss the ideas they would expect to see in the essay. Then ask students to read the sample essay carefully and discuss the answers to the questions with a partner. Elicit from students which of the four criteria for marking IELTS essays they think would apply to these questions (i.e. Task Achievement) and whether they think this essay would have scored highly in this criterion.

1 In part. The candidate makes it clear they believe social media to have had a positive effect. However, they do not answer the question that has been asked. As a result, the position they state relates to their argument, but not to the one that they should be writing about.

2 No. The candidate begins well, by describing how it has become easier for people to communicate at any time of the day. They go on to state what they see as a second reason for the usefulness/benefits of social media, but it does not relate to the question, which focuses on relationships between family and friends, not performers and their fans.

3 No. The example that the candidate gives does not actually relate to the question. Rather than explaining how useful social media is in strengthening relationships, they have actually written about how useful it is to own a mobile phone.

4 No. The candidate mentions that there are negative sides in both the introduction and conclusion, but the main body of the essay only discusses the positives. In any essay of this length, but particularly one that has two questions to answer, it is difficult to go into a great amount of detail. However, if you are going to state that there are negatives, you should aim at least to suggest what they are. Additionally, the candidate recommends a course of action for everyone to take, but this is not asked for in the question.

Ask students to close their books. Write 'Grammatical Range and Accuracy' on the board and ask students why they think this is important when answering IELTS Task 2 Writing questions (elicit that it is one of the four assessment criteria). Ask students what they think they need to do in order to get a high score for Grammatical Range and Accuracy. Note their answers down on the board, then ask them to open their books and compare their ideas with the information in the advice box.

Extension

It may be useful to refer students to the band descriptors for Writing Task 2. The Grammatical Range and Accuracy descriptor for Band 6 specifies that the candidate 'uses a mix of simple and complex sentence forms', and for Band 7, 'uses a variety of complex structures'. Therefore, students will need to practise and develop their use of complex structures in order to reach these bands for Grammatical Range and Accuracy.

05 Explain that in this exercise, students are going to focus on complex sentences containing concession clauses with 'despite' and 'although'. It may be necessary to explain the different between 'contrast' and 'concession' at this stage. Explain that contrast involves two opposing ideas, whereas concession involves an opposing idea that the reader may not expect. You could use the following example to illustrate this:

Contrast: I used to live in London, <u>but</u> now I live in Cambridge (a contrast between where I lived before and where I live now).

Concession: <u>Even though,</u> I live in London, I spend most of my time in Cambridge (a concession – it is surprising that I spend most of my time in Cambridge when I live in London) Tell students to read another sample answer and identify examples of sentences containing contrast and concession.

'In the past, people were able to talk to each other on the phone, but they had to make sure that they were both at home to make or answer the call at an agreed time.'

'Despite the fact that people need to communicate regularly with their loved ones in order to be happy, it appears that physical contact is not as vital as once thought.'

06 Explain to the students that it is possible to paraphrase concession clauses using different grammatical structures. Ask students to read the examples in the exercise and identify the correct grammatical structures.

> **1** and **3** *Despite* can be used with the following structures: Despite the fact that …; Despite + -ing verb; Despite + noun phrase (no verb)

07 Tell students that 'despite' and 'although' can sometimes be used interchangeably, but that this depends on the grammatical structure of the sentence. Ask them to look again at the three example sentences in Exercise 06, and to discuss in which cases 'despite' could be replaced with 'although'.

> **2** Although is usually followed by a normal sentence structure (subject + verb). Note that it can also be followed by a past participle or an adjective if the subject of both clauses is the same.

08 Tell students that they are going to practise identifying correct and incorrect use of sentences that contain concession and contrast.

Advice

It may be useful to explain at this point, that students will get a higher mark for Grammatical Range and Accuracy, not just for attempting to use complex structures, but also for accuracy. It may be useful to draw their attention to the descriptors for Band 6 ('makes some errors in grammar and punctuation but they rarely reduce communication') and Band 7 ('produces frequent error free sentences' and 'has good control of grammar and punctuation but may make a few errors').

> **1** Incorrect. Corrected version: In the past, although people were able to talk to each other on the phone, they had to make sure … Grammar point: Do not use *although* and *but* in adjacent clauses. They have the same function, so you don't need both.
>
> **2** Incorrect. Corrected version: *In the past, although the ability to talk to each other on the phone **was available**, people had to make sure … OR In the past, although **they had** the ability to talk to each other on the phone, people had to make sure …* Grammar point: *Although* is usually followed by a normal sentence structure (subject + verb). The only exception to this can be seen in sentence 4.
>
> **3** Incorrect. Corrected version: *In the past, **despite being** able to talk to each other on the phone, people had to make sure …* Grammar point: *Despite* can be used with the following structures: *Despite the fact that …; Despite + -ing* verb; *Despite + noun phrase (no verb)*
>
> **4** Correct. Grammar point: If both clauses have the same subject (in this case 'people') **and** the word *although* is followed by an adjective or past participle, it is

> not essential to have the subject in both clauses. For example: *Although (they are) concerned about how much time their children spend online, parents tend not to impose a time limit on them.*

09 Ask students to complete the exercise. Emphasize that they may need to change the structure of the sentence in order to make it grammatically correct. Encourage them to look back at examples from the previous exercises to do this.

> *Sample answers*
>
> **1** Despite wi-fi technology being cheaper than ever, certain parts of the world still have no internet access. OR Despite the fact that wi-fi technology is cheaper than ever, certain parts of the world still have no internet access. OR Although wi-fi technology is cheaper than ever, certain parts of the world still have no internet access.
>
> **2** Despite the fact that Virtual Reality headsets are now available to buy, most home computers lack the processing power to make them worthwhile. OR Despite Virtual Reality headsets being now available to buy, most home computers lack the processing power to make them worthwhile. OR Although Virtual Reality headsets are now available to buy, most home computers lack the processing power to make them worthwhile.
>
> **3** Although it is extremely important to learn at school, some students are better suited to studying arts subjects. OR Despite the fact that it is extremely important to learn at school, some students are better suited to studying arts subjects. OR Despite it being extremely important to learn at school, some students are better suited to studying arts subjects.
>
> **4** Despite its limited amount of government funding worldwide, space exploration has uncovered a huge amount of information about the way the universe works. OR Despite the fact that space exploration receives a limited amount of government funding worldwide, it has uncovered a huge amount of information about the way the universe works. OR Despite receiving a limited amount of government funding worldwide, space exploration has uncovered a huge amount of information about the way the universe works. OR Although space exploration receives a limited amount of government funding worldwide, it has uncovered a huge amount of information about the way the universe works.

In addition to using clauses containing contrast and concession, students will also learn how to use participle clauses; another type of complex structure which could help them to improve their score for GRA, particularly if they can use them accurately. Encourage students to read the advice box before moving on to Exercise 10.

10 Draw students' attention to the examples and ask them to discuss how the participle clauses have been produced.

> **1** The subject of both original sentences is the same (social media, *It*) and the verb in the first sentence is passive. Therefore, the writer has used a past particle clause to connect the two sentences. The words *Social media was first introduced* have been edited to form First introduced, while the subject *Social media* has been moved to replace *It* (the subject of the second clause). If the subject had been le as *it* (i.e. *First introduced to the internet around twenty years ago, it has since gone from strength to strength*) the reader would not know what was being discussed. It is therefore important to make sure that the subject is stated clearly, not referred to by a pronoun; this needs to happen after the comma that ends the participle clause.
>
> **2** Again, the subject is the same for both original sentences and the second original sentence suggests the reason for the first. In the second sentence, the verb is active, so the writer is joining the sentences together with a comma and a present participle clause, replacing the words *They argue with arguing*. Again, the presence of the comma is all-important. It would not be correct to write: Many critics have suggested that it is affecting the closeness of family relationships arguing that people spend too much time staring at screens rather than actually talking to each other. In this case, it is also possible to invert the order of these two clauses so we could begin this participle clause sentence with the second clause: *Arguing that …*

11 Tell students that they are now going to practise forming their own participle clauses. Ask them to work in pairs and then compare their answer with another pair. Emphasize that there may be more than one correct way of joining the clauses to produce a participle clause.

> **1** Greatly excited by social media, young people believe that it is a necessary way to keep in contact with their friends. OR Young people are greatly excited by social media, believing that it is a necessary way to keep in contact with their friends.
>
> **2** Some people argue that social media is the perfect tool for modern communication, drawing attention to the fact that family members and friends often find it impossible to spend time with each other. OR Drawing attention to the fact that family members and friends often find it impossible to spend time with each other, some people argue that social media is the perfect tool for modern communication.

12 Draw students' attention to the two sets of ideas and to the rewritten paragraph and ask them to identify the two complex sentences containing these ideas.

> **A:** <u>Although</u> it is possible to argue that it has created a society in which people spend less face-to-face time with friends and family, <u>social media has</u> revolutionised the way in which we relate to one another.

> **B:** Most people would not welcome a return to an old-fashioned style of communication, <u>being</u> more accustomed now to this convenient new form of interaction.

13 Remind students of the importance of organizing information logically and demonstrating clear progression though writing a clear conclusion (elicit that this will help them to improve their score for Coherence and Cohesion). Ask them to look again at the model essay and to choose the best conclusion. Ask them to compare their ideas with a partner and to explain their decision.

> Conclusion A is the best. It clearly restates the answers to both questions in the essay.
>
> Conclusion B only answers the second question in the essay. It does not sum up the reasons for social media's success.
>
> Conclusion C also only focuses on the second question and in fact contradicts the points made in Paragraph 3 about social media being on the whole a positive development.

EXAM SKILLS

14 Give students 40 minutes to attempt the practice Writing Task 2.

Refer students to the IELTS criteria specifically for bands 7 and 8 in the introduction to the Teachers' Book. Tell them to firstly determine whether they fully meet the criteria for band 7 and then check if they surpass it and can be judged to meet the grade 8 criteria.

Before students do this exercise, ask them to look back at the Tip boxes and Bullet boxes in this lesson.

Advice

Before students begin the task, remind them of the following:

- Read the question carefully, and ensure that both parts are answered
- Don't use the exact words from the rubric
- Try to increase your score for GRA by including some complex structures, including concession and particle clauses.

Feedback

When students have finished the task, ask them to swap essays with a partner. Tell students that they are going to focus on the Grammatical Range and Accuracy criterion. Ask them to find examples of complex sentences in the text, as well as any grammatical errors, and to provide some written feedback on GRA.

Extension

Show students the sample answer below. Ask them to focus on the GRA criterion, and highlight examples of complex sentences. Give students copies of the Band descriptors for GRA and ask them to try and identify which band score this essay would receive for GRA.

It would be difficult to imagine life without computers. Over recent years in particular, their use and potential have grown at an incredible rate and I strongly believe that this growth will continue as more innovative ways to use them are developed. Although there are definitely some downsides to their use, I do believe the positives outweigh the negatives.

Computers enable us to do a wealth of tasks that would have been unthinkable for previous generations. We can bank online, book holidays, do our weekly shopping – the list of labour-saving activities is almost endless. Given the speed at which they have evolved and altered the way we do things, I am convinced that this evolutionary trend will continue. Take, for example, the rise of virtual reality. We can already do amazing things with it, and, as a computer-based technology, it is only in its infancy. It has so many practical applications, from improving gaming to providing training for doctors or pilots to handle real-life situations. As computer processing power increases, so will its potential to enhance everything we do.

Despite this, there are dangers in relying quite so heavily on computers. So much of our daily lives is controlled by them, that without them, modern-day life as we know it would be impossible.

Furthermore, computers store all our important data and the risk of hacking exposes us to crimes such as fraud. However, I would argue that the technological advances made possible by computers have improved our world in so many ways. I believe that most people would argue that that any negative aspects of computers are outweighed by all the benefits they have brought.

In conclusion, I believe we will probably become more dependent on computers but that our lives will improve as the technology improves. While there is a negative side to such a dependency, there are many more positives that we can focus on. (*317 words*)

LISTENING

OUTCOMES

- complete multiple-choice questions with multiple answers and with single answers
- answer flow-chart completion tasks
- use less common phrases to explain cause and effect.

OUTCOMES

Ask students to focus on the outcomes. The first outcome concerns multiple-choice task types. Tell students that in the IELTS Listening exam students sometimes need to pick one correct answer from three possible choices and sometimes students need to pick more than one correct answer from many options. Tell students that in this unit they learn to use strategies to help them perform better with these task types.

The second outcome focuses on completing flow-charts. This is another relatively common IELTS Listening exam task-type. Students are advised how to complete these tasks in this unit in the best possible way. The final outcome is focuses on using less common ways to express cause and effect. This is linked in part to the previous outcome, as better usage and, therefore, understanding of these phrases can help with flow-chart completion, as well as general listening comprehension skills.

LEAD-IN

01 This exercise helps prepare students for the later listening task by asking them to think about related topics. Ask students to do this activity in pairs and monitor as they do this. Next invite students to volunteer answers and try to generate a class discussion by asking students to give reasons for their choices and to comment on what other members of the class suggest.

02 This exercise further prepares students for the listening task by discussing the festival schedule. This activity encourages them to use vocabulary and grammar that are likely to feature in the listening. Encourage students to use the grammar highlighted in the examples.

03 Exercises 03 to 09 focus on developing strategies to answer multiple-choice questions. Before students do this exercise, ask them to read the Bullet box.

Advice

Students should be aware that there are two types of multiple-choice question tasks in the IELTS listening exam. The first type is where students need to identify the correct answer from three options. The second type is where students have to select more than one correct answer from a longer list of options. Stress to students that the latter type may be more difficult because it tests their ability to understand opinions and arguments.

Exercise 03 focuses on students being able to identify similarities between what is said in the recording and the options. Then they should identify the answers from the options. Before students do this exercise, ask them to read the Advice/Bullet box.

Advice

Remind students that even though they may hear words related to all the options, they should listen carefully to identify the correct answers. Also, make sure students are aware that it is likely that the words in the recording will be different from the words in the question so it is advisable that students should try to think of synonyms or similar words in advance.

Now ask students to complete Exercise 03 in pairs. Monitor as students do this. Then invite them to volunteer answers or nominate students to do it. Before confirming answers, encourage other students to say if they agree with them or suggest alternatives.

| **A** 3,6 | **B** 4,8 | **C** 1,7 | **D** 5,10 | **E** 2,9 |

04 This exercise gives students practice of completing this type of listening exam task. Before students do this exercise, ask them to read the Tip Box.

Advice

Students should be reminded to read the question carefully as, in this case, students need to not only find which ones Tanya and Dylan agree with but also identify which the two most important concerns are.

Ask students to complete the exercise individually and then to compare answers with a partner. Monitor as students do this to check if they need to listen more than once. For feedback, follow the guidelines outlined in Exercise 03.

C and B

Transcript 45

Dylan: Hi, Tanya.

Tanya: Oh, hi, Dylan. How's your course going?

Dylan: Really well. I'm enjoying most of the lectures, and I'm looking forward to the Science and Technology Festival next week. Are you?

Tanya: Definitely. Although I haven't checked how much each talk costs to get in – I really hope it's not too much. If we do have to pay a lot on the door, I'll only be able to see one or two. My biggest worry is that there won't be anything related to my studies.

Dylan: You've got a point, but it's not so much that I'm worried about it being a waste of time for our course, and with a student discount we definitely shouldn't have any concerns about ticket prices. The real issue we've got is how to pick which ones to go to.

Tanya: I quite agree – there are so many interesting speakers, it's almost impossible to decide who to see. Plus, the lecture rooms around campus are pretty spread out, so I'm not exactly confident we'll be able to make it to each venue in time.

Dylan: That's absolutely true, neither am I. We'll have to look at the timings in the programme, but hopefully the organisers will have thought of that and won't be expecting everyone to run from one talk to another.

Tanya: I'm not sure about that. The schedule must be really tricky to plan; there are bound to be problems.

05 This exercise helps students to analyse the listening and supports them in identifying clues that were in the recording. Ask students to complete this exercise in pairs and monitor as they do this. Feedback can be given again as outlined in Exercise 03.

---

1 My biggest worry is

2 You've got a point

3 The real issue we've got

4 I quite agree

5 I'm not exactly confident

---

6 That's absolutely true

a concerns: 1, 3, 5; agreement/disagreement: 2, 4, 6

b You've got a point

c phrases 3–4 (option C); phrases 5–6 (option B)

Transcript 46

Tanya: If we do have to pay a lot on the door, I'll only be able to see one or two. My biggest worry is that there won't be anything related to my studies.

Dylan: You've got a point, but it's not so much that I'm worried about it being a waste of time for our course, and with a student discount we definitely shouldn't have any concerns about ticket prices. The real issue we've got is how to pick which ones to go to.

Tanya: I quite agree – there are so many interesting speakers, it's almost impossible to decide who to see. Plus, the lecture rooms around campus are pretty spread out, so I'm not exactly confident we'll be able to make it to each venue in time.

Dylan: That's absolutely true, neither am I.

06 Exercise 06 highlights different strategies students can use when answering multiple-choice questions, where they need to identify one answer from three options. Before students do this exercise, ask them to read the Tip box.

Advice

Emphasise to students that there are two ways that they can approach this question. The first is to read the questions and all of the options before the recording and then select the correct answer. Alternatively, students can read the questions and write their own answer when listening and finally use this answer to help them to pick the correct multiple-choice option.

Ask students to complete exercise 06. Monitor but do not give answers yet.

Student A: 1 *own answer* 2A

Student B: 1C 2 *own answer*

Transcript 47

Tanya: Anyway, which talks are you planning on seeing?

Dylan: Definitely the keynote speaker. I saw her present once before at a conference in Los Angeles, which was interesting because we had previously thought she only uploaded her talks onto the internet. When she presented to us, I couldn't believe how normal she seemed in real life, even a little shy, because she seemed to have such a big personality on those videos, and sometimes the content of the lecture got lost a little bit as a result.

Tanya: Sounds impressive. So she'll be opening the festival on Tuesday. What's her talk about?

Dylan: It'll be something about new technologies in Computer Game Design.

Tanya: Oh, perfect timing. I've got the first class of a Game Design module beginning next Thursday, so it would be good to get prepared for that. For example, I know my study skills aren't as good as they could be. I really should work on those, because I'll probably have forgotten everything by the time I go into class. The problem is finding the time for that and I'm too busy right now to work on them. I've bought the course books for the module already, and I'm definitely going to do some in-depth background reading beforehand. That has to be my priority.

07 Students can use their open written answers to help them identify the correct multiple-choice option from the choices that their partner has and vice-versa. Monitor and then provide feedback by inviting students to answer and comment on each other's answers before confirming the correct ones.

See answers for 06

08 This exercise encourages students to reflect on this process and to decide which strategy they preferred. Monitor to check students are on track. Then encourage a class discussion.

09 Students can now decide which strategy to follow when answering these multiple-choice questions. Ask students to do this individually before comparing in pairs after the recording. Monitor and complete feedback as outlined in Exercise 07.

3 C   4 C

Extension

Students can listen again and have a copy of the transcript to help them identify clues. Ask students to do this in pairs and then to reflect once again on the strategy they used to answer these questions.

Transcript 48

Dylan: Good idea. And my note-taking skills need work as well, but science and technology students don't seem to get much help. In laboratory tutorials, it sometimes seems like everyone's a little nervous about coming up with ideas for particular experiments, so I just start talking, even if I don't know what I'm talking about. I always feel like I'm dominating the conversation and speaking too much, but after I've made my point everyone else suddenly discovers what they want to say and we can relax.

Tanya: Mm, I know how you feel. Anyway, let's think about what to do after the keynote speech on Tuesday. There are two talks which immediately follow it, but neither of them look that interesting, so it would probably be a better idea if we used that time to decide which of tomorrow's lectures we should attend. Shall we grab a coffee while we're doing that?

Dylan: That's a great idea. Then we can go to that final lecture on virtual reality applications a bit more

refreshed. Once that one has finished, let's head over to that cheap Italian restaurant for something to eat. We'll be starving by then.

Tanya: You're on. And it's your turn to pay.

10 Exercises 10 to 12 focus on helping students to answer the flow-chart completion task in the IELTS Listening exam. Before students do this exercise, ask them to read the Bullet box.

Advice

Tell students that they need to fill in missing words in chronological stages. Remind students that they will need to use the exact words from the recording or choose answers from a list. Make sure students are aware that they need to pay attention to the word limit.

Ask students to do Exercise 10 in pairs. Monitor as students do this and then give feedback as outlined in Exercise 07.

1 noun (phrase)	**2** noun (phrase)	**3** verb (phrase)
that collocates with of	**4** noun (phrase)	**5** noun
(phrase)		

11 This exercise helps students to learn to deal with missing answers as they listen. Before students do this exercise, ask them to read the Tip box.

Advice

Students should look at the next two questions after their last answer so that they can cope with losing their place in the recording or missing answers.

Ask students to complete Exercise 11 individually and then to compare their answers in pairs. Allow students to volunteer or nominate them to answer in front of the class. Encourage other students to comment on the answers, before confirming the correct ones.

Extract 1 – Question 3
Extract 2 – Question 5
Extract 3 – Question 2
Extract 4 – Question 1
Extract 5 – Question 4

Transcript 49

1 We should try to review what we see as the main ideas, the most important technical features, that sort of thing. We'll then be able to decide together what …

2 Also, when we post it on the department web page, we'll need to show how it all relates to our courses. In order for us to get some feedback about this, we should probably contact our tutor …

3 That way, when we meet up again after the lecture, we'll be more able to compare notes, and to go over …

4 I've tried using those before. Diagrams are often a great way to learn or explain things in science, but they *can* make your notes a little difficult to follow.

5 Good plan. We agree what the most significant points are from each lecture, maybe even try to establish some of the common themes.

12 This exercise gives students practice of flow-chart completion. Before students do this exercise, ask them to read the Tip box.

Advice

Highlight to students that they should pay specific attention to the accurate use of singular and plural forms as this is one of the things that differentiates higher ability candidates from others.

Then ask students to complete this exercise individually and to compare answers in pairs. Monitor as students do this. Then provide feedback as outlined in Exercise 11.

> **1** bullet points **2** initial impressions **3** leave out
> **4** edited version **5** feedback

Extension

Students can listen again and have a copy of the transcript to help them identify clues. Ask students to do this in pairs and then encourage class discussion of the suggested clues.

Transcript 50

Tanya: We also need to consider what to include in our summary for the department web page.

Dylan: As neither of us are brilliant at taking notes, let's try to find a system that will work for us both.

Tanya: Well, so how about mind maps?

Dylan: I've tried using those before. Diagrams are often a great way to learn or explain things in science, but they *can* make your notes a little difficult to follow. I think it's better if we both opt for bullet points so that it's clear and consistent.

Tanya: OK, let's use those. That way, when we meet up again after the lecture, we'll be more able to compare notes, and to go over our initial impressions, stating what was particularly relevant. We should try to review what we see as the main ideas, the most important technical features, that sort of thing. We'll then be able to decide together what to include – and what to leave out – when we come to the summary.

Dylan: Good plan. We agree what the most significant points are from each lecture, maybe even try to establish some of the common themes. By doing so, we can then put together an edited version of these on a separate sheet of paper, and when we eventually come to write the summary, the main points will be even clearer.

Tanya: Also, when we post it on the department web page, we'll need to show how it all relates to our courses. In order for us to get some feedback about this, we should probably contact our tutor and send her a summary of the main points.

Dylan: OK, let's make sure we email her tonight, then.

13 Exercises 13 and 14 focus on the use of lesser common ways to express cause and effect. Before students do this exercise, ask them to read the Bullet box.

Advice

Explain to students that higher IELTS scores are awarded to students who are able to understand and use a range of less common and more complex expressions – in this case when speaking about cause and effect.

Exercise 13 gives students listening practice of these less common phrases for cause and effect. Ask students to do this individually and then to compare in pairs after the recording. Monitor and then provide feedback as outlined in Exercise 11.

> **1** That way
> *Cause*: use bullet points
> *Effect*: easier to compare notes
> **2** By doing so
> *Cause*: agree some significant points / establish common themes from lectures
> *Effect*: put together an edited version
> **3** In order for us to
> *Cause*: contact tutor
> *Effect*: get some feedback

Transcript 51

1 Dylan: I think it's better if we both opt for bullet points so that it's clear and consistent.

Tanya: OK, let's use those. That way, when we meet up again after the lecture we'll be more able to compare notes …

2 Dylan: Good plan. We agree what the most significant points are from each lecture, maybe even try to establish some of the common themes. By doing so, we can then put together an edited version of these on a separate sheet of paper …

3 Tanya: In order for us to get some feedback about this, we should probably contact our tutor …

14 This exercise focuses on grammatical accuracy and appropriate use of these types of phrases. Ask students to do this in pairs and monitor as they do this. Invite students to answer or nominate somebody. Allow students the opportunity to comment on their classmates' answers before confirming correct ones.

> **1** In order that she could / So as to / In order so
> **2** This way / The way / That way
> **3** For doing so / By doing so / After doing so
> The correct options in number 2 are better suited to speaking; those in numbers 1 and 3 are well suited to writing, but can be used in speaking as well.

Extension

You may want to give students more practice of the use of these phrases and confirm understanding by asking students to create their own sentences with the expressions above.

EXAM SKILLS

15 In this exercise, students are given exam practice to bring together all of the skills and knowledge learnt in the unit. Ask them to do this individually and then to compare answers. Monitor as students compare and then provide feedback as outlined in the previous exercise.

1/2 B, D	3 A	4 B	5 C	6 C	7 F	8 G
9 D	10 A					

Extension

Students can listen again and have a copy of the transcript to help them identify clues. Ask students to do this in pairs and then to reflect once again on the strategies they used to answer these questions.

Transcript 52

You will hear two students talking to their professor about the Science and Technology Festival they attended.

First you have some time to look at questions 1 to 6.

[pause]

Now listen carefully and answer questions 1 to 6.

Prof Dickens: Hi, Dylan, hi Tanya, thanks for coming to see me. I'm very interested to hear what you thought about the Science and Technology Festival.

Dylan: Well, we're both very pleased we went.

Prof Dickens: Glad to hear it. Was there anything you both found especially useful?

Tanya: Yes, definitely. I saw at least two lectures that directly relate to the subjects I'm studying in this first semester. I already feel a little more prepared than I did last week.

Dylan: There wasn't anything that had the same effect on me, but that wasn't my only focus. I saw the festival as a chance to explore new ideas and other subject areas, so I also tried to attend some lectures that looked interesting, rather than just the ones I thought would only be relevant to my course.

Tanya: I'm glad I didn't do that – I get too stressed when I don't concentrate on one thing. But <u>wasn't it great to be able to wander around the university and get a better idea of where everything is</u>?

Dylan: <u>Well, I certainly I feel more confident now I've explored the area a bit more</u>. And I also found it very easy to meet people who share the same interests as me. When I was waiting for some of the lectures to start, I just got talking to whoever was sitting next to me.

Tanya: I was too busy going through my notes to do that. I have to say, going to so many lectures in a short space of time has really <u>helped me to improve one area of study – my note-taking technique</u>.

Dylan: I wasn't so sure about that originally. But looking at my notes again this morning, <u>I could see how they got better as the week went on</u>.

Prof Dickens: I'm glad the week was of use to you. It seems to change focus annually; sometimes the emphasis is more on science, sometimes on technology, but there was an excellent balance this time. <u>It really brings these areas of study and research to the attention of the wider world and, for me, that's the primary reason the festival exists</u>. You may have noticed when you were there, and there were a number of university information stands set up around the campus. Did you see the free reference booklets that they were giving out?

Dylan: No, I assumed the stands were there to provide people with directions to each talk.

Prof Dickens: Well, <u>their aim was to encourage everyone to read some of the latest studies coming out of our labs and classrooms</u>. Many of the lecturers at the festival actually wrote the studies that were listed, so the talk and the booklets together are a great introduction to their work for anyone who attended. But the staff were certainly happy to point people in the right direction if it was needed.

Tanya: I have to admit, it was quite confusing, trying to follow some of the signs around the campus telling us where to go, so we used the map in the festival guidebook to find our way around. It was great for that. <u>And, although one or two of the talks actually started at different times to what was printed on the page</u>, one other thing I did like about the guidebook was that it wasn't full of adverts.

Dylan: Oh, I agree, but that's always the case with festivals now. I don't mind that, if it means that the festival is free to enter, as more and more of them are these days. And even if there is a fee for admission, the festival organisers hardly make any money from that, though they do tend to put the price of entry up each year. <u>They have to make money to run the festival somehow, so it makes sense to get the majority of that through ads</u>.

Tanya: That's a fair point.

Before you hear the rest of the conversation you have some time to look at questions 7 to 10.

[pause]

Now listen and answer questions 7 to 10.

Prof Dickens: So, what next? Do you still want to write something for the department website?

Dylan:	Oh, definitely. Can you give us some advice on how we do that?
Prof Dickens:	Well, it's a simple process, but it can mean a lot of work. First, you need to make sure that you have fully discussed and compiled the notes you made during the festival. For the next step I would recommend selecting a set number of principal theories that generate the most ideas and summarise those – four is probably the ideal number. Then you'll need to go to the website and go through what people have written before. These <u>posts</u> will help you to understand which style seems most appropriate – how academic in tone you need to be, or how informal, and so on. And as this is going to be a joint project, it's really important to make sure that you both come to a joint decision about the best way to divide up the <u>workload</u>. Believe me, arguments can happen. Further to that, you should also agree on exactly when you're aiming to publish it, so establish a <u>deadline</u>. Make sure you don't go past the agreed date, as it will become more difficult to finish if you do. Then, after all this is completed, you're ready to upload your summary and any other documents and post them onto the department website.
Tanya:	Wonderful, thanks so much, Professor Dickens. Hopefully we can come back to you if we need any more help..

SPEAKING

OUTCOMES

- improve your score for Grammatical Range and Accuracy (GRA)
- correctly use verb patterns in your answers
- develop strategies for buying time to answer more difficult questions.

OUTCOMES

Ask students to focus on the outcomes. The first outcome helps students to perform better in IELTS Speaking Part three by learning strategies to give them more time to answer more complex questions. This is important when answering questions in this part of the exam in a way that would be rewarded more highly, for example, with the use of complex grammatical structures and vocabulary. The second outcome provides students with a number of phrases that can be used in the speaking exam. Some can be used without the need to adapt them (fixed) and some can be adapted to suit the context (semi-fixed). Again, these are useful phrases for students to learn and be able to use in the exam to improve scores of

Lexical Resource and, to a lesser extent, grammatical range and accuracy. The third outcome helps with the latter criterion as it focuses on accurate use of verb patterns when speaking. The fourth outcome looks at more strategies to help students demonstrate greater grammar range and accuracy.

LEAD-IN

01 This exercise helps students prepare for the topic of the unit and tests their existing knowledge of related key vocabulary. Ask students to complete this exercise in pairs and monitor while students are doing this to check they are on task. Elicit answers from students and encourage other class members to say if they agree or not with the answers given before you confirm correct answers.

1	1783 = parachute
2	1843 = typewriter
3	1866 = dynamite
4	1798 = vaccination
5	1963 = computer mouse
6	1280 = eyeglasses
7	1710 = thermometer
8	2400 BC = abacus

02 This exercise provides students with less restricted speaking practice on this topic. Monitor as students complete this exercise in pairs and then invite or nominate students to give their answers to the class. Encourage other students to say if they agree or not with the answers given and if not, to say why.

Students' own answers.

03 Exercises 03 to 05 focus on strategies to score higher in the GRA criterion for Part one of the speaking exam Before students do this exercise, ask them to read the Bullet box and Tip box.

Advice

The key here is for students to understand that Part one of the exam, whilst being less difficult than the other two parts still provides a good opportunity for students to show the examiner their more complex and accurate grammatical knowledge. There are suggestions for how students can demonstrate this complexity in the advice box. You may wish to provide examples of each to clarify any lesser known grammatical structures.

The Tip box encourages students to consider how they can relate the question asked by the examiner to the various grammatical structures listed.

Exercise 03 tests students existing knowledge of tenses and also helps students to analyse an example speaking part one response. Ask students to complete Exercise 03 individually and then to compare answers in pairs. Monitor as students do this and then conduct feedback as outlined in Exercise 01.

2 – past and present simple

04 This exercise also encourages students to analyse an example speaking answer but this time is through listening to a recording. Ask students to listen individually and then to compare their answers in pairs after the recording. Monitor as students compare answers to see if the recording needs to be repeated. Provide feedback as outlined previously.

> 1 used to
> 2 'd be using
> 3 've been thinking
> 4 will be
> 5 have become
> 6 'm going to
> 7 if I didn't have one, I wouldn't have a
> The candidate has used a wide range of grammatical forms and structures correctly here in a very short space of time. If they continued in this way, they could expect a very high score for GRA.

Extension

If you feel students need more support, you can play the recording again and give students the transcript below. Students can then work in pairs to analyse the words and content used.

Transcript 53

Examiner: How often do you use your mobile phone?

Candidate: Not as much as I used to. After I first bought it, I'd be using it almost constantly, but I've been thinking that maybe I use it too often and should try to limit how long I spend on it. I don't know if that will be possible, though, they've become such a big part of everyone's lives these days, but I'm going to have to try. Not completely, though – if I didn't have one, I wouldn't have a social life.

05 Based on the analysis of the example answers in Exercise 03 and 04, students now have freer practice to demonstrate that they can use their knowledge of grammar to produce answers which will score more highly for the criterion of grammatical range and accuracy (GRA).

Refer students to the IELTS criteria specifically for bands 7 and 8 in the introduction to the Teachers' Book. Tell them to firstly determine whether they fully meet the criteria for band 7 and then check if they surpass it and can be judged to meet the grade 8 criteria.

Ask students to prepare answers individually and then to work in pairs to take turns in asking and answering the questions. Monitor as students do this. This time, make notes of anything you wish to discuss in feedback. This could be typical mistakes made by a number of class members but could also be examples of good practice you wish to discuss. Use any errors you noted down when you monitored. Write a list of these on the board (3-5 is manageable). Also, add 1-2 correct answers. Ask students to identify the correct answers and amend the incorrect

ones. This is a good way to recycle what has been learnt in the exercise and to also focus on responding to emerging student errors and needs.

06 Exercises 06 to 11 focus on Part two of the speaking exam and how to improve students' scores in the criterion of GRA. Exercise 06 helps students to prepare for speaking about this topic at length in subsequent exercises. Ask students to answer the questions in pairs and monitor as students do this. Provide feedback as outlined in Exercise 01.

> 1 A (the) radio; B electricity / bringing electricity to people's homes; C the aeroplane; D the compass
> 2/3 students' own answers

07 This exercise gives students exam style practice for questions related to this topic. Students should prepare individually and then take turns giving their answer. Again, monitor and take notes of anything you wish to raise in feedback. See Exercise 05 for details of how to use these during feedback.

Extension

After feedback, if you want to give students more practice, you can do the following open-pair practice. Select pairs from different parts of the classroom and then they do the pair work in front of the class. This allows everybody to hear the discussion or role-play and provides a model of good practice or, where errors occur, can give students an opportunity to correct their peers. This encourages greater student participation and peer learning.

08 This exercise looks at how Part two answers can be improved by accurate understanding of verb patterns. Before students do this exercise, ask them to read the Bullet box and Tip box.

Advice

Tell students that this particular grammar point concerns sentences where one verb follows another. Highlight the possible forms that could be taken and whether it can be used to introduce a 'that' clause or if it needs an object. Based on the grammatical knowledge of your students, you may wish to provide example sentences to further clarify this grammar point.

Exercise 08 allows students to analyse the written form of an example answer to the Part two question in Exercise 07. Ask students to do this in pairs and monitor to see how much they already know about this grammar point. Then play the recording and ask students to check individually before comparing answers in pairs. Conduct feedback as previously described.

> 1 I'd like to tell   2 let me begin   3 correct
> 4 correct   5 remember being taught   6 correct
> 7 managed to attach   8 can't help thinking
> 9 correct   10 imagine living   11 allow us to have
> 12 correct   13 remember to look it up
> 14 continue to be / continue being

Transcript 54

I'd like to tell you what I know about one of the most significant inventions in human history: the wheel. Why is it so significant? Well, let me begin by saying, first of all, it basically enabled us to develop whole civilisations, as we could for the first time start transporting goods from place to place, and this mobility really made trade grow at an incredible speed. I remember being taught about this at school. Our teacher told us not to see the wheel itself as the crucial invention, because it was actually the moment someone managed to attach a non-moving platform to two wheels that was critical. But I can't help thinking that you don't have to agree with everything you are told at school, and I would politely refuse to agree with him, if I was told this today. You see, without a wheel, a platform is just a bit of wood, essentially.

Anyway, wheels in everyday use. Well, can you imagine living without them? It's practically impossible. You wouldn't be able to drive anywhere, for one thing. What's more, wheels allow us to have a public transport system, and if wheels didn't exist, aeroplanes wouldn't be able to take often and land, and no one would be able to go on holiday.

How exactly a wheel works, I won't even attempt to explain, other than the fact that they go round. It's something to do with force. I've never been any good at physics, but maybe I should remember to look it up on the internet when I get home. But, overall, there's no question about how important the wheel is, and it will continue to be an integral part of our lives forever.

09 This exercise helps students to classify the verbs according to the pattern they follow. Highlight to students that some verbs can be put in more than one column. Ask students to do this in pairs and monitor. Provide feedback as described in previous exercises – avoid confirming correct answers until you allow other students to say if they agree or to suggest alternatives.

Verb + 'to' infinitive	Verb + gerund	Verb + object + to infinitive	Verb + object + bare infinitive (i.e. without 'to')
remember continue manage refuse attempt	remember continue can't help imagine	enable help tell allow	let

10 This exercise tests students' knowledge of the verbs which can take different forms and how that may change the meaning. Ask students to work in pairs and monitor. Encourage a class discussion during feedback and then confirm answers.

would like

would like + 'to' infinitive expresses a personal plan, hope, expectation, etc., e.g.

I would like to tell you about …

would like + object + 'to' infinitive expresses a plan, hope expectation, etc. of someone or something else, e.g. *I would like you to tell me about …*

continue

There is no difference in meaning between continue + infinitive and continue + gerund, e.g. *They will continue being / to be an integral part of our lives forever.*

remember

remember + gerund = the action expressed by the gerund happens first, e.g.

I remember (second action, now) *being taught* (first action, past) *about this at school. Do you remember learning your first words in English?*

remember + infinitive = the action expressed by the 'to' infinitive happens second, e.g. *I should remember* (first action) *to look it up* (second action) *on the internet when I get home. Did you remember to finish your homework?*

11 This exercise provides students with spoken exam style practice and builds on answers for Exercise 07. It is informed by the input on verb patterns. Students should prepare individually before taking turns saying their answers. Ask students to provide constructive feedback. Monitor as students complete this exercise, noting down things you want to raise in feedback.

12 Exercises 12 to 15 introduce the strategy of playing for time. Before students do this exercise, ask them to read the Bullet box.

Advice

Tell students that they won't lose marks if they do not know the answer immediately and pause but they will if they can't think of the correct words to use. Explain that it is a good idea to use strategies and phrases to give students thinking time especially for Part three questions.

12 This exercise helps students identify strategies used by candidates in the exam. Asks students to complete this exercise in pairs and monitor. Feedback can be provided as highlighted in Exercise 09.

| **1** B | **2** A | **3** C | **4** C | **5** B | **6** A | **7** C | **8** A |

13 This exercise builds on from the previous one by focusing on the grammatical accuracy of useful phrases to buy time in the exam. Ask students to complete this exercise in pairs. Monitor and provide feedback.

1 That's quite a tricky question.
2 It's never crossed my mind before.
3 I'm not entirely sure what you're driving at.
4 Sorry, I don't quite follow your question.
5 my mind has gone blank

Transcript 55

1 That's quite a tricky question to answer. Let me think.
2 I don't really know how to answer that. It's never crossed my mind before.
3 I'm not entirely sure what you're driving at. Can you rephrase the question, please?

4 Sorry, I don't quite follow your question. Do you mean with appliances, like kettles, or something like internet security?

5 You know, I'd usually be able to answer that question immediately, but my mind has gone blank.

14 This exercise helps students to build up a range of ways to buy time by adding to the examples provided in Exercise 12. Students can do this in pairs.

> **1** C   **2** C   **3** A   **4** A   **5** C

15 This exercise gives students spoken practice of using these strategies. Ask students to work in pairs and follow the instructions given. Monitor as students do this and note down anything you wish to bring up in feedback.

> *Student's own answers.*

EXAM SKILLS

16 This exercise gives students exam practice for all three parts of the IELTS Speaking exam. Remind students that it is unlikely that all three parts will be the same topic. Ask students to complete this exercise together. Monitor as they do this. Note down anything you wish to raise in feedback. You may also want to also provide open-pair practice (see Exercise 07 Extension). Reinforce good strategy use.

> *Student's own answers.*

Extension

Ask students to discuss together the strategies they used and to reflect on how effective they found them. With strategies, it is often good for students to reflect on their use to help them internalise them for use in the future.

Alternative

Students can create an audio recording of their answers on a smartphone or another device. Students can then listen to their recordings in class or for homework and then record an improved version. You can use these new versions in class or provide individual feedback.

READING

OUTCOMES

- locate and match information in a paragraph
- answer short-answer questions
- match sentence endings
- understand how the passive is formed and used in English.

OUTCOMES

This unit focuses on two IELTS reading task types: short answer questions and matching sentence endings. These are both tasks that require the candidate to first select the part of the text that contains the relevant information to answer the questions. Students will therefore focus on the skill of recognizing paraphrasing in the questions in order to locate the correct part of the text. Students will also focus on how the passive voice is formed and used, as the passive is a common feature of academic texts.

LEAD-IN

01 Ask students to close their books. Explain that they are going to read a text about the future of journalist. Begin by asking students to suggest definitions of the word 'journalist', then ask them what they understand by the term 'citizen journalist'. Then ask them to open their books and check their ideas with reference to the discussion questions. Finally give students five minutes to discuss the questions.

Alternative

Write the word 'journalist' on the board. Elicit from students some different types of journalist (e.g. news journalist, investigative journalist). When students have made some suggestions, add 'citizen' journalist to the list and elicit what students think a citizen journalist is / does.

02 Tell students that in many IELTS reading texts they will need to look for synonyms and antonyms of words in the text in order to answer questions. Tell them that they will identify synonyms and antonyms in order to better understand a text that they will read later. Ask students to identify which pairs of words are synonyms and which are antonyms.

1 S	2 S	3 A	4 S	5 S	6 S	7 A	8 S

03 Ask students to discuss the difference in meanings between the antonyms.

> **1** *Journalist* is a more generic word for anyone who works in media; a *reporter* is someone who writes or presents the news only.

> **2** This is dependent on context: for the news, *research* means looking at different sources to be clear on the facts of a story. *Investigate* implies a more active role of finding out information that was not previously known, or solving something.

> **4** same meaning – be the first to publish a news story

> **5** *Broadcast* is used for TV/radio and *publish* for printed stories.

> **6** A *media outlet* is a more generic organisation, for example a newspaper, magazine, or TV channel that offers a variety of information, whereas a *news agency* is just news focused.

> **8** An *eyewitness* is a person who was present and saw the events of the news story first hand. A *source* is a person or organisation that provides information for a news story.

04 Draw students' attention to the Bullet box. Explain that they are going to be looking at matching information questions, and that locating information in a text is a useful skill for this task type.

Tell students that they are going to skim read the paragraph and match each of the seven summaries with their corresponding paragraph. Explain that doing this will help them to locate the information that will help them answer matching information questions more quickly.

1 E	**2** G	**3** A	**4** C	**5** F	**6** B	**7** D

05 Ask students to scan the paragraphs to locate the information. Draw their attention to the information in the Bullet box and explain that they may need to look for information from the questions that has been paraphrased.

> **A** a camera **B** Ohmynews! **C** CNN, The Times
> **D** 2021 **E** educational, economic, social, cultural
> **F** rioters, looters **G** their critical faculties

06 Ask students to focus on the underlined words and phrases and identify the synonyms or paraphrases in the text that helped them identify the answers to the questions.

> **A** possessed – owned **B** a Korean news site – one of South Korea's most influential online sources
> **C** media outlets – news organisations **D** half – 50%
> **E** obstacles – barriers **F** criminals – offenders
> **G** audiences – readers and viewers

07 Explain to students that they are going to test their knowledge of the text so far. Ask them to cover up the text and to identify whether the information in this exercise can be found at the beginning, middle or end.

> *Students' own answers*

08 Tell students that they are going to attempt the exam task. Explain that having identified the main areas of the text where the information is located, they should now find it easier to locate the paragraphs where the information can be found.

1 D	**2** F	**3** G	**4** A	**5** B	**6** E

Focus students' attention on the advice box. Ask them to read the information carefully and then close their books. Ask them some concept-check questions (e.g. 'Will the information be in the same order in the questions as it is in the text?' / 'Which words in the question will it be useful to underline?').

09 Ask students to look at the questions and underline the question words and key words. Explain that doing this will help them to think about the kind of answer they are looking for in the text, and should help them to locate the answers more quickly.

> **2** <u>What</u> was the <u>subject of the story</u> given as an <u>example</u> of an <u>amateur journalist scoop</u> before it was reported by a <u>major news agency</u>?
> subject – probably a noun
>
> **3** From <u>which group of people</u> have the <u>media establishment</u> begun to <u>hire staff</u> ?
> group of people – a plural or collective noun
>
> **4** <u>What mainstream media</u> traditionally had seen their <u>role</u> in <u>news reporting</u> as being?
> role – a noun

10 Now ask students to answer the questions using no more than three words from the text. When they have finished, ask them whether underlining the key words and predicting the types of word in the answer made it easier to locate the answers. Emphasize that this is a strategy that can be used for this question type in the IELTS reading exam.

> **1** eyewitness   **2** space shuttle Columbia
> **3** (amateur) (news) bloggers   **4** gatekeepers

11 Tell students that they are going to try to answer some short-answer questions that have multiple-choice options. Explain that although MCQs are a different IELTS task type, considering the alternative options will help students to find evidence from the text to support their choice of answer. Ask students to work in pairs and discuss which options are correct / incorrect and why.

> **7** **A** correct **B** incorrect – the text says critical thinking is desirable, not a 'risk' **C** incorrect – the words are not in the text
>
> **8** **A** incorrect – too many words **B** correct **C** incorrect – the authorities *are* the police
>
> **9** **A** incorrect – this is the old model **B** correct **C** incorrect – We media is not a 'model' of broadcasting

12 Tell students that now they have practised using some strategies for answering short-answer questions, they are going to practise finding some further short-answer questions. Encourage them to continue to underline key and

questions words in the questions and to consider the types of word that might form the answers.

> **1** Independent Media Center / Indymedia
> **2** democratisation
> **3** reduce inequality

The difficulty of this task for candidates is that a number of different answers will fit grammatically and appear to make sense, but the correct answer must match the exact information from the text. Before students do this exercise, ask them to read the Bullet box.

Advice

Emphasize to students that they will have to locate the part of the text containing the information in order to choose the correct sentence half.

13 In this exercise students are given the correct part of the text, which means that they will be able to focus on matching the information with the two possible sentence halves. Ask them to complete the task and to discuss the reasons for their answers with a partner.

> B

14 Tell students that they are now going to practise locating information in the text in order to answer matching-sentence-endings tasks correctly. Encourage them to underline key words and ideas in the sentence endings to help them locate the information in the text. Make them aware that there are more options than they need, so they will also need to identify the endings that do not match with the stems.

1 C	**2** E	**3** B

Tell students that the passive voice often features in academic texts, as they are written with a more impersonal tone. Tell them that they are going to focus on some examples of use of the passive in the text.

15 Focus students' attention on the example sentence from the text, and ask them to identify each part. It may be necessary to elicit from students that the 'agent' means the person / group / thing responsible for a particular action (i.e. replacing).

> **1** The traditional 'filter then publish' model
> **2** 'publish then filter'
> **3** replaced
> **4** has been
> **5** by

16 Elicit from students which tense is used in the example in the previous exercise. Explain that the passive voice can be used in any tense and that they are going to practise writing the example sentence from Exercise 15 in different tenses.

> **Present continuous**: The traditional 'filter then publish' model is being replaced by 'publish then filter'.
>
> **Past perfect**: The traditional 'filter then publish' model had been replaced by 'publish then filter'.

Future simple: with *will* The traditional 'filter then publish' model will be replaced by 'publish then filter'.

17 Tell students that now they have focused on the form of the passive, they are going to think about when it may be used. Ask them to work in pairs and discuss whether the statements about the passive are true or false.

> **1** F. Some sentences would not make sense or would sound very wrong. For example, the active sentence *I passed the IELTS test* would sound wrong in the passive (*The IELTS test was passed by me*).
>
> **2** T. The passive allows us to shift focus from the person or thing doing an action to the person or thing affected by the action.
>
> **3** F. It is used a lot. However certain forms of the passive, such as those that use *It* as a subject (*It is believed …, It has been estimated …*) sound very formal when spoken.
>
> **4** Sometimes it is not important or relevant to say who does the action. For example, *My bicycle was stolen*, we don't need to say *by a thief* because this is understood.
>
> **5** T. For example, the passive is commonly used in scientific texts and language as it expresses the objectivity for a situation.

Extension

Give students some examples of sentences from the text written in the active voice (e.g. Participatory journalism represents the democratization of the media). Ask them to write them in the passive voice, paying attention to the tense that was used in the active voice.

EXAM SKILLS

18 Tell students that they are going to attempt an IELTS exam practice task which will include short-answer and sentence-ending tasks.

Advice

Remind students of the following:

- It is necessary to locate the information in the text in order to answer both short-answer and matching-sentence-endings tasks.
- Use key words and/or question words in the questions in order to locate the part of the text that contains the information needed to answer the question.
- For short answer questions, try to predict the type of word(s) that they answer will be.
- For matching-sentence-ending tasks, locate the part of the text that contains the information in the sentence stem, and remember that there will be more endings than are needed to answer the questions.

> **1** B **2** D **3** D **4** C **5** A **6** B
> **7** educational (type) **8** (their) personality
> **9** (the) producer(s) **10** (the) confessional
> **11** E **12** A **13** D **14** C

WRITING

> ## OUTCOMES
>
> - describe a pie chart
> - describe percentages and fractions
> - improve your grammatical range and accuracy
> - use the passive voice.

OUTCOMES

In this unit, students will learn how to describe pie charts in IELTS writing Task 1. In order to improve their score for lexical Resource, they will need to use a variety of language for describing fractions and percentages. This unit focuses on useful language for doing this, as well as use of the passive voice and the importance of checking for errors in order to get a better score for Grammatical range and accuracy.

LEAD-IN

Tell students that they are going to focus on some different ways of visually presenting information that they may see in IELTS Writing Task 1 questions. Elicit from students what types of visuals they might see in this task types (e.g. bar chart / table / pie chart). Explain that they are going to focus specifically on how to describe information in a pie chart.

01 Focus students' attention on the pie chart in Exercise 01. Elicit the type of information that the pie chart shows, then ask students to predict which section of the chart represents which type of media. Ask students to discuss the reasons for their predictions in pairs.

02 Tell students that they are going to focus on language that can be used to describe information presented visually in pie charts. Ask them to match the descriptions with the different sections of the chart.

> **a** 3 (online) **b** 1 (TV) **c** 2 (not specified) **d** 5 (radio)
> **e** 4 (print)

03 Give students five minutes to discuss these questions. Explain that they are going to be looking at examples from an IELTS Task 1 question on this topic and that it will therefore be useful for them to consider their own ideas on the topic.

Explain to students that in order to answer IELTS Task 1 questions on pie charts, they will need to be aware of a variety of language for describing percentages and fractions. Explain that using this language will help them to improve their score in the Lexical Resource criterion of the IELTS writing marking criteria.

04 Ask students to close their books. Elicit which types of word or number they may use to describe percentages and fractions. Then ask them to open their books and compare their ideas with the information in the Tip box and in Exercise 04. Then ask students to complete the task.

> **1** b **2** d **3** e **4** c **5** f **6** a

05 Tell students that they are going to practise identifying different ways of expressing percentages. Explain that this is a useful skill for avoiding repetition and therefore improving their score for Lexical Resource.

1 80%	**2** 66%/67%	**3** 10%	**4** 40%	**5** 25%

06 Tell students that they are going to practise describing different sections of a pie chart without using numbers. Encourage them to use the modifiers in the box where appropriate.

Feedback

When students have finished the task, ask them to swap descriptions and give each other peer feedback. Ask them to look carefully at the language used to describe the percentages, and to make corrections where necessary. As students are doing this, monitor and make a note of examples of good phrases for describing percentages, as well as examples that contain errors.

Extension

Write up examples of good phrases and those containing errors on the board. Ask students to identify the correct ones and to correct the ones that contain errors.

> *Sample answers*
> Almost two fifths of adults in the USA never read news on social media.
> Just under a fifth often access news on social media.
> About / Approximately / Roughly a quarter of people sometimes get their news from social media.
> A little under a fifth hardly ever access news on social media.

Tell students to close their books. Ask them what they already know about how to describe a pie chart in IELTS Writing Task 1, and any advice that they have for getting a high score. Make a note of their ideas on the board, then ask them to open their books and read the advice box. Ask concept-check questions (e.g. 'How should you begin your answer to this task?', 'What type of information should you include from the charts?' etc.)

07 Ask students to look at the two pie charts and to discuss with a partner what they think the key features of the data are.

> *Sample answers*
> More than half of Brazilians access news online.
> TV is a popular way to get the news in both countries.
> Print and radio are both much more popular in the UK.
> Very few listen to the news on the radio in Brazil.

08 Focus students' attention on the sample answer. Ask them to read through and identify examples of the different features. Before students do this exercise, ask them to read the Bullet box.

Advice

Emphasise that including these different features will help students to improve their score for the Task Achievement criterion in the IELTS Writing marking criteria. It may be useful to show students the band descriptors for IELTS writing and to point out how they refer to these features.

1 The two nations show broadly similar patterns, though there are some differences, both significant and minor.

2 53%, 3%, 15% and 6%

3 over a third of people, more than half, two fifths of the UK population

4 broadly similar patterns
while in the UK … , in Brazil more than half
3% fewer
one major difference over twice as many people
compared with
Similarly
three times more
are used less
in comparison with

5 *Introductory sentence*: The pie charts show the principle ways of finding out the news in two different countries, the UK and Brazil.
Concluding sentence: Overall, it can be said that the high levels of internet use in Brazil mean that other methods such as radio and print are used less in comparison with the UK.

6 main (ways) – principle   it is clear – it is apparent
generally (similar) – broadly   preferring – favouring
key (features) – most   each one / in that order –
prominent   respectively

Ask students to close their books. Write Grammatical Range and Accuracy on the board. Ask students why they think this is important when completing IELTS writing tasks (elicit that it is one of the 4 marking criteria for IELTS writing). Then ask students what common grammatical errors they think students may make when describing pie charts. Ask them to open their books and compare their ideas with the information in the advice box.

09 Ask students to look at the example description of the pie chart and to find and correct the errors.

> *Corrections are underlined*
> The pie chart shows the frequency with which adults in the US use social media to obtain news. Overall, it is clear that less than half use it on a regular basis. One of the most significant points in the data is that just under two fifths of people report that they never access the news via social media. To be precise, 38% of respondents gave this response, which is the highest of all categories. The second highest category is those who sometimes find out the news from social media sites. Around a quarter (26%) of those surveyed selected this response, which is 12% fewer than the 'never' group. Finally, there was a tie for the least common response. Equal numbers of respondents 'hardly ever' and 'often' use social media to find out what is going on in the world. To conclude, social media is used to get news often or sometimes by just 44%. It is evident from the data that the majority of citizens do not read news on these sites.

10 Ask students to put the errors from Exercise 09 into the appropriate category. Tell them to look at the categories and to try and identify any of the errors that they think they make frequently. Explain that being aware of the types of error that they make will help them to be more accurate in future.

> 1 are using, was never accessed
> 2 social medias, category, citizen
> 3 frequency, regular basis, highest, majority
> 4 news was never accessed by them, were selected, is use
> 5 the pie chart show, adults in the US, uses those who sometimes finds, majority of citizen(s) does not
> 6 US, response, equal
> 7 in regular basis, highest from, by the data, in these sites
> 8 highest, 12% less, less common response

11 Focus students' attention on the first pair of sentences. Ask them which they think would score the highest in an IELTS writing exam and why. Before students do this exercise, ask them to read the Tip box.

ADVICE

Using the passive voice will help students to demonstrate that they are able to use a good range of grammatical structures, and with flexibility, in line with the band descriptors for level 6 and 7. However, there are times when it is more appropriate to use the active voice, and candidates should be able to determine which feels more natural in a variety of situations.

> 1 Sentence A is more natural. Sentence B, whilst grammatically possible, feels unnatural. Verbs for describing visual data such as *indicate, show, reveal, demonstrate, suggest* are intransitive in this context and rarely used in the passive in this way.
> 2 Sentence B. Using we in *One thing we can see* has a more informal feel. Using the passive here gives a more objective tone and demonstrates the use of modal passive forms.
> 3 Sentence A is more natural. Sentence B gives the impression that somebody made the number of subscriptions increase. We don't usually use verbs of increase or decrease (*rise, fall, go up/down, reduce*, etc.) in the passive in this kind of report.
> 4 Sentence A is more natural. (see answer 1)
> 5 Sentence B. Sentence A gives the impression that somebody doubled the number of over 40s rather than it simply increased. See point 3 for other verbs that we probably wouldn't use in the passive in this kind of essay.

EXAM SKILLS

12 Tell students that they are now going to attempt and IELTS Task 1 writing task. Give them 20 minutes to answer the question.

Refer students to the IELTS criteria specifically for bands 7 and 8 in the introduction to the Teachers' Book. Tell them

to firstly determine whether they fully meet the criteria for band 7 and then check if they surpass it and can be judged to meet the grade 8 criteria.

Advice

Advise students to do the following. They should:

- begin the description with a brief overview
- identify key features of the data to describe
- use a variety of language for describing percentages and fractions.
- use the passive voice where appropriate.
- be aware of the types of error they are most likely to make, and allow time before the end to check for them.

Sample essay

The pie charts represent which sources the citizens of two countries, Germany and Nigeria, turn to first in order to access the news. It should be noted that the figures for Nigeria do not include figures for rural areas of the country. Overall, it is clear from the data that the two countries have vastly different tendencies when it comes to news sources.

For Germans, the primary news source is newspapers, with just under half of the population using them, followed in second place by television with 30 percent. In Nigeria, however, television is the dominant first news provider, more than doubling the German figure with 63 percent, and whilst newspapers are a relatively popular source of first news in Nigeria, only 13 percent use them in this way. The second most popular first news provider in Nigeria is actually radio, with numbers approaching a quarter of the population. In Germany, however, the figure is less than half that, only reaching 10 percent. In fact, the internet is more commonly used by Germans than radio, with 11 percent of the population turning to it first. This contrasts sharply with Nigerians, of whom only 1 percent say that they use it for initial news access. In summary, it can be said that whilst television is one of the favoured first news providers for both countries, the two countries otherwise exhibit very different first news consumption habits. (*232 words*)

Extension

Give students the sample answer to read. Ask them to find examples of the following:

- Good language for describing fractions and percentages
- Use of the passive voice

LISTENING

OUTCOMES

- **make use of signposting language in talks**
- **handle sentence completion tasks**
- **complete flow-charts.**

OUTCOMES

Ask students to focus on the outcomes. The first outcome concerns helping students to identify key words and phrases when listening in order to follow what a speaker is saying. Tell students that in this unit they will learn to make better use of this signpost language. The second outcome focuses on the exam task of sentence completion. In the IELTS Listening exam, students need to fill in the gaps to complete sentences using words from the recording. Tell students that they will learn strategies in this unit to help them do this. The final outcome also involves a typical IELTS exam task – flow-chart completion. This is a visual representation of what the speaker is saying and students need to complete it using words from the recording. Students will learn useful strategies for this in this unit.

LEAD-IN

01 This exercise prepares students for the topic of the listening. Ask students to do this in pairs and monitor to check they are on task. As there will be a variety of answers, try to generate a class discussion during feedback.

02 Exercises 02 and 03 focus on making use of signpost language. Before students do this exercise, ask them to read the Bullet box.

Advice

In part 4 of the listening exam, students will hear a speaker give a talk. It is likely that the speaker will use signpost language to help structure the talk and this can be used by listeners to help them follow and answer the questions.

Exercise 02 helps students to identify these typical signpost phrases which appear in a talk. Students should listen individually.

Alternative or extension

Ask students to number the phrases as they hear them. Students can predict together first in pairs (if this is used as an alternative to Exercise 02). Then students should listen individually and then compare in pairs. Monitor as students discuss their answers. Then give students a copy of the script below for them to check their answers.

Transcript 56

OK, everyone, I'd like to start by introducing myself. My name is Warren Short and I'm a freelance news reporter. So, what that means is that news agencies hire me to go to different parts of the world and report on on-going stories as they develop. The reason I've been asked to speak to you is to give you some tips on making your own news reports, which I know is something you have to do for your media course.

Let's begin our talk with a few general points. The first one is know your audience. By that I mean, are they older or younger viewers, where are they from, what are their values, ideas or beliefs, what level of education do they have? The reason we try to find out as much as possible about the audience is that we want to interest them. If they can't engage with or relate to the stories we choose or how we present them, they'll choose another news channel. The same story can be presented in different ways for different audiences. So, for example, if there's an oil spill

into the sea, will our audience be more concerned about the environmental or the economic consequences?

The next general point I want to make is that pictures are as important as words. You need to choose very carefully what you're going to show, in what order and for how long. The first and last shots the audience sees are the ones that make the most impact. The last of my general points is that you must be fair and balanced. The reputation of the TV station is at stake here, so it's crucial not to give the impression that the station is trying to push its own agenda. If you interview someone from one side of a debate, you should then interview someone from the other side. Without this balance, you will definitely get complaints from viewers.

Right, so I'll just repeat those general points for you before we move on. Get to know your audience, choose your pictures wisely and avoid bias.

[pause]

OK, so let's take a simplified look at the process of making a news report. As with any project, the first stage is planning. What you have to remember is the five Ws: Who, What, When, Where and Why. These are the five questions you need to have answers to. Once you've gathered the information about the story, you need to put together a script. The key advice here is keep it simple or you may lose your audience. As part of writing the initial script, try to visualise the report in your mind. Make sure you're clear on who you're going to interview, where this interview will take place, the questions you want to ask, and what shots you're going to include.

After that it's time to get the camera rolling. A news report begins with the reporter talking to the camera and giving a brief introduction to the story. Keep it snappy. Don't go into unnecessary detail or say things that will be covered by the interviewees. Just outline the story that your report will tell in a straightforward and appealing way.

The next stage of the report is the interview or interviews. Choose someone directly affected by the story who can put their ideas across in a clear and concise way. This could be, say, a witness who observed the events of the story directly. The ideal place to interview them is somewhere that reveals something about the person or the events of the story. For example, if he or she works in a factory affected by the story, interview him or her inside the factory with machinery and workers in the background. On the other hand, there shouldn't be too much going on in the background as that would detract from the story.

OK, moving on to the second interview. This person's views should contrast with those of the first speaker. I've already mentioned the need to avoid being accused of bias, and that's why his or her position on the story must be different. So, if the first person was a worker in the factory explaining why jobs must be saved, the second interviewee could be one of the factory managers giving their perspective on why job cuts are necessary.

Now, depending on the length of your report, you might or might not have time for other views and shots. But the piece should finish with the reporter on camera again, rounding up the story, and if possible saying something about the possible next steps in this story. For example, if the story is about a court case, when the verdict is expected.

So, that's about it. To sum up, be fair, be balanced and be interesting. Now, are there any questions?

03 This exercise helps students identify the function of the signpost language. Ask them to do this in pairs and monitor. For feedback, invite students to volunteer answers or you can nominate. Before confirming answers, encourage other students to say if they agree or not with the answers their classmates have given and to suggest alternatives, if necessary.

beginning or ending	c, n
sequencing / moving on	d, e, f, h, j, k, l
referring back	m
summing up	g, n
emphasising	i
giving reasons	b

04 Exercises 04 to 09 focus on strategies for sentence-completion tasks. Before students do this exercise, ask them to read the Tip box.

Advice

Students should be aware that the gaps are often at the end of the sentences but can sometimes be in the middle. Sentences will be in the same order as in the recording. Make sure students know that there is a word limit for each gap and that this will be made clear in the question. Tell students that the answers will be the same words as in the recording.

Exercise 04 helps students to predict what the missing words potentially are. Before students do this exercise, ask them to read the Tip box.

Advice

Students should use their time wisely in the exam. They can do this by thinking about the topic and then looking at the gaps in the sentences to make predictions based on the context and their own grammatical knowledge. This will help them when they listen and try to answer.

Ask students to work in pairs to predict the missing words. Monitor and for feedback, follow the procedure outlined in Exercise 02.

Sample answers
1 professional, freelance, sports – adjective
2 national/local/international newspapers, television channels, news agencies, media outlets, news websites – plural noun phrases

05 Students have the opportunity to listen to check their answers. Ask them to listen individually and then to compare in pairs. Monitor as students discuss their answers and then provide feedback.

1 freelance
2 news agencies

Transcript 57

OK, everyone, I'd like to start by introducing myself. My name is Warren Short and I'm a freelance news reporter, So, what that means is that news agencies hire me to go to different parts of the world and report on on-going stories as they develop. The reason I've been asked to speak to you is to give you some tips on making your own news reports, which I know is something you have to do for your media course.

06 This exercise emphasises the need for correct spelling and grammar for answers given. Before students do this exercise, ask them to read the Tip box.

Advice

Remind students that they need to spell their answers correctly, use correct grammar and the right number of words. Tell students that they will lose marks otherwise.

Students should complete this exercise in pairs. Monitor and provide feedback.

1 **A** correct **B** wrong spelling **C** words from question repeated (which also means the answer exceeds the word limit) **D** the word is spelt correctly but should be the adjective form
2 **A** singular form **B** correct **C** too many words – the candidate has added a word which fits grammatically but is not in the audio **D** 'agencies' alone is not suffnembers icient, two words are permitted and both words are needed

07 Exercise 07 helps students to understand that the question sentences will be paraphrased versions of what is said in the recording and helps them to deal with this. Before students do this exercise, ask them to read the Tip box.

Advice

Remind students that they need to use the exact words from the recording. However, emphasise that the questions use paraphrased words. This means students need to be able to recognise when the paraphrased words in the questions relate to what is in the recording.

Students should do this in pairs. Monitor and provide feedback as before.

1 d	2 a	3 b	4 c

08 Students now have the opportunity to practise sentence completion when listening. They should listen individually and then check in pairs. Monitor as students compare their answers to see if they need to listen again. Provide feedback but do not confirm answers until other students have had the opportunity to answer - as outlined previously.

1 your/the audience
2 interest them
3 news channel
4 consequences

Transcript 58

Let's begin our talk with a few general points. The first one is <u>know your audience</u>. By that I mean, are they older or younger viewers, where are they from, what are their values, ideas or beliefs, what level of education do they have? The reason we try to find out as much as possible about the audience is that <u>we want to interest them</u>. If they can't engage with or relate to the stories we choose or how we present them, <u>they'll choose another news channel</u>. The same story can be presented in different ways for different audiences. So, for example, if there's an oil spill into the sea, will our audience <u>be more concerned about the environmental or the economic consequences</u>?

09 Students have further practice of sentence completion in this exercise. Follow the instructions from Exercise 08.

1 pictures	2 reputation

Transcript 59

The next general point I want to make is that <u>pictures are as important as words</u>. You need to choose very carefully what you're going to show, in what order and for how long. The first and last shots the audience sees are the ones that make the most impact. The last of my general points is that you must be fair and balanced. <u>The reputation of the TV station is at stake</u> here, so it's crucial not to give the impression that the station is trying to push its own agenda. If you interview someone from one side of a debate, you should then interview someone from the other side. Without this balance, you will definitely get complaints from viewers.

Right, so I'll just repeat those general points for you before we move on. Get to know your audience, choose your pictures wisely and avoid bias.

10 Exercises 10 to 14 focus on the completion of flow-charts Before students do this exercise, ask them to read the Bullet box.

Advice

Explain to students that flow charts are visual representations of what they speaker says in the listening exam. Tell them that sometimes they need to select answers from a list – there will always be more possible answers than are needed if this is the case – or they need to use words from the recording. They must, as always, respect the word limits. Point out to students that the skills required to fulfil this task are similar to those used for table, sentence and note completion.

Exercise 10 helps students choose which words can or can't be used to complete the flow-chart (questions 1-3). This is a good way to help them narrow down their options and look for grammatical clues. Students should do this in pairs. Monitor and then provide feedback.

1	A	NP – wrong grammar
	B	P
	C	NP – wrong grammar
	D	NP – doesn't go with the preposition by

2	A	NP – a not an before gap
	B	P (but is a repetition of the previous stage)
	C	P
	D	NP – not logical here
3	A	NP – information is uncountable
	B	P
	C	P
	D	P

11 Students have practice listening to complete a flow-chart (questions 1-3), using the advice from the previous exercise. Students should do this individually and then compare in pairs. Monitor and provide feedback.

1 planning	2 script	3 detail

Transcript 60

OK, so let's take a simplified look at the process of making a news report. As with any project, <u>the first stage is planning</u>. What you have to remember is the five Ws: Who, What, When, Where and Why. These are the five questions you need to have answers to. Once you've gathered the information about the story, <u>you need to put together a script</u>. The key advice here is keep it simple or you may lose your audience. As part of writing the initial script, try to visualise the report in your mind. Make sure you're clear on who you're going to interview, where this interview will take place, the questions you want to ask and what shots you're going to include.

After that it's time to get the camera rolling. A news report begins with the reporter talking to the camera and giving a brief introduction to the story. Keep it snappy. <u>Don't go into unnecessary detail</u> or say things that will be covered by the interviewees. Just outline the story that your report will tell in a straightforward and appealing way.

12 This is a repeat of Exercise 10 but for questions 4-6. This time, options are not given. Ask students to do this in pairs and monitor. For feedback, try to generate a class discussion of the possible answers and rationales for them.

Possible answers
4 singular noun for a person: *victim, police officer, witness, politician*
5 verb: *disagree, differ, conflict, contrast*
6 plural noun phrase: *(future) developments, participants*

13 Students repeat the listening task but for questions 4-6. Follow the instructions from Exercise 11.

4 witness	5 contrast	6 next steps

Extension

Give students a copy of the script and play the recording again to help them identify where the answers are.

Transcript 61

The next stage of the report is the interview or interviews. Choose <u>someone directly affected by the story</u> who can put their ideas across in a clear and concise way. <u>This could be, say, a witness</u> who observed the events of the story directly. The ideal place to interview them is somewhere that reveals something about the person or the events of the story. For example, if he or she works in a factory affected by the story, interview him or her inside the factory with machinery and workers in the background. On the other hand, there shouldn't be too much going on in the background as that would detract from the story.

OK, moving on to the second interview. <u>This person's views should contrast with</u> those of the first speaker. I've already mentioned the need to avoid being accused of bias, and that's why his or her position on the story must be different. So, if the first person was a worker in the factory explaining why jobs must be saved, the second interviewee could be one of the factory managers giving their perspective on why job cuts are necessary.

Now, depending on the length of your report, you might or might not have time for other views and shots. But the piece should finish with the reporter on camera again, rounding up the story, and if possible <u>saying something about the possible next steps</u> in this story. For example, if the story is about a court case, when the verdict is expected.

So, that's about it. To sum up, be fair, be balanced and be interesting. Now, are there any questions?

EXAM SKILLS

14 This exercise gives students exam practice of the task types and use of strategies outlined in this unit. Students should do this individually and compare after each task type or at the end. Monitor as students compare their answers. Provide feedback as outlined previously.

1	anything new
2	more selective
3	personal relevance
4	audience
5	the competition
6	E
7	B
8	F
9	A
10	H

Extension

Give students a copy of the script and play the recording again to help them identify where the answers are. In addition, add a reflective element to this task by asking students to work in pairs or small groups to compare together what they found easier or more difficult, the strategies they used and whether they were helpful. Then ask students to say what strategies they would use again. This will help them to internalise useful strategies and use them automatically. It will also help you to identify what students have learnt. Generate a class discussion after students have done this.

Transcript 62

You will hear someone giving a talk about writing for a newspaper and the printing process. First you have some time to look at questions 1 to 10.

[pause]

Now listen carefully and answer questions 1 to 10.

Good afternoon, everyone. So today's talk is divided into two parts. In the first part I'm going to try to explain the decision-making process behind choosing what stories to publish in a newspaper. Later, in the second part of my talk, I will explain the process of producing a print newspaper.

So, first of all, I'd like to consider the question 'What is news?' It's a question I get asked all the time. Well, to put it in very simple terms, <u>it is 'anything new'</u>. However, that definition is extremely vague and open to interpretation. In other words, it doesn't really help a newspaper editor decide what stories to include. So a better question would be 'What factors help newspaper editors decide which stories make it into their newspaper?' Well, of course, it's a slightly different process for TV news programmes because <u>TV editors have to be more selective</u> about what to include. TV news shows are restricted by length and can be as short as five minutes. Newspapers don't have these restrictions but even with print or online newspapers, there are many more stories vying for attention than those that actually appear in the final edition.

Returning to the question then, what makes a news story newsworthy? <u>What is it that grabs the attention</u> and makes you want to interact with the story? Basically, <u>it is anything with personal relevance</u> for the reader. This presents us with two more questions: How do we as newspaper editors decide what is relevant and what is not? And what is it that makes a story personal? The answer is that <u>it very much depends on your audience</u>, and a good newspaper editor chooses stories based on their relevance and personal interest to their audience. He or she needs to know what sells their newspaper because at the end of the day, if our newspapers don't sell, we don't have a job. A successful editor doesn't just think about their audience, <u>they also need to keep an eye on the competition</u>, and this is the final factor I want to address in this part of my talk. To clarify, the competition is other newspapers or news channels. If a story is getting a lot of attention and coverage elsewhere, then, as an editor, you need to find a way to include it in your newspaper.

[short pause]

So, now to move on to the second part of my talk, which is the process of putting together an edition of a printed newspaper. The first stage is a continuous process in which journalists are collecting and writing up stories and the marketing people are positioning the advertisements, and this is known as the <u>news gathering</u> stage. As soon as an article is finished, it's passed on to the second stage of the process, editing. Both content and language have to be edited. Facts may need to be checked and changes made to the language to ensure the tone of the piece fits the style of the newspaper and the message the editor wants to convey. There may be a number of different editors, depending on the size of the newspaper, and each editor needs to use a contrasting colour to edit so that it's easy to see who has made the changes. For example, sub-editors use red, the chief sub-editor uses blue and the editor uses green.

Once all the editing is finished, we move on to the next stage, which is called pre-press. This stage is concerned with layout. Each page of the newspaper is laid out and designed with stories, pictures and adverts. A prototype – or first version – of each page is made. Nowadays, these are then transformed into digital form by graphic designers.

The pre-press stage is followed by the press or lithographic stage. Traditionally, and in places where digital printing isn't used, the stories and adverts are registered on a plate – an iron sheet in the size and shape of the newspaper.

Next comes the impression stage. The plates are hung on the printing press and the final copies are printed out. For some of the national newspapers this can run to thousands of copies that need to be collected and put in order before the final stage – circulation, when the newspapers are sent out to be distributed across the country.

Although digital technology now plays a part in this whole process, it's actually remarkably similar to the way it has always been done. The process from beginning to end typically takes about 12 hours as it's a very fast moving business.

SPEAKING

OUTCOMES

- talk about TV programmes
- correct yourself and clarify while speaking
- stress words correctly when correcting yourself
- use the passive when speaking

OUTCOMES

Ask students to focus on the outcomes. The first outcome concerns a topic that is fairly common and may appear in either Part 2 or Part 3 of the IELTS Speaking exam. The nature of this topic means that language functions, grammatical structures and vocabulary may well be transferable to other topics. The next outcome concerns a strategy when speaking which helps students self-correct any errors that they make and clarify what they are trying to say. This is a good way of avoiding being marked down for errors and is acceptable to some extent even in bands 8 and 9 of the IELTS Speaking exam under the fluency and coherence criterion. By doing this effectively, students can avoid lower marks in the other three criteria. The final outcome helps students with using the passive voice when speaking. This grammatical structure, while being less common in spoken English than when written, is seen as more complex.

LEAD-IN

01 This exercise tests students' existing knowledge of vocabulary related to the topic area and will also help students when they speak about this topic in later exercises. Ask students to work together in pairs and monitor as they do this to check they are on task and to offer support if

necessary. Then invite students to give their answers. There will be a lot of variation with answers so encourage students to give details about their answers to check understanding or you can ask concept-check questions to clarify that students understand the words in the box.

Students' own answers.

02 This exercise further tests and builds upon students' existing vocabulary knowledge – this time concerning expressions to describe TV programmes. Again, ask students to do this in pairs and monitor. During feedback, invite them to volunteer answers or nominate students to do so. Before confirming correct answers, encourage classmates to say if they agree with the answers given or to suggest an alternative.

Positive
gripping
inspirational
intriguing
absolutely hilarious
a definite 5 star rating
compulsive viewing
I watched it in one sitting.
It has/had me on the edge on my seat.
I was glued to the screen
Negative
pointless
utter garbage
a complete waste of time
It's not my cup of tea.
Neutral
I can take it or leave it.
It gave me food for thought.
It was nothing to write home about.

03 This exercise provides students with freer spoken practice of the vocabulary from Exercise 01 and 02. Ask students to work in pairs and take it in turns to speak about TV programmes. Monitor and note anything you feel you want to bring up in feedback. This could be typical mistakes made by a number of class members but could also be examples of good practice you wish to talk about. Use any errors you noted when you monitored. Write a list of these on the board (3-5 is manageable). Also, add 1-2 correct answers. Ask students to identify the correct answers and correct the incorrect ones. This is a good way to recycle what has been learnt in the exercise and also to focus on responding to emerging student errors and needs.

04 Exercises 04 to 08 focus on the speaking strategy of correcting and clarifying when speaking. Before students do this exercise, ask them to read the Bullet box.

Advice

Tell students that they should not feel concerned about correcting themselves when they make a mistake. Explain that this is actually quite common even for native speakers. Even at IELTS bands 8 and 9, some correction is seen as acceptable and this is certainly preferable to making mistakes without attempting to self-correct. In addition, tell students that they should try to clarify what they are saying by giving more information or explaining what they are saying in different words if they feel it is necessary, for example if the examiner seems confused by what the student has just said.

Exercise 04 gives students the opportunity to listen to an example student answer for Part 2 in order to identify how this student corrected and clarified himself. Ask students to listen individually and then to compare answers together in pairs. Monitor as students do this. Follow the feedback instructions outlined in Exercise 02.

He corrects himself or clarifies 12 times:

One of my favourite programmes is *Fear Factor*. (1) <u>Actually</u>, I would <u>say</u> it's a programme that I love to hate! (2) <u>What I mean by that is</u> – I love, it but at times the things on there are awesome, (3) <u>sorry, I meant to say</u> *they are awful*. So the type – (4) <u>or rather</u> *the genre* – of show is reality but also it's a competition. What happens is that there are four people – (5) <u>well, you know</u>, four competitors – and they has to do, (6) they have to do a series of tasks. Sometimes they have to dive into – (7) <u>or actually</u> *they dive under* water and open a box – (8) <u>I mean</u> *unlock a box*, or they have to climb up a high building. In the second task, there are nasty animals – (9) <u>not animals as such</u>, but things like cockroaches or snakes which they must to, (10) they must lie in a box with or something. So, I don't like it, but it's compulsory. (11) <u>I'll rephrase that.</u> I watch it even though I don't want to. It's compulsive. It's on Thursday nights on a channel called Reality. I usually watch with my brother – *both my brothers*, (12) <u>actually</u>.

Sometimes we play our own version of it and make each other do silly tasks, but not as bad as the ones on the TV.

Transcript 63

One of my favourite programmes is *Fear Factor*. Actually, I would say it's a programme that I love to hate! *What I mean by that is* I love it but at times the things on there are *awesome, sorry, I mean to say they are awful. So the type – or rather the genre –* of show is reality but also it's a competition. What happens is that there are four people – *well, you know,* four competitors – and they has to do, they have to do a series of tasks. Sometimes they have to *dive into – or actually they dive under* water and open a box – *I mean unlock a box,* or they have to climb up a high building. In the second task, there are nasty animals – *not animals as such*, but things like cockroaches or snakes, which *they must to, they must lie* in a box with or something. So, I don't like it, but it's compulsory. *I'll rephrase that.* I watch it even though I don't want to. It's compulsive. It's on Thursday nights on a channel called Reality. I usually watch with my brother – *both my brothers*, actually. Sometimes we play our own version of it and make each other do silly tasks but not as bad as the ones on the TV.

05 This exercise gives students practice of self-correcting using a selection of phrases. Before students do this exercise, ask them to read the Tip box.

Advice

It's important for students to understand when to use different phrases. Some of the phrases are more appropriate for correcting grammatical errors (e.g. '*I mean*') and others are more appropriate for clarifying what you are saying ('*let me put that another way*').

Ask students to complete this exercise in pairs. Each person should take it turns to read the sentence and then correct or clarify. Monitor as students do this. This time, make notes of anything you wish to discuss in feedback. This could be typical mistakes made by a number of class members but could also be examples of good practice you wish to talk about. In feedback, use any errors you noted when you monitored. Write a list of these on the board (3-5 is manageable). Also, add 1-2 correct answers. Ask students to identify the correct answers and correct the incorrect ones. This is a good way to recycle what has been learnt in the exercise and to also focus on responding to emerging student errors and needs.

Sample answers

1 I mean, they're not very *interesting*.
2 What I meant to say was the *presenter* is very good.
3 Let me start again. It's a show which gives people makeovers.
4 I'll rephrase that. It's a programme where you get to see inside celebrities' homes.
5 Sorry, what I intended to say was most people in my country watch this show.
6 Let me put that another way. I like game shows, especially when there are big prizes.

---

06 This exercise focuses on pronunciation and particularly the use of stress when using phrases to self-correct or clarify. Before students do this exercise, ask them to read the Tip box.

Advice

Explain to students that the corrected word, phrase or idea is usually stressed. Show students the example sentence in Exercise 06 to help illustrate this.

Now ask students to work in pairs to complete this exercise. Students can then check their answers when listening and compare their final answers in pairs. Nominate or invite students to give their answers. Before confirming correct answers, encourage other students to either say they agree with the answer given or to suggest alternatives.

---

1 Watching TV is a time of waste. Sorry, I'll rephrase that – <u>a waste of time</u>.
2 Comedic shows, or rather <u>comedy</u> shows, are not very popular in my country.
3 I can't understand why realism TV is so popular. Let me start again. I can't understand why <u>reality TV</u> is so popular.
4 The popularity of sports programmes, especially football series, I mean football <u>highlight shows</u>, makes no sense to me.
5 One thing that I dislike about TV is the amount of publicities. Oh, did I say publicities? I meant to say <u>commercials</u>.

Transcript 64

Example I absolutely hate watching the new. Sorry, I meant to say <u>news</u>.

1   Watching TV is a time of waste. Sorry, I'll rephrase that – <u>a waste</u> of <u>time</u>.

2   Comedic shows, or rather <u>comedy</u> shows, are not very popular in my country.

3   I can't understand why realism TV is so popular. Let me start again. I can't understand why <u>reality TV</u> is so popular.

4   The popularity of sports programmes, especially football series, I mean football <u>highlights shows</u>, makes no sense to me.

5   One thing that I dislike about TV is the amount of publicities. Oh did, I say publicities? I meant to say <u>commercials</u>.

07 This exercise gives students practice of clarifying and explaining what they are saying. Ask them to look at the example and then to complete the exercise in pairs. Monitor as students do this. Invite students to give their answers and encourage class mates to comment and to provide constructive feedback if necessary. You can then provide your own feedback.

> *Sample answers*
>
> 2   I think TV is a very positive thing. Let me explain. Children can improve their imaginations and learn a lot from watching TV.
>
> 3   Children should be allowed to watch TV online unsupervised. To put that another way, I don't think it's very practical to expect parents to supervise their children all the time they are online.
>
> 4   Watching TV online is far superior to watching conventional TV. What I mean by this is you can choose when you're going to watch and watch anywhere you like.
>
> 5   The standard of TV programmes is so much better these days. Let me clarify that. In the past, there wasn't much to see at the weekends but nowadays we have so many channels, we can always find something to watch.

08 This exercise provides students with freer practice of self-correcting or clarifying. Ask students to do this in pairs and to take turns. Encourage students to provide constructive feedback. Monitor and take notes of anything you want to bring up during feedback. Follow the feedback guidelines outlined in Exercise 05.

Alternative

Ask students to record their answers on a smart phone or other recording device. These can then be used for peer or self-appraisal. Then encourage students to rerecord their answers and to email them to you. You can use these for future class material or to provide individual feedback.

09 Exercises 09 and 10 focus on the use of the passive voice in the speaking exam. Tell students that this grammatical structure can help them achieve higher scores for the *grammatical range and accuracy* criterion in the exam. Before students do this exercise, ask them to read the Bullet box.

Advice

Remind students that in Part three of the IELTS Speaking exam they need to speak about less familiar and more general topics. Often it is necessary to talk impersonally and the passive voice structure using *it* is a good way to do this.

Now ask students to complete Exercise 09 individually.

> *Sample answers*
>
> 1   It has been said/reported that children who watch a lot of TV are less sociable.
>
> 2   It is believed / thought / widely accepted that most newspapers are biased.
>
> 3   It has been proved that TV can damage your eyesight.
>
> 4   It has been estimated that by 2025, 80% of TV viewing will be done online.

10 This exercise gives students the opportunity to practise using the sentences from Exercise 09 to start a short discussion in pairs. Students can take turns doing reading and reacting to the sentences. Monitor as students do this and note down anything you wish to talk about during feedback.

Extension

After feedback, if you want to give students more practice, you can do the following open-pair practice. This is where pairs are selected from different parts of the classroom and they do the pair work in front of the class. This allows students and you to hear the discussion or role-play and students can get a model of good practice or, where errors occur, they can help to correct their peers. This encourages greater student participation and peer learning.

1. Select a student from one side of the classroom.

2. Select a second student from the other side of the classroom.

3. Ask the selected students to complete the activity so that everyone can hear.

4. Thank the two students and if correct, confirm this to the class– this provides a good model.

5. If a student is incorrect, give him or her an opportunity to self-correct. You can gently ask students to do this by repeating the incorrect word(s) with a questioning intonation.

6. If that student can't self-correct, ask other students to help and confirm to all students what the correct answer was.

7. Repeat as desired.

EXAM SKILLS

11 This exercise gives students exam practice and encourages students to use the strategies and grammar highlighted in this unit. Remind students that in the IELTS Speaking Exam, the three parts will not be about the same topic. Ask students to complete this exercise in pairs. Students should give each other constructive feedback. Write the following descriptor from the IELTS *fluency and coherence* criterion on the board or on a document for students to use when giving feedback:

Does your partner…

…speaks fluently with only occasional repetition or self-correction?

Monitor as students do this and note down anything you wish to raise in feedback.

Refer students to the IELTS criteria specifically for bands 7 and 8 in the introduction to the Teachers' Book. Tell them to firstly determine whether they fully meet the criteria for band 7 and then check if they surpass it and can be judged to meet the grade 8 criteria.

Alternative and extension

You can ask students to record their answers as explained in Exercise 08 or follow the open-pair activity guidelines as explained in Exercise 10. It is also a good idea after feedback for students to reflect on the strategies used in this exercise. Give students a few minutes to discuss what strategies they used, what was more effective and which strategies they will use in future.

READING

OUTCOMES

- review reading skills
- review reading task types
- use relative clauses.

OUTCOMES

The purpose of this unit is to review the reading skills and task types that have been covered in the book so far, and to remind students of the strategies that they can use to answer a range of IELTS reading task types. Students will be reminded of what each task type entails and the importance of using skimming and scanning skills in all IELTS reading task types. They will practise a number of different tasks types based on several texts on the topic of culture, and will finish with a final exam practice task containing two task types. In addition, they will learn how to recognize and use both defining and non-defining relative clauses, which occur frequently in IELTS reading texts.

LEAD-IN

01 Tell students that they have practised a number of different reading exam task types, they are going to assess their knowledge of test procedure. Elicit what this means (e.g. how the test is carried out / how long they have to complete each task. Then ask students to work in pairs and complete the true / false questions.

> **1** F (60 minutes only – no transfer time is given)
>
> **2** T
>
> **3** F (the texts are from a variety of sources but all written for a nonspecialist audience)
>
> **4** F (each question is worth one mark)
>
> **5** T

02 Ask students to close their books and write a list of as many IELTS task types that they can think of. Ask them to compare their lists with a partner, and then open their books and check their lists against the list of task types in Exercise 02. Focus students' attention on the example, then ask them to work in pairs and write explanations for the other task types.

Extension

Divide the class into groups of three. Give each group three tasks each and ask them to write an explanation for each one. Then ask each group to join with another in order to test each other on their task types.

> **1** Choose from options A–D or choose two or more options from a larger list.

> **2** Decide if statements about factual information in the text is confirmed by the text (True), contradicted by the text (False) or not included (Not Given).
>
> **3** Decide if statements about views or claims in the text are mentioned (Yes), contradicted by the text (No) or not included (Not Given).
>
> **4** Match information from the text with the paragraphs that contain it.
>
> **5** Match main ideas with paragraphs or sections.
>
> **6** Match statements with people, places or things mentioned in the text.
>
> **7** Complete sentences about the text, choosing from a list of options with distractors.
>
> **8** Complete sentences about the text, using words from the text, keeping to a word limit.
>
> **9** Complete information in note, table, or flow-chart (process) formats, using words from the text, keeping to a word limit.
>
> **10** Complete missing information in a diagram, either choosing from a list or using words from the text, keeping to a word limit.
>
> **11** Answer *What/Where/Why/When/How* questions, keeping to a word limit.
>
> **12** Complete a summary of part of the text, either choosing from a list or using words from the text, keeping to a word limit.

03 Ask students to close their books, look back at the list of reading tasks from Exercise 02 and check the explanations that they originally gave on how to tackle them. Ask them to now write down the types of reading skill that they think they will need to use for each task and then to write down any skills that they think are needed for all reading task types. After discussing students' answers as a group, ask them to open their books and check their ideas against the tips in the advice box.

Draw students' attention to the passage on youth subcultures, then give them two minutes to skim it and answer the questions.

> 1, 3, 4 (2 and 5 are false because in the last paragraph the writer expresses regret at the passing of some youth cultures, and says 'those of us who recall,' which tells us he/she remembers them personally.)

04 Tell students that now they have practised skimming the text for general information, they are going to scan the text for some more specific information. Elicit from students whether they think they will find the exact words in the questions in the text or whether the words will be different but with the same meaning (i.e. paraphrased). Ask students to look at the first statement and to try to think of a way that it could be paraphrased in the text. Ask them to scan the text and first identify the paragraph in which the information can be found, and then identify the paraphrased information. Finally, ask students to complete the task.

1 F *There is one subculture that seems to have endured better than the others: the bikers.*

2 C *It was a time when conventional social values were being questioned and […] young people found themselves with more freedom. Fuelled by American culture, Britain's youth suddenly had something to say and a desire to express themselves.*

3 E *made possible by the internet. They […] share information about demonstrations on social media. They take part in charity events […] to raise awareness as well as money.*

4 A *(the whole paragraph)*

5 C *… Elvis Presley and the advent of Rock and Roll generated the Teddy Boys in the UK, who in turn influenced both Mods and Rockers.*

6 D, G
The second half of paragraph D, beginning *Although the younger generation of today has been called 'identity-less', that is not actually the case …*
and in paragraph G: *Rather than being without identity as a generation, today's youth are typically broad-minded and well informed, each individual having created their own unique style and set of beliefs*

7 B *It was in the 1990s that many older commentators started to point out that the youth movements had lost their fire and had become conventional.*

8 D, E *the development of the internet and its widespread availability from the 1990s onwards has fundamentally changed how young people interact with the world (paragraph D); Today's young people are more tolerant and international thanks to globalisation (paragraph E)*

05 Tell students that they have skimmed and scanned the text for information, and that they are going to focus on another reading task type. Ask them to look at Exercise 05 and to identify the task type from the list in Exercise 02. Tell them to read the instructions carefully and then ask some concept check questions (e.g. 'Will you need to use all of the headings to complete the task?'). Before students do this exercise, ask them to look back at the Bullet box.

Advice

Elicit from students which strategies they will need to use to complete this question. Remind them that they will need to read the whole paragraph to find the correct heading, and that they should not rely on key words in the heading, which may occur in more than one paragraph.

Give students 15 minutes to complete the task, then check answers with the group.

1 iv   2 ii   3 vi   4 viii   5 x   6 ix   7 i

06 Ask students to read Exercise 06 and to identify the task type from the list in Exercise 02. Before students do this exercise, ask them to read the Bullet box.

Advice

Elicit from students which strategies they will need to use in order to answer this task type in the IELTS reading exam. Remind them of the kind of information that they will need

to identify in the text - i.e. information which supports the statement (true) contradicts it (false) or does not say anything about it, in spite of being closely linked to the topic (not given). Remind students to look for paraphrased information in the text, and also to pay attention to modifiers which may alter the meaning of the question.

1 Y   2 N   3 NG   4 Y

07 Ask students to close their books. Write the two sentences from Exercise 07 on the board. Underline the relative clauses in each one and ask students which grammatical feature they think the underlined sections show. After discussing students' answers, tell them to open their books and compare their ideas with the information in the advice box.

Then ask students to look again at the two examples and decide whether they are defining or non-defining relative clauses.

1 defining – no commas, relative clause can't be omitted

2 non-defining – commas, relative clause can be omitted

08 Ask students to find another example of each type of relative clause in the text. Elicit that looking for relative pronouns and use of commas may help them to do this. Before students do this exercise, ask them to read the Bullet box.

Advice

Emphasize that both types of relative clause occur frequently in academic texts, and that they will often occur in IELTS reading texts. Explain that being able to identify relative clauses may help students to identify specific information, to enable them to answer a number of different IELTS reading task types.

Sample answers
Defining: *… we need to look at the reasons why conditions were ripe for the emergence of youth cultures in the mid-twentieth century*
Non-defining: *Hippies, who emerged in America and spread across the world, represented a more peaceful group.*

09 This exercise introduces students to relative pronouns that can be omitted if they refer to the object of the sentence rather than the subject. Ask students to look at the examples in pairs and answer the questions.

1 *The identities* is the object of the defining relative clause and so the relative pronoun can be omitted.

2 *that* and *which* could be added between *identities* and *they*.

3 No. In both cases the relative pronoun is the subject of the relative clauses.

10 Tell students that they are going to practise writing some relative clauses of their own. Emphasize that being able to write relative clauses correctly is likely to help them to get a better mark for Grammatical Range and Accuracy in their IELTS writing exam.

1 American culture had a major influence on Britain's youth, who copied the style and music but made their own version of it.

2 One of the more memorable groups of the 1970s was the Punks, whose drainpipe jeans, kilts, safety pins and extraordinary hairstyles made them instantly recognisable.

3 The younger generation of today has been called 'identity-less', which is not actually the case.

EXAM SKILLS

11 Tell students that they are going to practise two more IELTS reading tasks from the list in Exercise 02. Ask them to read the tasks and identify which task type they are.

Advice

- Questions 1-5 are Information matching tasks, similar to those practised in Unit 6. Remind students that to complete this task they will firstly need to identify the part of the text that contains the information in the question, and then find paraphrases of the information in the question in the text.

- Question 6 is a global multiple-choice question. Emphasize that to answer this question correctly, students will need to use their knowledge of the whole text to choose the correct option. This will involve using skimming skills to identify the writer's purpose, looking for key ideas which support the correct option.

Give students 20 minutes to answer the questions, then check answers as a group.

1 D

2 B

3 C

4 B

5 A

6 D (A is wrong as there is no comparison of success. B is wrong as backpacking culture is only mentioned in the first paragraph as a modern example of the desire to travel. C is wrong as the text does mention that society has 'a confused and contradictory relationship with travellers' but the writer does not criticise any particular attitude.)

Extension

As you check the answers, nominate students to give reasons for their choice. Use the explanations above to help students understand the reasons for the correct answer in Question 6.

WRITING

OUTCOMES

- describe a process in Task 1
- give opposing views and your own opinion in Task 2
- write a complete essay.

OUTCOMES

In this unit, students will learn how to write process descriptions for Task 1 and to write essays giving opposing views and their own opinion for Task 2. They will focus on using a variety of vocabulary, the passive voice and sequencing linkers in Task 1 and expressions for giving their opinion in Task 2. They will also practise using relative clauses in sentences, in order to help them improve their score for Grammatical Range and Accuracy.

LEAD-IN

Ask students to close their books. Write the word 'culture' on the board and have students discuss what it means for them. Tell them to note down their answers in the form of a mind map. Then, after discussing their ideas in a group, ask them to open their books and look at Exercise 01.

01 Ask students to read the definitions of culture carefully and then compare the ideas in the definitions with the ideas they noted down previously. Ask students to discuss which definition they prefer and why.

02 Ask students to complete the task individually, and then compare ideas as a group. Explain that they will be writing about this topic later in the lesson, and that noting down their ideas about their own culture at this stage will support them in their own writing later.

03 Ask students to close their books and write 'describing a process' on the board. Explain to students that this is an IELTS writing task type. Elicit from students whether they think that this is Task 1 or Task 2 in the IELTS writing exam and what they think the task will look like (i.e. will it contain visual information?). Then ask them to reopen their books and read the advice box carefully.

Draw students' attention to the task in Exercise 03. Ask them to imagine that they are going to write about this process of making lanterns, and to think of verbs, nouns and adjectives that they may need to use. Encourage them to look carefully at the illustration in order to work out the types of words that they might need. Before students do this exercise, ask them to read the Bullet box.

Advice

Refer students to the IELTS criteria specifically for bands 7 and 8 in the introduction to the Teachers' Book. Tell them to firstly determine whether they fully meet the criteria for band 7 and then check if they surpass it and can be judged to meet the grade 8 criteria.

VERBS	NOUNS	ADJECTIVES
cut	scissors	coloured
make	lantern	colourful
tie paste / glue	glue	main
/stick / attach	bamboo sticks	
insert	square	
need repeat	triangle frills	
decorate hang	tissue paper	
	frame top	
	bottom/base	

04 Ask students to close their books. Elicit which grammatical structure they think they would use when describing a process. Ask them whether they think that the style they would use to describe a process in the IELTS reading test is likely to be quite formal or quite informal. After discussing the answers as a group, ask students to open their books and compare their ideas with the information in the Tip box.

Ask students to look at the examples written in the active voice and to rewrite them using the passive.

> **2** Next, the square and triangular tissue paper shapes can be stuck onto the frame.
>
> **3** The lantern is then ready to be hung on a lightbulb.

05 Tell students that they are going to look at a sample answer to the question. Ask them to read it carefully and not worry about the spaces. Tell them to identify any of the vocabulary that they wrote down in Exercise 03. Have them look at the words in the box and elicit what types of words they are (i.e. sequencing linkers). Refer them to the Tip box and then have them fill in the spaces with sequencing linkers from it.

> **1** followed by
> **2** To begin with
> **3** then
> **4** This stage
> **5** Then / Next / After that
> **6** Once
> **7** Then / Next / After that
> **8** Finally

06 Ask students to read the sample answer again and complete the task. Elicit what imperatives are (i.e. verbs in the infinitive form which are used to give commands or instructions). Before students do this exercise, ask them to read the Tip box.

Advice

Emphasize that using a range of grammatical structures such as those in Exercise 06 will help students improve their score for the Grammatical Range and Accuracy criterion. It may be worth showing them the band descriptors for this criterion (Band 6: uses a mix of simple and complex structures. Band 7: uses a variety of complex structures)

> **1** Yes. The second sentence in the first paragraph.
> **2a** relative clauses: *which is used to decorate it / which will give you the basic frame of the lantern / which correspond to the squares and triangles on the frame*
> **2b** passives: *is used to decorate it / Four of the sticks are then tied together / The remaining two squares are then tied in place / Once your frame is completed / the tissue paper shapes should be attached onto the frame / The squares at the top and bottom of the frame should be le empty / The lantern is then ready to be hung on a lightbulb.*
> **2c** imperatives: *take brightly coloured tissue paper / cut out eight triangles / fold and cut paper / decorate the base of the lantern*

07 Tell students to close their books and write 'giving opposing views and your own opinion' on the board. Elicit from students whether they think this would be an IELTS Task 1 or Task 2 question type. Ask them what they think they will have to do in this task type. After discussing the answers as a group, ask them to open their books and read the Bullet box carefully.

Tell students to look at the essay question and identify the two opinions. Elicit from students whether they agree with one opinion more than the other. Ask them to look at the extracts and label them as opinion A or opinion B.

> **1** B   **2** A   **3** A   **4** A   **5** A   **6** B

08 Ask students to look again at the extracts and identify the phrases used to give an opinion.

Advice

Emphasize that using expressions like these can contribute to the overall Coherence and Cohesion of the answer, which is another of the IELTS marking criteria. It may be useful to draw students' attention to the band descriptors for Coherence and Cohesion (Band 6: arranges information and ideas coherently and the is clear overall progression. Band 7: Logically organizes information and ideas: there is clear

> **1** In my experience
> **2** what I believe is that
> **3** It is evident to me that (used to present an opposing opinion)
> **4** The reality is that (this is preceded in the previous sentence by the phrase Some people are of the opinion that which presents an opposite opinion)
> **5** We cannot deny that
> **6** I strongly believe that

09 In this task students practise expressing their opinions using a range of appropriate language. Before students do this exercise, ask them to look at the Bullet box again.

Advice

Remind students that expressing their own opinion in this task type will help them to improve their mark for Task Achievement. Emphasize that in order to do this, they will need to show that they have fully answered all parts of the question and that they have included details, examples and/or evidence to support their views. It may be useful to show them the band descriptors for Task Achievement (Band 7: addresses all parts of the task / presents a clear position throughout the response / presents, extends and supports main ideas, but there may be a tendency to overgeneralise and/or supporting ideas may lack focus. Band 6: addresses all parts of the task although some parts may be more fully covered than others / presents a relevant position although the conclusions may become unclear or repetitive / presents relevant main ideas but some may be inadequately developed/unclear)

Feedback

Ask students to write their ideas on the board. Encourage them to look at each example and provide some peer feedback both on the language and the quality of the supporting details and examples.

Sample answers

1 My own view is that any language is a reflection of culture and contains words and phrases that are specific to that culture. For example in English, there is an expression 'It's not my cup of tea', meaning 'It is not to my taste', which I think reflects the fact that the British are predominantly a nation of tea drinkers.

2 However, it seems to me that what affects our lives most are issues on a local or national level rather than on a world level.

3 On the other hand, our lives are so inundated with aspects of other cultures – restaurants, music, fashion, to name but a few examples, that it is sometimes impossible to separate the culture of one nation from another.

10 Tell students that they are going to look at a checklist for writing a complete essay. Before showing them the checklist, ask them if they have any idea what it might include. Then after students have discussed their ideas, have them complete the check list with the missing words from the box. Before students do this exercise, ask them to read the Bullet box.

Advice

Emphasize the importance of planning answers carefully. Explain to students that they have longer (40 minutes) for Task 2 because they need to write more (250 words) and use their own ideas. Also point out that they will find it much easier to write a well-organized, coherent answer with good supporting detail, if they have made a plan.

1 highlight
2 plan; paragraphs
3 outline
4 topic sentence; examples
5 opposing
6 cohesive
7 conclusion
8 proof-read

11 Tell students that they are going to look at a sample answer to Task 2. Ask them to work with a partner and answer the questions.

Advice

The questions in Exercise 11 are all focused on the features of an IELTS Task 2 essay that will help candidates to score higher marks. Ensure students understand that should be following the items on the checklist when they write an IELTS Task 2 answer.

Sample answers

1 Yes. The candidate gives a definition of culture, mentions both views but clearly states their own opinion on the question.

2 At the end of the introduction (*I would lean towards the latter*) and again in the conclusion (*My own view is that while we are influenced by our nationality, in this globalised world, one's country of origin is only one aspect of our collective culture.*)

3 Opinion A. The topic sentence is: *If someone is born and raised in a place, they will be heavily influenced by it.* There are three reasons/ examples: the psychologist argument, the cuisine of a country and the music of a country.

4 Opinion B. The topic sentence is the first one. The candidate has probably decided to include this argument here because it supports his/her opinion given in the introduction, and having it at the end makes her conclusion stronger.

5 *Personally speaking, my own view is* and *To my mind*.

EXAM SKILLS

12 Tell students that they have an hour to complete a whole IELTS writing exam task, including Part 1 and Part 2.

Advice

- Tell students that they will need to spend 20 minutes on Task 1 and 40 minutes on Task 2.
- For Task 1, advise students to make a list of the vocabulary they might need to answer the question. Remind them to use sequencing linkers and the passive voice.
- For Task 2, advise students to make a plan before they start writing. Make sure they make their position clear and use details and examples to support their ideas

Sample answers

Task 1

The diagram shows the traditional techniques used for carving wooden shoes known as clogs. The process consists of six main stages, which are done by hand rather than using automated processes.

The first stage is to obtain wood from either poplar or willow trees. The wood is cut into pieces of the correct size using a saw. Next, outlined each clog is roughly shaped using an axe. After this, the clog maker takes a long knife to cut the shoe to the exact shape it should be. Once the exterior is finished, the next stage in the process is to bore out the interior of the clogs using a spoon drill to make space for the foot.

Once this is done, the shoes are nearly finished. Sandpaper is used to smooth down the wood on both the interior and the exterior of the clog. The final task for the clog maker is to decorate the completed wooden shoe using various different colours, although this is an optional stage. The clog is then ready to be worn.

This completes the process of making traditional wooden footwear, or clogs, by hand. (*188 words*)

Task 2

Today we live in a globalised world and the development of global culture is often at the expense of local traditions. There are certainly many people that show indifference to local customs in favour of embracing global ideas, but there are still many who see the value in maintaining them, myself included.

It is easy to argue that people are strongly influenced by the effects of globalisation. Technology in particular seems to dominate the leisure time of young people, whether it be gadgets or the internet. As a result, there are trends which can be described as global in all aspects of culture. For instance, many people now prefer listening to music by Ed Sheeran or Beyoncé rather than the traditional music of their country, which is often seen as outdated by comparison. Similarly, many would rather try exotic 'foreign' foods than use traditional recipes, which they might see as dull or old-fashioned.

However, it would be a mistake to think that everyone thinks this way. Many people are turned o by technology, which they see as culturally empty. Older people especially feel nostalgia for how things used to be done. For example, in the UK, the Royal Family are as popular as ever, and thousands of people turn out to see them wherever they go. It should also be remembered that many of today's global pop stars were themselves inspired by more traditional genres of music. Ed Sheeran, for example, embodies many musical traditions, such as folk music and busking. In the same way, it is still common to see performances of more traditional forms of music, such as classical and jazz.

My own opinion is that there is truth in both views. There are certainly people so focused on global trends that there is no space in their lives for, or interest in, preserving the past. On the other hand, there are many who prefer to live their lives more nostalgically and value the traditions that have been handed down. I would say that I belong more to this second group of people, although I admit I would struggle without the internet. (*343 words*)

Feedback

After students have done the task, tell them to use the checklist from Exercise 10 to carry out peer correction on another students' Task 2 essay.

LISTENING

OUTCOMES

- use notes to follow a talk
- do note completion and sentence completion tasks
- check your answers
- use prepositions in relative clauses.

OUTCOMES

Ask students to focus on the outcomes. The first two outcomes are related. For note completion tasks, students should use the notes to help them predict what the speaker will say which will help them to answer the questions. This is particularly useful for the IELTS Part four listening when a speaker talks at length in an academic-style lecture. Students will be given practice of and further advice for this task type as well as sentence completion questions. Outcome three helps students to improve the accuracy of their answers by looking at how they can check their answers. The final outcome focuses on the use of prepositions in relative clauses. This will help students to better understand when they are used in the listening exam.

LEAD-IN

01 This exercise helps students to prepare for the topic of the listening by looking at different word forms related to globalisation. There is also a grammatical focus and this too will help students with the listening topic and language used. Ask students to complete this exercise in pairs and monitor as they do it. Provide feedback by inviting students to give their answers and to comment on answers given. Then confirm correct answers.

1 globally	**2** global	**3** globalised	**4** globe
5 globalisation			

02 This exercise provides more specific preparation for the listening topic. Students should do this in pairs. Monitor as they discuss their opinions together. Then encourage a class debate.

03 Exercises 03 and 04 focus on using notes in note completion tasks in order to predict lecture content and help students to answer and complete this type of exam task more successfully . Before students do this exercise, ask them to read the Bullet box.

Advice

Remind students that they should use the time before the recording to read the notes. In addition to predicting possible content using contextual and grammatical clues, tell them that for the longer Part four academic style lectures especially, there are not many long pauses during the listening and between answers so it may be easy to get lost. By looking at the notes before the listening, this can help students avoid this.

Students should complete this exercise in pairs. Monitor as students do this to make sure they are on task. Provide feedback as outlined in Exercise 01.

> The headings in bold tell you what the structure is: Definitions of culture – Negative view – Positive view – Effect of the internet – Conclusion

04 Students practise using the notes to follow the listening. Ask students to do this individually and just to reflect in pairs on how easy or difficult it was. Monitor and then encourage a class discussion to highlight what were the clues and strategies students used to help them.

Transcript 65

Good afternoon, everyone. Today we continue our series of talks about globalisation, and today's talk is on the globalisation of culture. This is quite a complex topic as there are lots of different ways in which we can look at culture. To begin with, there is no agreed consensus on how best to define culture. Culture can cover both visible aspects, such as music, clothes, food and architecture, as well as less visible ones such as value and belief systems. An important point I want to stress from the beginning is one that anyone who studies culture needs to understand. It's not enough to just look and see what's happening on the surface. You need to look beneath the surface to understand the meanings that people assign to cultural phenomena. Let me give you an example. The American film Titanic proved hugely popular in China when it was released in 1998. When this was studied in detail by sociologists, it was found that it had nothing to do with the popularity of American culture. The film was understood by the Chinese purely in terms of their own historical circumstances. So, the whole idea of cultural globalisation needs to be looked at beyond the superficial level.

(Stop to check if students are following notes.)

OK, let's move on to discuss some different views on the globalisation of culture. For some it's seen to be a very negative thing indeed. Many critics see it as an extension of global capitalism. They see capitalism attempting to extend its influence to all corners of the globe through advertising and marketing, creating needs people didn't know they had in order to sell their products and services. One of the main criticisms of this economic approach is that it has led to corporations trying to find uniform answers to the needs of everybody, a kind of one-size-fits-all approach to products and services they produce. In other words, this approach does not consider or cater to the different personalities that different cultures have, and therefore either ignores or is detrimental to their individual needs. Some even see this process as a form of corporate imperialism, comparable perhaps to the colonisation of the 'new world' by European powers in the 15th to 19th centuries. This can lead to a form of cultural extinction; long-held customs and traditions slowly disappear or die out. This is a fear that many nations have expressed. In 1999, for example, a survey in France found that 60% of people in that country felt that globalisation was the greatest threat to the French cultural way of life.

Many people, however, view globalisation in a much more positive light. Some see it as giving people more options to choose from and improving life for everyone. For example, we can get the benefits of Japanese technology, Italian food, British music, American films and Swedish interior design wherever we live in the world.

(Stop to check if students are following notes.)

The fact that a Chinese family eats out at an American burger restaurant once a month doesn't alter the fact that on the other 30 days, they make and eat their traditional food at home. Although Japanese businessmen dress in British suits, they still do business in a very different way from their Western counterparts. In this view of cultural globalisation, people are viewed as world citizens who knowingly choose from a menu of options when it comes to music, food, clothes and so on. In other words, we have much more variety to suit our individual needs, thanks to such influences. It should also be remembered, though, that when it comes to the more deeply rooted aspects of culture, these are less susceptible to change. We can change the music we listen to, but our deeper profound beliefs about society cannot be altered so readily.

(Stop to check if students are following notes.)

To add another point to the discussion, I believe that the internet and other media that have led to a so-called 'global culture' can actually work to the advantage of national and regional cultural groups. The internet helps spread information about these cultures and contributes towards preserving not only their customs, but also their languages. For example, many Native American tribes have used social media to re-engage younger tribe members with the skills to learn and use their mother tongues.

In concluding my talk this afternoon, I would like to emphasise the part that education can play in this discussion of the globalisation of culture. If we can all learn to respect other cultures and *appreciate* their differences rather than fearing them, it is perfectly possible for them to flourish alongside a shared global culture. Now, does anyone have any questions?

05 Exercises 05 to 08 focus on note completion tasks. Before students do this exercise, ask them to read the Bullet box and Tip box.

Advice

Tell students that this is a common task during Part four of the IELTS Listening Exam. Also, highlight the fact that there may be up to ten gaps in the notes and that there could just be a short pause in the middle of the listening.

Exercise 05 gives students structured support in terms of identifying potential and impossible answers. Before students do this exercise, ask them to read the Bullet box.

Advice

Remind students to use the words from the recording and that the questions will be paraphrased and not contain the words in the actual recording. However, students need to use their grammatical knowledge to help them to fill in the gaps accurately.

Ask students to complete this exercise in pairs. Monitor and provide feedback.

1 C – the gap needs a verb
2 A – the gap needs a singular or plural noun
3 A – exceeds word limit

06 This exercise gives students further practice of identifying potential answers by examining grammatical clues within the notes. Students can do this in pairs. Monitor and then provide feedback. Encourage students to explain the reasons for their answers.

4 A   **5** B   **6** C

07 This exercise provides less structured practice of identification of potential words to fill in the gaps. Follow the procedure highlighted in the previous exercise.

> *Sample answers*
> **7** the comma suggests it will be a noun, someone who is able to choose
> **8** noun: e.g. *politics, economics, religion*
> **9** noun: e.g. *knowledge, appreciation*
> **10** noun: e.g. *the internet, conflict, nationalism*

08 Students have practice of listening and completing the notes. They should listen individually and then compare their notes in pairs. Monitor as students do this and then provide feedback.

> **1** visible **2** meanings **3** historical
> **4** capitalism **5** individual **6** 60% / 60 percent
> **7** citizens **8** society **9** languages **10** education

Extension

Give students a copy of the script and play the recording again to help them identify where the answers are.

09 Exercises 09 and 10 focus on sentence completion. Before students do this exercise, ask them to read the Bullet box.

Advice

Tell students that this task is similar to note completion but that these sentences are different to the notes as they are grammatically complete and may not be as connected to each other as the notes are.

Ask students to complete this exercise in pairs. Monitor and provide feedback. Ask students to give their reasons for their answers.

> 1 plural noun or noun phrase (the verb *help* suggests it will be plural)
> 2 verb (related to the effect one language can have on another)
> 3 noun or noun phrase, related to a particular context or aspect of life
> 4 noun or noun phrase, one that collocates with the preposition *into*
> 5 adjective or adjective phrase OR verb phrase in gerund form
> 6 singular countable noun or noun phrase, beginning with a consonant

10 Students have practice of sentence completion using their predictions from the previous exercise. Ask students to listen individually and then to compare their answers in pairs after the recording. Monitor as students do this. Provide feedback by encouraging students to give their answers, to comment on classmates' answers and provide alternative answers where necessary. Then confirm correct answers.

> *NB do not reveal these answers until students have completed exercise 11.*
> **1** ancient monuments **2** dominate **3** business
> **4** integration **5** getting older **6** complete course

Extension

See Exercise 08 Extension.

Transcript 66

Language is more than a collection of words and sounds. It is an essential part of a culture that helps not only with communication, but is a reminder of a culture's heritage. It can give us a valuable insight into the beliefs and the way a group of people think, in the same way ancient monuments give us insight into the past. Currently, the UNESCO Atlas of World Languages believes that there are 575 languages that are in danger. This includes languages that have just a handful of speakers such as Yagán in Chile and Ainu in Japan, but also some languages where there are still thousands of speakers. For example, it is estimated that there are around 170,000 speakers of Navajo, but the language is still in danger as younger generations are not learning it.

So why are so many languages dying out? Why are fewer people learning the languages of their ancestors? One explanation is globalisation. When a language becomes socially, politically and economically stronger than a native language, we often see displacement – the stronger language will dominate at the expense of the so-called weaker ones. One example of this can be seen in East Africa, where Swahili is spoken by 100 million people across Tanzania, Mozambique and Kenya. In other words, it has become the lingua franca for this pocket of Africa and in particular the language of business for these nations. This has led to other languages in the region coming close to extinction. By extension it will probably become the language of art and culture as technology increases in the region.

Another factor of globalisation that affects language is the movement of people. As people move to other countries to find work and education possibilities, immigrant parents tend to be less likely to teach their children the language and customs from the 'old' country. However, it's not clear if this is because these parents are driven by concerns about theirs and their children's integration into the new culture and local language or just that as immigrants they may have to work hard to establish themselves and not have the time to teach their children.

Nevertheless, there are some ways in which languages that may have died out in the past are being saved, and this is thanks to the globablisation and technology that have threatened languages in the past. For example, Joshua Hinson, a member of the Chikasaw tribe in North America, was concerned about the fact that the tribe members who could speak the language well were getting older and the younger members were not interested. He therefore developed an app that taught the Chikasaw alphabet and language. This was a great success with the younger members and they have formed a Youth Speaking Language

Club and <u>are partnering with language experts to produce a</u> <u>complete course</u>, which they hope to make available in the near future.

11 This exercise focuses on encouraging students to check their answers effectively. Before students do this exercise, ask them to read the Bullet box.

Advice

Students are encouraged to double check answers as they transfer them to the answer sheet. Spelling, grammar, accurate transfer and legibility should be prioritised and students are recommended to guess any unknown answers at this stage by using clues in the question. It's important to tell students that the IELTS exam does not deduct marks for incorrect answers.

Ask students to read the checklist and follow it as they transfer their answers.

Extension

Ask students to swap their answer sheet with a partner to evaluate. Ask partners to say whether the checklist has been followed and to give constructive feedback. Then ask students to discuss together in pairs which of the checklist guidelines they already follow, which they think are particularly useful and which they will definitely use next time. Encourage class discussion of this.

12 Exercises 12 and 13 focus on the grammatical use of prepositions in relative clauses. Before students do this exercise, ask them to read the Bullet box.

Advice

Tell students that prepositions are sometimes used if the relative pronoun is the object of the relative clause. Ask students to look at the example sentence in Exercise 12. Explain to them that the location can differ depending on whether it is produced when speaking (at end of the relative clause) or more formal settings e.g. writing (just before the relative pronoun). Highlight the use of whom for the relative pronoun after prepositions but explain that this is no longer always used.

This exercise focuses on grammatical analysis of the use of prepositions in this context. Ask students to do this in pairs and monitor. Provide feedback by first asking students to give their answers, comment and discuss if they agree with answers given. Then confirm correct answers.

> **1** subject: *we*; object: *which*   **2** (the) world
>
> **3** before it   **4** to the end of the relative clause: *the world (which) we live in*

13 This exercise helps students to understand the use of prepositions with relative pronouns in both more formal and spoken settings. As students are making the sentences less formal, these are likely to be the structures that students will hear when listening.

> **1** The man (who) you need to speak to is Mr Brodie.
>
> **2** Chapman Brothers, the company (which) I worked for for 20 years, is closing down.
>
> **3** Camilla Stark, with whom I went to school, is now a well-known actor.

> **4** Yasmin demanded the goods for which she had paid.
>
> **5** Christmas is the holiday which children wait for all year.
>
> **6** The man whose life the film is based on died a long time ago.

EXAM SKILLS

14 This exercise gives students exam practice of some of the task types and strategies identified in this unit. Students should complete this exercise individually and compare after each task type or at the end. Monitor as students compare their answers. Provide feedback as outlined previously.

> **1** independent country   **2** urban areas / cities
> **3** social groups   **4** contact   **5** yellow paint
> **6** (river) spirits   **7** (terrifying) masks   **8** tourists
> **9** government   **10** natural

Extension

You can again give students a copy of the script and replay the recording to help them identify where the answers are. In addition, it's a good idea to add a reflective element to this task. Ask students to work in pairs or small groups to compare together what they found easier or more difficult, the strategies they used and whether they helped them and if they would use them again. This will help students to internalise and make automatic useful strategies and will help you to identify what students have learnt. Generate a class discussion after students have done this.

Give students a copy of the script and play the recording again to help them identify where the answers are. In addition, add a reflective element to this task by asking students to work in pairs or small groups to compare together what they found easier or more difficult, the strategies they used and whether they were helpful. Then ask students to say what strategies they would use again. This will help them to internalise useful strategies and use them automatically. It will also help you to identify what students have learnt. Generate a class discussion after students have done this.

Transcript 67

You will hear a talk about the island of New Guinea and some of the people of Papua New Guinea. First you have some time to look at questions 1 to 10.

[pause]

Now listen carefully and answer questions 1 to 10.

Today's talk is about the fascinating culture of New Guinea, an island divided in two politically but with huge diversity in both parts. For those of you who don't know, New Guinea is located in Oceania, in the south western Pacific Ocean, north of Australia. <u>Since 1975 the eastern side has been</u> <u>the independent country of Papua New Guinea</u>, while the western side consists of the Indonesian administered provinces of Papua and West Papua. Papua New Guinea has 7 million inhabitants and is an incredibly rural country with <u>only 18% of the population living in urban areas</u>. It has 852 known languages and is one of the least explored terrains on the planet.

Now, one of the reasons that Papua New Guinea, and indeed the whole of New Guinea, is such an interesting place is that it's home to hundreds of traditional tribes – perhaps better described as distinct social groups, each one numbering hundreds or even thousands of members. In the Indonesian part of New Guinea, that is the provinces of Papua and West Papua, there are 312 different tribes, including around 44 uncontacted ones. These are tribes who up until now hadn't had any contact with the outside world, even with other neighbouring tribes. Of course, everyone is most curious to know about these tribes, but, by definition, we have little or no information on them.

[short pause]

I am now going to talk about the tribes of the Papua New Guinea highlands. These people only rarely had contact with the outside world until the 1960s, so they are still relatively isolated. When we start to examine the tribes, we see a common theme, which is the use of various methods to intimidate other groups so as to protect their own tribe. Let's look first at the Huli-Wigmen, a tribe of about 40,000 from the Tari Highlands of Papua New Guinea. They have given their faces a very distinctive look by using yellow paint, and they wear belts made of pigtails, aprons made of leaves, and wigs, which are a sort of hat, made from their own hair. This look is designed to scare o outsiders, which they also do with their bird dances which mimic the birds of paradise that inhabit their land.

Another highland tribe, the Asaro mud men, have the same intention as the Huli-Wigmen – to ward o outsiders. By smearing themselves in clay and mud they adopt the form of the river spirits, which are known to terrify their enemies. Their elaborate appearance is further supplemented with extended finger nails and they wear terrifying masks which serve to accentuate their ferocious look. The Asaro mud men were discovered by the outside world less than 80 years ago, but have now become a symbol of Papua New Guinea and make an important contribution to the tourist trade.

A third tribe that has become well known is the Chimbu, who live high in the mountains. The Chimbu skeleton dancers used to dance to intimidate their enemies. This tribe traditionally lived in male/female segregated houses, though they're now increasingly living in family groups. This group too now display their traditional dances not to scare o other tribes, but more to entertain tourists.

An interesting event, the Mount Hagan Sing-Sing, takes place every year, involving over 50 tribes. This came about due to the constant fighting between tribes, which became a serious problem for the Papua New Guinea government, so in 1961 it came up with the idea of a cultural show which would bring together as many tribes as possible in peace and pride in their cultural heritage.

The Mount Hagan Sing-Sing is a wonderful opportunity for Papua New Guinea to showcase its fascinating cultural heritage. At this event, tourists and locals alike can witness the spectacular costumes, including six feet high headdresses made of flowers, shells and feathers. Inevitably, there is some loss of authenticity associated with this kind of event. For example, chemical dyes are now used instead of the natural ones the tribes used earlier. However, a poor,

developing country has to exploit whatever resources it has, and the wealth of this region is its tribal peoples.

SPEAKING

OUTCOMES

- review all parts of the Speaking test
- review speaking skills
- use relative clauses with indefinite pronouns, *some-, every-, any-, no-*

OUTCOMES

Ask students to focus on the outcomes. The first outcome concerns further practice of all three parts of the IELTS Speaking Exam. This will help students practise strategies highlighted in the book and to further familiarise students with the Speaking exam. The second outcome helps students to review the speaking skills and strategies developed in this book. This will help students to perfect these strategies and encourage them to use them. The final outcome concerns the use of relative clauses with indefinite pronouns. This helps students to score more highly in the criterion of *grammatical range and accuracy*.

LEAD-IN

01 This exercise gives students the opportunity to think about advice for the speaking exam in order to identify good and bad advice. Ask students to work in pairs to complete this exercise. Monitor to check they are on task. Then encourage a class discussion of the advice before you confirm answers.

> **1** B Students who have rested before an exam tend to do better. In addition, the language you need for the exam is very different from what you would hear in movies. What's more, by doing this you are practising listening, not speaking.
>
> **2** B There is a big risk in memorising answers in the exam. It is highly unlikely you will be asked a question that corresponds exactly to what you memorised and the examiner will most likely realise what you are doing and this could lower your score.
>
> **3** G Many students are not aware of mistakes they make when they speak, but recording yourself gives you the chance to notice consistent errors and correct them.
>
> **4** G Smiling makes you seem more confident and friendlier, and eye contact helps you focus on what the examiner is asking you, as you can see their body language. It also stops you mumbling (speaking unclearly).
>
> **5** G You are already stressed on the day of the test, so don't add to this by risking being late.
>
> **6** B Fluency is not just about speed, but also clarity. It is more important to speak clearly and accurately, so try not to rush your answers. Use phrases for buying time to allow you to think of good answers rather than saying the first thing that comes into your head.

02 This exercise helps students add to the list of advice from Exercise 01. Students should do this in pairs and then compare with another pair or group. Again, encourage a class discussion and write down good advice on the board.

Sample answers

Good advice: Practise functions like comparing and contrasting, speaking hypothetically, speculating, and learn different language structures for these functions.

The best way to improve your speaking is to speak more often, especially by doing practice tasks under test conditions.

Don't panic if you make a mistake. One mistake will not ruin your overall score, and, if you realise, why not correct yourself so the examiner sees you realise the mistake?

Bad advice: Ask other students who did the test recently what questions they answered, and learn your own answers by heart. Keep your answers short and your grammar simple so that you avoid mistakes.

Don't ask the examiner any questions, even if you are unsure what to do.

Keep talking, even if you are not answering the question, because you want the examiner to hear your English.

03 This exercise focuses on reviewing strategies outlined in the book. Ask students to do this in pairs and monitor. Invite or nominate students to answer. Confirm answers only after encouraging students to comment on their class mates' answers – particularly in terms of whether they agree with answers given or suggest alternatives.

1 b	**2** d	**3** e	**4** a	**5** f	**6** c

04 This exercise helps to further check students' understanding of the above strategies. Students can do this in pairs. Monitor and follow the feedback guidelines identified in the previous exercise.

Sample answers

1 Furthermore, Nevertheless, Despite this, On the other hand, What's more, …

2 In my view, To my mind, Clearly, The reason for this is …

3 That's right. Not really.

4 That's not an easy question to answer. Let me think …

5 Could you explain what you mean? So what you're saying is …

6 Sorry, I'll start again. I mean, …

05 Students can practise using the strategies outlined in the previous exercises. Students should do this in pairs and record their answers if possible. Monitor as students do this and note anything you wish to bring up during feedback. Use any errors you noted when you monitored. Write a list of these on the board (3-5 is manageable). Also, add 1-2 correct answers. Ask students to identify the correct answers and correct the incorrect ones. This is a good way to recycle what has been learnt in the exercise and to also focus on responding to emerging student errors and needs.

06 If students have recorded their answers on a smart phone or other recording device, these can then be used for peer or self-appraisal. Ask students to look at the criteria and listen to their partner's recording. Encourage students to use the criteria to give constructive feedback.

Extension

Encourage students to rerecord their answers and to email them to you. You can use these for future class material or to provide individual feedback.

07 Exercises 07 to 13 focus on further familiarising students with all parts of the IELTS Speaking Exam. Ask students to complete Exercise 07 individually and to compare with a partner after the recording has finished. Monitor as students discuss their answers. Conduct feedback as outlined in previous exercises.

1 call him	**2** his identification	**3** work/job
4 music	**5** eclectic	**6** food	**7** sweet food(s)/
desserts / cheesecake, pancakes		

Transcript 68

Examiner:	Good morning. My name is Paula Brady. Can you tell me your full name, please?
Luis:	Yes, it's Luis Moreno Gonzalez.
Examiner:	Thank you. And what shall I call you?
Luis:	You can call me Julio.
Examiner:	Thank you. And can you tell me where you're from?
Luis:	I'm from Cordoba in the south of Spain.
Examiner:	Can I see your identification, please?
Luis:	Yes, here it is.
Examiner:	Thank you. … Now, Luis, in this first part, I'm going to ask you some questions about yourself. Let's talk about what you do. Do you work or are you a student?
Luis:	At the moment, I'm working, but I'm hoping to go to the UK to do my Master's next September.
Examiner:	What do you like most about your job?
Luis:	Well, I work in IT and, in fact, I will have been at my company for three years in March, so I know my job really well. The part I like best is helping people with their computer problems. Sometimes they're quite stressed, but when they call me and I tell them how to solve the problem, they calm down. It can be quite rewarding.
Examiner:	And is there anything you don't like about your job?
Luis:	Yes! The hours! As I said, my job involves helping people having computer problems and obviously these can happen at all times of the day and night, so sometimes I have to work on evening and night shifts. The problem is that my sleeping patterns are affected.
Examiner:	Would you like to change jobs in the future?

Luis: Yes, but I want to stay in IT. As soon as I get a Master's, I can become a manager and I think my work will be more varied and interesting. And less disruptive for my sleep.

Examiner: OK, Luis, now let's move on to talk about music. How much time do you spend listening to music?

Luis: Oh, lots of time. Probably about three or four hours a day on working days, and a lot more on my days off.

Examiner: And what type of music do you listen to?

Luis: I would say my taste in music is … eclectic. I like all types, really, although I'm not so keen on classical music, but all types of modern music – pop, rock, R and B, hip hop, dance music. I always keep up to date with new releases and follow the charts.

Examiner: Where do you usually listen to music?

Luis: Everywhere! I have a stereo in my car and also I have music on my phone, which I listen to when I'm walking or travelling by bus or train. I listen at home and even at work sometimes.

Examiner: Is music important in your culture?

Luis: Yes, definitely. Spanish music, especially guitar music, is known all over the world. It's very haunting music about love and tragedy. The words are very poetic and of course people dance our traditional dances to it. We really like to express our culture through music and it's important in all our festivals.

Examiner: OK, now we're going to talk a little about food. What are your favourite types of food?

Luis: Er, well, I'm quite adventurous when it comes to food. I'll try anything. But I have a really sweet tooth, so I suppose my favourite food has to be desserts … like cheesecake or pancakes.

Examiner: Do you prefer eating out or eating at home?

Luis: Without a doubt, I prefer eating out! In our culture it's very normal to eat out several times a week. I like it because I can go with my friends and try new dishes. I'm not a very good cook, so eating at home is hard for me.

Examiner: How often do you eat with your family?

Luis: I try to have lunch with my parents every weekend. We usually have a huge feast, prepared by my mother, all the family are there, and we spend hours sharing our news and catching up on the gossip. But I can only do this at weekends. I really wouldn't have time for such a big meal with my parents if I visited them during the week!

08 This exercise helps students to analyse the grammar used in the recording so they are aware of what they should include when answering part one of the exam. Before students do this exercise, ask them to read the Tip box.

Advice

Remind students that they should try to use complex grammatical structures in order to receive higher scores for the criterion of *grammatical range and accuracy*.

Ask students to listen individually and to compare answers in pairs. Monitor as students do this. Conduct feedback as outlined previously.

---

1 future perfect: *I will have been at my company for three years in March*
2 passive voice: *The problem is that my sleeping patterns are affected.*
3 first conditional: *As soon as I get a Master's, I can become a manager and I think my work will be more varied and interesting*
4 relative clauses: *and also I have music on my phone, which I listen to when I'm walking*
5 second conditional: *I really wouldn't have time for such a big meal with my parents if I visited them during the week!*

Extension

If students need more support, play the recording again and give them a copy of the script for support.

09 Exercise 09 helps students to analyse Part two of the IELTS Speaking exam. Ask students to listen individually and then to compare their answers together in pairs. Monitor as students do this to see if the recording needs to be repeated additional times.

Sample answers

why it interests you: Neighbouring country but different, his city has a cathedral that used to be a mosque

how you learnt about it: At school and he has been there

what you know about it: Food is tasty, spicy and healthy, couscous and flat bread, stews cooked in tagine

plans to visit this country: Casablanca in spring with friends Luis gives a very good performance. He covers all the points on the card and speaks for the correct amount of time. He also gives an appropriate answer to the examiner's follow-up question.

Transcript 69

Examiner: Right, Luis, now I'm going to give you a topic and I'd like you to talk about it for one to two minutes. Before you talk, you'll have one minute to think about what you're going to say and you can make some notes if you wish. Do you understand?

Luis: Yes.

Examiner: Here's a pencil and some paper for making notes and here's your topic. I'd like you to describe a country that interests you.

[the examiner times one minute]

Examiner: OK, remember you have one to two minutes for this, so don't worry if I stop you. I'll tell you when the time is up. Can you start speaking now, please?

Luis: OK, so the country that interests me is Morocco. It's <u>one of our neighbouring countries</u>, and yet in many ways, <u>it's worlds apart from</u> Spain. I learnt about it in many different ways. At school, first of all, but also I've been over to Tangier a few times as <u>it's only a short boat ride away</u>. In my city, Córdoba, we have a cathedral called La Mezquita because it used to be a mosque. So, <u>dating back to my childhood</u> I've been exposed to aspects of the culture of the Arab world.

I guess I learnt most by visiting. <u>I remember very vividly</u> my first trip to Tangier. I walked around a Moroccan market. The sights and sounds were so different, and the smell of those ingredients <u>made my mouth water</u>. I only spent the day there the first time, but when I went back a few years later, I spent several days there.

One thing that fascinates me is Moroccan food. It's spicier than the food we eat at home, and they use different ingredients – couscous rather than rice, for example, and their bread is flatter than ours. Their <u>cuisine</u> is healthy and delicious, with lots of vegetables and pulses. They cook stews in a tagine, a kind of clay cooking pot, which makes the food come out smelling and tasting amazing.

As for my travel plans, well, next time I go to Morocco, I want to <u>travel a little further afield</u>, maybe Casablanca, which I think must be a really romantic and fascinating city. I'll probably go with some of my friends and stay at least a week. I don't have any definite plans yet, but I was thinking of going next spring, as the summer may be too hot.

Examiner: Thank you. And are you interested in other countries in the same region?

Luis: Yes, I would be interested in visiting Algeria and Tunisia as well, as they are culturally quite similar to Morocco. Oh, and Egypt – I've always wanted to see Giza and the Valley of the Kings.

10 This exercise gives students the opportunity to evaluate and analyse Part two of the exam but this time focusing on the vocabulary. Before students do this exercise, ask them to read the Tip box.

Advice

Encourage students to use a wide range of vocabulary accurately. Tell students that for the criterion *lexical resource* students are rewarded for using a wide range of vocabulary.

Students should listen individually before comparing their answers in pairs. Monitor and then conduct feedback by encouraging students to volunteer answers and then asking classmates to comment on whether they agree with the answers given or to suggest alternative. Then confirm correct answers.

> **1** our neighbouring countries **2** it's worlds apart from **3** a short boat ride away **4** dating back to my childhood **5** I remember very vividly **6** made my mouth water **7** travel a little further afield **8** cuisine

11 This exercise helps students to analyse part three of the exam. Students should listen individually before answering the questions in pairs. Monitor as students compare answers and then provide feedback.

> **1** Two sub-topics: language and culture; culture and change
>
> **2** So, do you think when we learn a language we need to learn the culture as well?
>
> But isn't there a culture associated with the language itself?
>
> Can you give me an example of that?
>
> Do you think globalisation has changed Spanish culture at all?

Transcript 70

Examiner: We've been talking about a country you would like to visit and I'd like to discuss with you one or two more general questions related to that. First, let's talk about the importance of languages in culture. How do you think language helps us to understand a culture?

Luis: <u>Personally speaking</u>, I would say it helps a lot. I feel quite bad that I don't know any Arabic at all. I think that's the reason we find countries like Morocco so strange and exotic. I'd feel more at home there if I knew at least the basics of their language. And also, <u>in my view</u>, it's kind of a mark of respect to be able to greet someone and say thank you, that kind of thing.

Examiner: So, do you think when we learn a language we need to learn the culture as well?

Luis: Well, <u>it depends</u>. <u>The thing is</u> that languages like Spanish, English and even French are not associated with just one country. <u>Take Spanish, for example</u>. In a class, different students might be planning to use their Spanish in Spain, in Argentina, Venezuela, Colombia, so many places with different cultures. With English, the countries that use it are even more diverse, as it's spoken not only in the UK, the US, Australia and countries like that, but also places further afield <u>such as</u> India, Singapore, Hong Kong and African countries. <u>Given this fact</u>, English is quite separate from any culture.

Examiner: But isn't there a culture associated with the language itself?

Luis:	Well, I suppose there is to some extent. So, in Spanish, we have different forms of address for different people I mean, there's a more respectful form if you are speaking to older people or a stranger. In English, it seems to be part of the language to be very polite all the time, you know, say 'please', 'thank you' and 'excuse me' a lot, but I don't know if that's true everywhere that English is spoken.
Examiner:	OK, let's talk about how cultures change. What aspects of culture do you think are most resistant to change?
Luis:	That's a good question. Obviously, anything embedded in the language is not going to change quickly and also anything connected to religion. I would say the most deeply rooted aspects of culture are those we cannot see.
Examiner:	Can you give me an example of that?
Luis:	Well, I suppose things like the fact that the Spanish are eternally optimistic. It's a kind of belief that good will triumph over evil or everything will be alright in the end. What you see is people always smiling, singing and dancing, but underneath the belief is that life is basically good.
Examiner:	That's interesting. Do you think globalisation has changed Spanish culture at all?
Luis:	Er, let me think. No, I wouldn't say so. Not the culture at least, which is something we Spanish are very proud of. It has changed things superficially, and these days you'll notice the presence of more international businesses and chains. There are more international films and TV programmes available, and younger people probably listen to more international music than, for example, when my parents were children. But deep down, we are the same. We still do things our own way.
Examiner:	Thank you very much, Julio. That's the end of the Speaking test.

12 This exercise helps students to further analyse part three of the exam. Students this time focus on the language used and analyse the functions of the vocabulary used. Students should do this in pairs. Monitor and then provide feedback.

Showing agreement / disagreement	Giving examples	Buying times	Giving opinions	Explaining / clarifying
I wouldn't say so to some extent it depends	such as Take Spanish, for example	Let me think That's a good question	Personally speaking In my view Obviously	I mean The thing is

13 Students now have the opportunity to practise all three parts of the exam using the questions asked to Julio. Students should take turns being the candidate and examiner. Give students the criteria of *fluency and coherence, lexical resource, grammatical range and accuracy* and *pronunciation*. Use the band 7 and 8 from the IELTS descriptors (detailed below)

Refer students to the IELTS criteria specifically for bands 7 and 8 in the introduction to the Teachers' Book. Tell them to firstly determine whether they fully meet the criteria for band 7 and then check if they surpass it and can be judged to meet the grade 8 criteria.

Ask students to use the above criteria to evaluate their partner's answer and to provide constructive feedback. Monitor as students do this and note down anything you wish to bring up during feedback.

Alternative

Ask students to record their answers. These can then be used for peer or self-appraisal. Then encourage students to rerecord their answers and to email them to you. You can use these for future class material or to provide individual feedback.

14 Exercises 14 to 16 focus on clauses with indefinite pronouns. Before students do this exercise, ask them to read the Bullet box.

Advice

This language structure not only demonstrates a good range of grammar, but is ideal for part three of the exam where more impersonal information is needed. These pronouns (*some, every, no, any*) can be used with defining relative clauses to give a more objective and impersonal feel to part three answers in particular.

Ask students to complete this exercise in pairs. Monitor and then conduct feedback as outlined previously.

1 everywhere	**2** anyone	**3** Someone	**4** nothing
5 everybody	**6** something	**7** anything	**8** nowhere

15 This exercise gives students freer practice of using this grammatical structure. Students should do this individually.

Sample answers
1 Everyone who visits my country loves the food.
2 I am someone who is very dedicated to their career.
3 Cultural difference is something that we all need to respect.
4 Somewhere that I'd really love to visit is Argentina.
5 I don't know anybody who doesn't use social media.

16 Students now have the opportunity to talk in pairs about the sentences they completed for themselves in the previous exercise. Encourage students to add more detail to their answers and for the non-speaking partner to give constructive feedback. Monitor as students do this and make a note of anything you want to bring up in feedback.

EXAM SKILLS

17 This exercise gives students exam practice and the opportunity to use the skills and advice given in this unit to help students improve their answers. Ask students to work in pairs and take turns asking and answering the questions where appropriate. Monitor as students do this and then provide feedback.

Alternative and extension

Ask students to record their answers for later self-appraisal or peer feedback. Students should then re-record their answers. These can then be sent to the teacher to use in class or evaluated.

It is also a good idea after feedback for students to reflect on the strategies used in this exercise. Give them a few minutes to discuss what strategies they used, what was more effective and which strategies they will use in future.